WITHDRAWN

D1305664

HC
147
L66

STAMFORD BRANCH LIBRARY

UNIVERSITY OF CONNECTICUT

SCOFIELDTOWN ROAD

STAMFORD, CT 06903

UCONN STAMFORD

a 34012 0287595582b

OEMCO

The Economic
Development of Panama

Robert E. Looney

The Praeger Special Studies program—
utilizing the most modern and efficient book
production techniques and a selective
worldwide distribution network—makes
available to the academic, government, and
business communities significant, timely
research in U.S. and international economic, social, and political development.

The Economic Development of Panama

The Impact of World Inflation on an Open Economy

Stamford Branch Library
University of Connecticut
Scofieldtown Road
Stamford, Conn. 06903

Praeger Publishers   New York   Washington   London

PRAEGER SPECIAL STUDIES IN INTERNATIONAL ECONOMICS AND DEVELOPMENT

HC
147
L66

Library of Congress Cataloging in Publication Data

Looney, Robert E
    The economic development of Panama.

    (Praeger special studies in international economics and development)
    Bibliography: p.
    Includes index.
    1. Panama—Economic conditions. 2. Inflation (Finance)—
Panama. 3. Inflation (Finance) I. Title.
HC147. L66   330. 9'7287'05   74-33038
ISBN 0-275-05390-3

PRAEGER PUBLISHERS
111 Fourth Avenue, New York, N.Y. 10003, U.S.A.

Published in the United States of America in 1976
by Praeger Publishers, Inc.

All rights reserved

© 1976 by Praeger Publishers, Inc.

Printed in the United States of America

In 1974 the author spent the summer in Panama, with the assigned task of examining the economic benefits that Panama would derive from a proposed road connecting Tocumen (the international airport) with Chorrera, a residential city on the opposite side of the Canal Zone from the airport. The purpose of the road was not only to relieve traffic congestion in Panama City, by bypassing the city, but to integrate the economy on both sides of the canal. The assigned task was to examine the economic resources at work in Panama City for the purpose of making a long range forecast of the economy.

The author had long been interested in the continuing debate over what should be done with the canal and the Canal Zone, but like most Americans knew little of the facts involved. At first the issue seemed to boil down to the fact that the Panamanians "wanted the canal back" and that for trade, military, or strategic reasons—or perhaps simple stubborness—the United States was not going to "give it back." After several weeks, suspicions arose 1. that the Panamanians really did not want the canal back, but were interested only in obtaining more money from the United States; 2. that the issue was clearly political—there were few economic implications for either the United States or Panama—and; 3. that somehow all this would be decided after endless political jousting with Washington. The result was fairly predictable. The United States would keep the canal and in return would probably agree to buy the Panamanian banana crop at twice the world price for the next fifty years, or as long as General Omar Torrijas, president since 1968, kept the students calm (they had rioted over the canal in 1964).

In examining the economy of the country, it became apparent that economic issues were really at the heart of the matter; not economics in the sense of extracting more money from the United States, but economics in the sense that the canal and related treaties had created economic forces that over time had totally shaped the economy of Panama in a manner that was perhaps constraining the country's future growth. The popular press in the United States, by concentrating on the issue of sovereignty over the canal, had blurred the significance of the negotiations with the United States and had distorted the

Panamanian position. Existing books on the subject were no more instructive.[1] They tended to concentrate either on the legalistic relations between the Republic of Panama and the Canal Zone or on a narrow segment of the economy. Statements from public officials were not very enlightening:[2] none had examined the economic impact that the canal has had on the economy of Panama—an analysis essential to a complete understanding of one of the most important and complex foreign policy issues confronting the United States.[3] This book is designed to clarify those economic issues. Together with those issues, it takes into consideration the constraints which the current treaty has placed on the economy. It does not, however, undertake to speculate on those treaties now being negotiated. Such a study would be a major undertaking in itself.[4]

The book will be of special interest to all those concerned with the current Panama issue, while the new treaty is being negotiated by the two countries.

NOTES

1. For example, a recent book by William C. Merrill, Lehman Fletcher, Randall Hoffman, and Michael Applegate, Panama's Economic Development: The Role of Agriculture (Ames: Iowa State University Press, 1975) does not even include the canal or Canal Zone in the analysis of the overall economic situation in Panama.

2. See Thomas M. Franck and Edward Weisband, "Panama Paralysis," Foreign Policy no. 21 (Winter 1975-76): 168-87.

3. Stephen S. Rosenfeld, "The Panama Negotiations—A Close Run Thing," Foreign Affairs 54, no. 1 (October 1975): 1-13.

4. Robert E. Looney, "The Impact of Alternative Treaties on the Economy of Panama," (1975).

ACKNOWLEDGMENTS

I am indebted to far more individuals than can be conveniently identified. However, I would like to thank Robert Davenport of Stanford Research Institute; Jorge Espino and Raul Cisneros of the Ministerio de Obras Publicas; Nicolas Ardito Barletta; Jose B. Sokol and Jarilaos Stavrou of the Ministerio de Planificacion y Politicia Economica; William Byerts, Arnold Harberger, and Larry Sassjad of the University of Chicago; Mario Belotti, Father William F. Donnelly, S.J., Peter Van den Dool and Daniel Dick of the University of Santa Clara; Professor Emilio F. Clare, Universidad de Panama; Raul Auzmendi, Frank Ryan, Derish Wolff, and Tony Ohlin of Louis Berger International; Herman Rodriguez of the Ministerio de Commercia; Walter West of the United States Embassy in Panama; Michael Applegate of Iowa State University; and Juan Manuel Caballero, Carlos Brugiati, and Edilma De Lopes of the Direccion de Estadistica y Censo Contraloria General de la Republica Panama.

Francisco Andrade was most helpful as both critic and researcher. Special thanks are given to my parents for their help and encouragement, to Christine Tapley for her invaluable assistance in conceptualizing and organizing the study, to my wife Anne for her assistance in the computations, and to Marlene Plumb for her excellent typing of the final draft.

CONTENTS

LIST OF TABLES

xiii

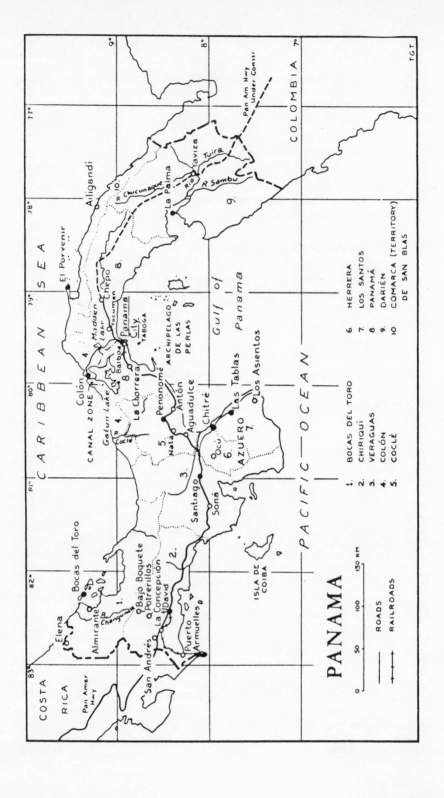

PANAMA

ROADS

RAILROADS

0   50   100   150 KM

1. BOCAS DEL TORO
2. CHIRIQUÍ
3. VERAGUAS
4. COLÓN
5. COCLÉ
6. HERRERA
7. LOS SANTOS
8. PANAMÁ
9. DARIÉN
10. COMARCA (TERRITORY) DE SAN BLAS

COSTA RICA

CARIBBEAN SEA

COLOMBIA

PACIFIC OCEAN

Gulf of Panama

Elena
Pan Amer Hwy
San Andrés
Bocas del Toro
Almirante
Changuinola
Bajo Boquete
Potrerillos
La Concepción
David
Puerto Armuelles
ISLA DE COIBA
El Porvenir
Alligandí
Colón
CANAL ZONE
Gatún Lake
Miraflores
Madden Lake
Chepo
Tocumen
Panamá City
Balboa
TABOGA
La Chorrera
ARCHIPELAGO DE LAS PERLAS
Penonomé
Antón
Aguadulce
R. Coclé
Natá
Santiago
Soná
Chitré
AZUERO
Ocú
Las Tablas
Los Asientos
La Palma
R. Chucunaque
R. Tuira
R. Tavíza
R. Sambú
Pan Am Hwy Under Constr

T.G.T.

The Economic
Development of Panama

1

PANAMA—
THE COUNTRY
AND THE PEOPLE

Panama is a small country of roughly 29,000 square miles (slightly less than the area of South Carolina), but its strategic position, by virtue of the canal, has raised it to the status of international importance. The country consists largely of low mountain ranges, thick jungles, and fertile valleys and plains. Jungles cover much of the eastern part; agricultural land lies largely in the south and west.[1]

The population of about one and a half million is largely mestizo, an amalgam of Spanish, Indian, and Negro, with smaller elements of white, Indian, Negro, and Oriental. About half of the inhabitants live on small farms or in country villages and make their living in agriculture, stock raising, and fishing.

Education is free. By law all children between the ages of seven and fifteen must attend school; however, only one-third of school age children attend, especially in the country areas. About one-fourth of the people cannot read or write.

The government, since the coup d'etat of 1968 when the National Guard assumed control, has comprised a president, his cabinet, a Supreme Court of Justice, and a number of autonomous agencies. It maintains the National Guard, but has no regular army.[2]

The balboa and the U. S. dollar are legal tender; they are of equal value, although the balboa exists only in the form of coins. Inflation tends over time to be the same as that in the United States.[3]

The country is influenced by the United States in many other ways, largely stemming from the treaties that have existed between the two countries. The first of the treaties was negotiated in 1903,[4] when the Republic of Panama granted to the United States "in perpetuity the use, occupation, and control of the lands and waters necessary for the construction, maintenance, operation, sanitation and protection of a strip 10 miles wide to the distance five miles on each side of the interoceanic waterway" in return for payments of $2 million annually.

Since that time the canal has been the most important factor in Panama's economic life. Aside from the annual payment of $2 million, the United States employs seven out of every 100 Panamanians; and the gross national per capita income of $800 in 1973 (in 1960 balboas) was mostly derived from activities related to the canal. Those activities accounted for 50 percent of the value of all goods and services; in contrast, commercial agriculture, the second most important sector, accounted for less than 20 percent.

Other treaties followed that of 1903, a monetary agreement in 1904 and revisions of the 1903 treaty in 1936 and 1955. Basically, however, the original treaty has had no substantive changes, with the exception of several meaningful concessions, such as closing down U. S. commercial manufacturing plants in the Canal Zone and allowing the Panamanian government to tax the incomes of Panamanians working in the Canal Zone. But although the treaties have acted to the advantage of both countries, many Panamanians now feel that they have become a constraint on the country's continued economic growth.

The country's economy has traditionally depended on the growth of world commerce. Indeed, since 1968 it has developed into a major international financial center, capitalizing on its liberal banking laws, its location, good communications, transportation facilities, and absence of exchange controls.

Until very recently its economic development has been at a high rate, with relatively little inflation. Both private business and government have played key roles in this process: private business mainly through heavy reinvestment of profits in expanded plant and capacity, and government through the building of social overhead capital—schools, an improved transportation network, and better communications.

But in spite of its economic growth the country faces many problems: one of the highest population growth rates in the world, massive migration from rural areas to the terminal cities of Panama City and Colon, and significant problems of unemployment and overcrowding.

The history of its economic growth is roughly divided into four distinct periods: * (1) the pre-World War II period; (2) the immediate post-World War II period (1945-55) of depression and recovery; (3) the boom period 1955-65; and (4) the recent period (1966-75) of consolidation (1966-68), revolution (1968), and decelerating growth and inflation (1970-75).

NOTES

1. An excellent description of the geography of Panama is given in Preston E. James, Latin America 4th ed. (New York: Odyssey Press, 1969).

2. Background on the country can be obtained in Thomas E. Weil, et al., Area Handbook for Panama (Washington D.C.: U.S. Superintendent of Documents, 1972).

3. Larry Sjaastad, "Prices and Wages in Panama," (Panama City: U.S. Agency for International Development, 1973), pp. 1-4.

4. The original treaty, together with subsequent amendments, is to be found in U.S. Department of State, Friendship and cooperation; General Treaty Between the United States of America and Panama, and Exchange of Notes, signed at Washington, D.C., March 2, 1936. Treaty Series No. 945 (Washington: U. S. Government Printing Office, 1939): U. S. Department of State, Mutual Understanding and Cooperation: Treaty, with Memorandum of Understanding Reached Between the United States and Panama, signed January 25, 1955. Treaties and other International Acts Series No. 3297 (Washington, D.C.: Government Printing Office, 1956). A good summary of the Panamanian--U. S. relations is given in "United States Policy Toward Panama, 1903--Present: Questions of Recognition and Diplomatic Relations and Instances of United States Intervention," Department of State Bulletin (April 22, 1974). The current debate over a new treaty and the various positions of leading United States officials is summarized in "Controversy Over Proposed Revision of the Panama Canal Treaty", Department of State Bulletin (November 1972), pp. 257-288.

---

*This is somewhat arbitrary. The text makes a case for considering the postwar period strictly in terms of constraints on the economy. Under this criterion the postwar period is broken into three major periods: (1) 1946-55, (2) 1955-65, and (3) 1966-73.

2

ECONOMIC TRENDS
THROUGH 1955

Nature has endowed Panama with little physical wealth apart from a favorable location for facilitating world trade. But the Panamanian people, through their energy and resourcefulness, have created a relatively prosperous economy that has been sustaining a healthy rate of growth for over two decades. Because of the paucity of its natural resources, its unique location relative to the canal and its historical relations with the United States, both commercial and cultural, the economy has developed into one oriented toward trade, commerce, and services.

Agriculture, however, remains backward and maunufacturing has been neglected, with the result that the country is self-sufficient in relatively few products.[1] But Panama has the canal, its principal and in fact its only important natural resource It is the canal that accounts for Panama's relative well-being; and it is the canal that has made the nation a trader, an entrepot, and an international financial center.

But the old adage that one does not get something for nothing is true of the canal. It is a tremendous source of political tension and distraction, continuously raising basic issues involving such diverse matters as sovereignty, the rights of Panamanian workers, and smuggling. To a large extent these issues concerning the canal have diverted the country's attention and energy away from building an economy capable of self-sustained growth in its own right.[2]

Also because of the political influence wielded by commercial interests, Panama has developed a mercantilist mentality. And with this historical emphasis on commerce,

4

there has been an unbalanced utilization of resources. Before
1968, the country had developed under a series of governments
with a largely laissez-faire economic approach to government's
role in the economy. Very conspicuous in the past was an economic philosophy that little more than exploiting the nation's
geography needed to be done. Historically, this has resulted in a
tendency for many North Americans to view Panama as unique
in Latin America—as Switzerland is in Europe. There has also
been a tendency within Panama to follow a "fast-buck" approach
to economic development, with incentives to tax-haven corporations,
numbered bank accounts to attract foreign capital, tax exemption
for the registry of ships, and casinos (but very little else) to
attract tourists. [3]

In 1964 the joint tax program of Organization of American
States and the Inter-American Development Bank (OAS/IDB) noted
that the Panamanian efforts toward development did not constitute
the real substance of economic development. They did not provide
the foundation for the type of economic society likely to have
consistent growth and in which the fruits will be shared equitably.
Rather, they resulted in a type of economy that advances in fits
and starts, depending on such variables as world inflation and
economic activity, the level of canal traffic, and the number of
new tax-haven corporations. "And for this type of economy it
matters little for much of the population whether the economy as
a whole is advancing or standing still. The Panamanian economy
reminds one of a ballgame in which only the stars are allowed to
play. One cannot help but wonder how long the other contestants
will be content to sit on the bench. "[4]

They did not wait long. When the present Panamanian
government came to power in October 1968 by overthrowing the
long entrenched oligarchy, it announced plans for a fundamental
transformation of the pattern of development in the country;[5]
the excessive dominance of the Canal Zone would be broken, the
country's dependence on the United States would be lessened, the
very unequal distribution of wealth and income would be changed,
and a genuine popular participation in the national development
would be promoted; new exports would be developed, and as
rapid an economic growth would be sought as would be compatible
with the government's social goals (which clearly had first priority). The government has encountered a number of problems,
however, in attempting to alter Panama's traditional pattern of
development.

Starting in the early 1970s the country has experienced
a marked slump in economic activity, accompanied by inflation

and a rapid deterioration in the balance of payments. Currently, the country is in a recession, its economic infrastructure is strained, and there is reason to doubt the ability of the public sector to keep social overhead capital growing in line with the country's needs. For the first time in several decades there is some question as to whether Panama can continue to sustain high growth rates and at the same time provide sufficient growth in employment opportunities for a population that is rapidly leaving the crowded agricultural areas in search of employment in the terminal cities.

The problems the government is encountering in implementing its program can best be understood in historical context. While it is true that the causes of many of Panama's economic problems also exist in other Latin American countries,[6] it is the combination and intensity of a number of growth-inhibiting factors in Panama that make its future development uncertain.

THE PRE-WORLD WAR II PERIOD

During the period between completion of the canal (1914) and World War II, the Republic of Panama was transformed from a subsistence-agrarian economy to one with an infrastructure and market-oriented economic system organized to facilitate international traffic and trade. During the 1920s and 1930s intensification of these activities took place during periods when world trade was booming, or when large-scale construction works were being carried out on the transisthmian route. To a large extent the country remained dependent on the Canal Zone, with little change taking place in the rest of the country.[7]

During this period nearly all the initiative for the growth of the Panamanian economy came from the private sector. It is easy to maintain that the freedom and openness of the economy characterizing the prewar period in Panama was achieved by default, partly because of the inertia of those in power who continued along the paths established by the original canal treaties, partially because of their inability to institute competent administration for proper direction and control of the economy, and partly because of subservience to private business interests or complicity in the gains therefrom. There is some truth to this observation. But the restriction of government economic intervention and the reliance on private initiative arose basically, and in great measure, from a conscious conception on the part of policymakers of what they believed to be in the best interests of the country.

Given Panama's unique geographical location, businessmen have long recognized the advantages the country possesses for trade, commerce, tourism, and financial and other services. Those in high

office, in both the executive and legislative branches—many of them
businessmen, or lawyers with business orientation—shaped public policy to accommodate this private thrust into trade, finance, and services. As a consequence, the movement of capital goods and persons
has been subjected, from the initial days of the country's existence, to
minimal restrictions. Similarly, the government pursued a policy of
freedom in dealing with international flows of capital and private investment. It also favored a preponderantly conservative fiscal policy
whereby taxes were kept low and expenditures nearly always fell short
of revenues. Government administration was kept on a relatively small
scale and suffered perennially from inefficiency and corruption.

The openness of the Panamanian economy was one of its outstanding characteristics during this period. [8] The openness brought
certain advantages: easy access to foreign technology (greatly facilitated by the widespread use of high-quality English); and access to
foreign capital goods and high-quality industrial inputs from abroad.
Without these, the progress made up until World War II would probably not have been possible.

Thanks to rapidly growing world trade during the 1920s this
openness was one of the factors making possible an exceptionally high
standard of living for the residents in the terminal cities—Panama
City and Colon. Of course, the country's specialization was coupled
with the risks typical of economics exposed to changing world economic
conditions. The decline in world trade resulting from the economic depression of the 1930s posed serious problems for the policy makers
who wanted to maintain a high rate of growth. Any stimuli to productive
activity that might have been encouraged by increased government
expenditures were frustrated by the lack of basic social capital in
general and of a national transportation network in particular, by the
subsistence nature of the greater part of the agricultural sector, and
by the fact that the economy was completely exposed to external competition. These factors, together with the fixed parity between the
Panamanian monetary unit (the balboa) and the U.S. dollar (imposed by
the 1904 treaty), guaranteed (and still do) that world deflation and inflation will be eventually and inescapably transmitted in full measure
to the Panamanian economy; that is, the country cannot prevent fluctuations in world markets and economic conditions from determining
the rate and level of domestic prices and economic activity. [9]

Many of Panama's employment problems arose during this
period from the fact that the country's monetary system ties the rate
of growth of domestic expenditure to that of exports. By checking the
expansion of domestic expenditure, the expansion of employment was
also restricted. The traditional way of achieving a degree of economic
independence through import replacement was restricted by the country's limited opportunities for achieving low-cost production levels

(economies of scale) and by the country's natural resource limitations.
All of these facts combined to give the country its worst period of
stagnation in the early and middle 1930s. Since reliable statistical data
are not available for this period, only a few general observations can
be made.

Panama's prewar geographical pattern of development became
extremely concentrated, with most of the country's economic activity
located in the two terminal cities—a situation that had attracted
workers from the rest of the country. Since most of the government's
revenues came from the canal, these were spent in improving the
social infrastructure of the terminal cities, especially Panama City.
Given the government's limited revenues, little public expenditure
was undertaken in areas outside the immediate vicinity of the Zone.
Since communications to the rest of the country had not been developed,
the demand for goods generated by the residents of the Canal Zone and
the terminal cities was incapable of stimulating production in the rest
of the country. Nearly all the industrial and commercial activities
were concentrated in the metropolitan areas (the provinces of Panama
and Colon). The economy was thus split into two distinct sections:
over one-third of the population lived in urban areas near the terminal
cities, with relatively high incomes, better transport, and more advanced social services. The remaining two-thirds who were still
living in the countryside were largely outside the monetary economy
and were living at subsistence levels.

By the 1930s, therefore, the structure of the economy had
been molded by the canal. Most of the Republic east of the Canal Zone,
and nearly all the north coast to the west, remained virgin tropical
forest. Population increased rapidly in the south and west, but towns
in those areas were still small—some even smaller than before 1800,
particularly in the rural areas.[10]

The social system of those years had changed little from the
time of the original Spanish settlements. Incomes of most of the
people were not only low but very unevenly distributed; most of the
adults in the rural areas were illiterate; and the country was politically
in the hands of several of the more prominent families.

Finally, the economy was highly sensitive to international
developments. Exports consisted almost exclusively of services to the
Canal Zone and the export of a few primary products. Little industrialization had taken place because the country maintained unrestricted
trade with the rest of the world. As a result, the country depended
heavily on imports for most of its nonfood items. Many industries
were unable to compete against imports because the government gave
local entrepreneurs only limited protection from foreign producers,
and the country's poorly developed transportation system made it
cheaper for residents of the Zone and terminal cities to purchase

imports rather than domestically produced goods.

The government was incapable of picking up the slack in demand by increasing its expenditures, since its tax base was very low. * Forty percent of the urban labor force during the 1930s was employed in the Zone. Import tariffs on most consumer durables and clothing were negligible. Since a substantial part of the population had access to the Canal Zone commissaries (which imported goods duty free), most Panamanians could obtain these goods either through family or social ties. Although an income tax was enacted in 1934, the wages paid by the Zone authorities to Panamanians were exempted from the tax by the treaty of 1903. Consequently the burden of taxation fell on the rest of the employed population in the republic. These workers, however, had much lower wages, and hence provided a much more limited source of revenue than those working in the Canal Zone. Over 50 percent of tax revenues stemmed from import duties on essential consumer goods. Another 30 percent came from excise taxes on gasoline and domestically produced liquor, with the remainder mainly from corporate profit and personal income taxes.[11]

Until World War II, therefore, Panama had gone through several expansionary phases during periods of high demand for its exports. Those periods were rather short lived, however, both because of the country's inability to develop a diversified structure of domestic production and its inability to compete with imports. Those booms, therefore, had been mere fleeting periods of prosperity and when they ceased, the country reversed to its more common state of unemployment and slow growth.

It is clear that the free-market mechanisms relied on for the country's growth were unable to correct the country's numerous economic problems. The structure of the economy was essentially the same as in the decades immediately following the construction of the canal: Canal Zone activities still provided the essential demand needed to maintain growth. No other new source of growth of any significance had emerged. At the same time the Canal Zone activities and lack of government protection from foreign goods inhibited industrialization; that is, imports expanded rapidly so that the growth of domestic industries was checked. What was needed was a more direct involvement of the government in the growth process.

---

*At this time the government was not permitted to tax the incomes of Panamanians working in the Canal Zone but residing in Panama. See Chapter 9 of the text for a more detailed description of this problem.

THE POSTWAR PERIOD—1945-56

With World War II and the increased activity in the Canal Zone
associated with the operation and defense of the canal, prosperity re-
turned: the demand for locally produced goods and services rose substantially; the resident population (both military and civilian) of the
Zone expanded as did Panamanian manpower employed in that area. In
addition, the war led to an exceptional increase in the number of pas-
sengers in transit. The net effect of these developments was a rapid
expansion of demand for domestically (Panamanian) produced products.
For the first time in its history the country's domestic markets became large enough to enable entrepreneurs to produce profitably a
number of products previously imported.

The high growth rates experienced during World War II, however, were somewhat illusory. Manufacturing was still a minor component of GDP (8.2 percent in 1945). In addition, much of the increase
in the domestic product was not equated with higher standards of living; it merely offset the increasing costs involved in urbanization—that
is, food had to be brought farther, and city transport and water supplies
had to be expanded.

At the end of the war the economy still revolved almost exclusively around the Canal Zone. Services to the Canal Zone accounted
for 21.0 percent of the gross domestic product (GDP) in 1945, but only
7.7 percent in 1950. The fall in export receipts to the Zone had a major
deflationary effect on the economy. Fortunately, the accumulation of
funds by Panamanian workers during the war and the reduction in domestic prices relative to imports helped pick up the slack in demand by
facilitating high levels of domestic consumption expenditures. The
stabilizing effect of private consumption on aggregate demand was particularly important during the depression phase of the years 1946-51—
when these expenditures expanded from 222.6 million in 1946 to 253.0
million in 1951. During this period the gross national product (GNP)
declined from 274.4 million balboas (B/274.4 million) to B/271.1 million, reaching a low of B/255.5 million in 1947, (Table 2.1)

After the war, Panama's pattern of development began to
change. External competition was eliminated in certain areas as the
government began to control imports through tariffs and quotas. The
public authorities also encouraged the development of domestic production and embarked on a series of investment projects designed to
expand the country's social overhead capital. This in turn stimulated
private expenditure. This expansion in domestic expenditure, both
public and private, not only mediated to a certain degree the depression
after the war, but—which is much more important in the long run—
broadened the internal market and thus stimulated for the first time
the growth of production for the domestic (non-Zone) market; the

TABLE 2.1

Trends in the Panamanian Economy, 1945–56

(in millions of 1950 balboas)

	1945	1946	1947	1948	1949	1950	1951	1952	1953	1954	1955	1956
Private consumption	164.3	191.8	206.2	188.5	194.4	212.6	221.7	232.4	230.4	242.1	256.8	264.4
Public consumption	28.6	30.8	29.6	28.1	27.0	31.6	31.3	34.1	35.6	39.8	38.4	41.3
Total consumption	192.9	222.6	235.8	216.6	221.4	244.2	253.0	266.5	266.0	281.9	295.2	305.7
Private investment	22.0	30.5	29.7	31.2	26.6	19.9	21.9	23.9	32.1	33.6	35.9	36.2
Public investment	14.5	11.5	11.7	6.0	4.1	8.6	5.9	7.7	7.5	6.3	8.9	13.0
Total investment	36.5	42.0	41.4	37.2	30.7	28.5	27.8	31.6	39.6	39.9	44.8	49.2
Exports (E)	131.7	124.7	83.8	83.8	86.0	78.0	70.0	71.7	78.5	85.3	92.5	92.4
Imports (M)	86.7	103.8	103.8	82.1	78.1	80.4	79.7	89.0	87.3	93.9	98.0	103.9
E – M	45.0	20.9	-19.0	1.7	7.9	-2.4	-9.7	-17.3	-8.8	-8.6	-5.5	-11.5
Savings	81.5	62.9	21.5	38.9	38.6	26.1	18.1	14.3	30.8	31.3	39.3	37.7
Gross National Product	274.4	285.5	257.3	255.5	260.0	270.3	271.1	280.8	296.8	313.2	334.5	343.4

Source: Compiled from United Nations Economic Commission for Latin America, Analysis and Projections of Economic Development, VII, The Economic Development of Panama (Panama City, 1959): 23.

early 1950s therefore denote the period when the government began to
play a relatively active role in the economy.

Panama's experience during the war had proved the country's
capacity to achieve a respectable rate of national economic growth
during periods of heavy canal traffic or strong world demand for Panama's exports. But this economic growth could not be sustained if for
any reason Canal Zone or export activity slackened.

In the early 1950s the government's major concern about the
future development of the country arose from a changing pattern in the
traditional elements of Panama's economic growth. Historically, the
foundations of the economy were built up largely as a natural, unaided,
and unguided process. The country's growth had been mainly the result of the expansion and enterprise of the population in an attractive
and undemanding environment oriented toward serving the needs of the
Canal Zone. The transit trade and revenues obtained from the Panama
Canal had been the mainstays of the economy. Yet after the war these
activities began to slacken and there was little indication that they
would be a driving force in the economy as they had been in the past.
Changing world trade patterns and new sources of internal demand
dictated a change in the government's policies toward the economy.
It was at this point that questions arose concerning the ability of the
public sector to obtain more control over the economy, and its desirability.

CONSTRAINTS ON GROWTH, 1945-56

The economic trends experienced by Panama through the
period 1945-56 suggest a number of forces that shaped the economic
structure of the country: (1) the behavior of individuals and the
country's institutions:* (2) imported technological know-how:
(3) policies of the government; and (4) exogenous factors (or forces
outside the country's control). It is possible to express a number of
these in quantitative terms.

Developments in the Panamanian economy during this period
were characterized by generally low and uneven growth rates, by an
almost chronic balance of payments deficit, a very low rate of
inflation, rising unemployment, and serious difficulties in diversifying
exports. Yet there were elements of stability in the economy; private

---

*In general the word "institutions" is used in the text as
referring to the treaties with the United States.

consumption demand remained high, as did investment. The model developed here tries to identify some of the interrelationships between these factors; it also serves as the basis for comparing the structure of the economy in 1945-56 with that of other time periods, thus enabling an identification of the country's major structural changes over time.

In examining the changes in growth patterns in Panama over time it is useful to make a distinction between the various types of constraints on the country's economic growth. At the macro level it is possible to make a distinction between two major factors (domestic savings and imports) whose scarcity may have at one time or another caused the country to grow at a rate lower than its potential. The rate of investment in the Panamanian economy appears to be a function of the willingness and ability of entrepreneurs to mobilize savings. It is possible that the Panamanian willingness to save, though it appears substantial, may at times have been impaired by the inability of entrepreneurs to channel these funds into investment, that is, to acquire through international trade the imports necessary for domestic investment.[12]

The inability of the country to transform its domestic savings into investment stems from the low level of economic integration in Panama after World War II. For example, domestic savings might not be converted into additional foreign exchange earnings either because increased export production or increased production of import replacements, or both, were not economically viable at the time. This picture of the economy is consistent with its structure—a country exporting mainly consumer goods and importing mainly capital goods and intermediate products necessary for domestic production.

Because of the rigidities in the economy (for example, deficiencies in transport)the country was unlikely to be in a position to adjust, after the war, to sudden changes in world demand for its exports, and thus might not have obtained the imports necessary to facilitate the required level of investment for sustained growth.

If the attainment of a given level of national income in Panama requires a minimum flow of imports of goods and services to achieve a certain level of investment, a trade gap could exist. This gap would be equal to the excess of required imports over the existing level of exports. Similarly a savings gap could exist. This would be represented by the amount by which intended or potential savings fall short of investment needs. By the national income accounting conventions used in Panama, the two gaps must be identical; the net inflow of foreign capital—that is, the excess of imports over exports— would be equal to the excess of investment over savings, and to the excess of resources used by the economy over the resources supplied by it.[13]

In terms of the levels of imports needed by entrepreneurs and the amount of savings desired by individuals, however, it is quite likely that the two gaps would be numerically different during any given periods of time (again the actual or realized levels are equal because they are defined that way in the national income accounts). The difference in the desired magnitudes would be a reflection of any disequilibrium in the economy, a disequilibrium that might have persisted over several years because it took a long time for the productive structure of the Panamanian economy to adjust fully to changes in international market forces. In a changing world, therefore, it is possible that the intentions of Panamanians to save, invest, import, and export are not mutually consistent. They are made by different individuals and no mechanism may exist to bring about their equality over a given period of time. This is a direct consequence of the fact that the economy lacks the ability to alter its production methods or production structure in a relatively short period of time. This hypothesis is tested and the mechanisms and constraints on Panamanian growth[14] are identified in Appendix A.

It is also possible that foreign capital inflows might reduce domestic savings in Panama.[15] If this is the case, the net benefits of foreign capital to the economy may be significantly less than their absolute magnitudes would suggest. Since foreign inflows are a major item in the Panamanian balance of payments, it is important to determine the impact on domestic savings and thus the country's growth. A significant result of the analysis is that they are completely complementary (as evidenced by the negative sign and value of -1.0 coefficient of F in equation A.11 in Appendix A).

The foreign exchange constraint on Panamanian development implies that during this period (1945-56) the country could neither increase its exports (or their rate of growth) nor reduce its imports (or their rate of growth). If these changes were possible, the excess of the foreign exchange gap over the savings gap could have been reduced and possibly eliminated. Apparently both export possibilities and import requirements were determined by technical considerations and world market forces, and were thus not under the influence of the Panamanian planners. During this period the country had a productive structure that was built almost exclusively around the Canal Zone. It might be thought that labor-intensive manufactured goods would have provided a way of expanding exports. But many of these types of exports require special labor skills and in any case the high wage levels in Panama (as a result of wage scales in the Zone) placed the country at a distinct disadvantage for these types of products.

On the other hand, since the country's required import level was also inflexible in the short run, one might argue that the nation's strategy would have been to restrict luxury imports. This avenue would have been soon exhausted, however. Techniques, especially in the industrial sector, were inflexible and the capital goods industry was too primitive to allow more than a small proportion of the required machines and intermediate goods to be made domestically. All of these factors combined to place Panama in a position where its growth was totally limited by its inability to increase exports.

Despite problems in the foreign sector, a number of stable relationships existed in the Panamanian economy. These allowed the country to survive the sharp fall in postwar export earnings. The major sources of demand—consumption and investment—did not decline significantly during the temporary drop in the overall rate of GNP growth. This is indicated by equations A.1, A.2, and A.4 in Appendix A.

CONCLUSIONS

By 1955 Panama had developed a distinct set of characteristics that were to establish the pattern of development in the country for some time. First, structural transformation still had a long way to go—in spite of the country's relatively high level of per capita income. Second, the economy was very dependent, not only structurally in the sense that there was a high ratio of foreign trade to GNP, but also there was great reliance on foreign capital inflows to sustain growth. The inability of the country to finance levels of imports necessary for domestic investment was the chief limitation on the country. Third, because the population had begun to taste the fruits of development as a result of the high levels of economic activity during the war, any slowing down in the pace of development was fraught with dangers of social and political unrest. The development effort in the years ahead had to be intensified in order to accommodate the rising population with their heightened expectations of material improvement and in order to compensate for the expected decline in the rate of growth of the Canal Zone.

The government was somewhat limited, however, in playing a very active role in the economy: only two development approaches were available to it: (1) a pattern of development based on import replacement, and (2) a pattern based primarily on export growth. These strategies of development can be illustrated in terms of the following simple algebra:

$$\frac{\Delta Y}{\Delta t} > \frac{\Delta E}{\Delta t} \qquad \text{and} \qquad (2.1)$$

$$\frac{\Delta Y}{\Delta t} \leq \frac{\Delta E}{\Delta t} \qquad\qquad\qquad (2.2)$$

where Y = GDP (which by the assumption of no net capital movements is equal to gross domestic expenditure), E = exports (which by the assumption of no net capital movements and no net payments of profits abroad = imports), t = time, and Δ = the change during a specified time period.

Panamanian growth up to the middle 1950s had been almost entirely by the mechanism expressed in equation 2.1. The question facing the country in the early 1950s was how much scope did the government have for modifying the relationship expressed in equation 2.2. It seems there was some limited scope, for protection of local import—replacing industry was not the only means of modifying the existing relationship between the rate of growth of domestic expenditure and the rate of growth of exports. For example, the construction sector—especially housing (whose output is obviously not tradable in international markets) had the potential to be a more propulsive sector of the economy. Analytically the government had at its disposal two mechanisms for effecting this. One was the deliberate changing of private consumption patterns away from imported goods either by trying to influence individual decisions or by the use of its policy instruments. This strategy would not result in a strain on the balance of payments since there would be a shift from expenditure on imports to expenditure on housing, and thus the constraint placed on growth by the trade gap could be eased. The other alternative was some limited application of direct financing of construction expenditures through expansion of the money supply and some limited measure of controls to suppress inflationary pressures and to prevent a strain on the balance of payments. This would, of course, involve more autonomy in the conduct of monetary management than the government possessed.

But even after allowing for increased monetary autonomy (which would require a change in the 1904 treaty), an expansion of government expenditure, and limited application of controls over prices and imports in order to give the government greater domestic control to expand employment and to mobilize resources, the fact still remained that Panama's size alone made the country dependent on foreign trade and on foreign private capital inflows for sustained growth. This fact ruled out the implementation of a system of trade and price controls of the extreme form often practiced in many of the large and medium-sized countries.[16]

NOTES

1. See William C. Merrill, et al., Panama's Economic Development : The Role of Agriculture (Ames: Iowa State University Press, 1975), Chapters 3 and 4.

2. An interesting point made by Louis Harris in "Panama," in Political Forces in Latin America, ed. Ben G. Burnett and Kenneth F. Johnson(Belmont, California: Wadsworth, 1968),chapter 5.

3. This is changing with the creation of the Instituto Panameno de Turismo. See the Institute's Estudios Sectoriales: Potencial de la Industria de Turismo (Panama City: Direccion General de Planificacion y Administracion de la Presidencia, Departamento de Planificacion, 1970.)

4. Joint Tax Program of the OAS/IDB, Fiscal Survey of Panama: Problems and Proposals for Reform (Baltimore: Johns Hopkins Press, 1964), p. 3.

5. An excellent summary of the post-1968 Government's aims and objectives is given by Nicolas Ardito Barletta in Que Presenta a la Asamblea Nacional De Representantes de Corregimentos (Panama City: Ministerio De Planificacion y Politica Economica, October 1973).

6. For Latin America in general see Alexandre Kafka, "The Theoretical Interpretation of Latin American Economic Development," in Economic Development for Latin America, ed. Howard Ellis (London: Macmillan, 1963), pp. 1-28.

7. An excellent description and bibliography of this early period is given by Emilio Clare. See his "Apuntes de Politica Economica", mimeographed (Panama City: Universidad de Panama, Facultad de Administracion Publica y Comercio, 1970).

8. The word "openness" as used here is defined in Ronald I. McKinnon and Wallace E. Oates, The Implications of International Economic Integration for Monetary, Fiscal, and Exchange-Rate Policy (Princeton, N.J.: Princeton University, International Finance Section, Department of Economics, 1966); and Marina von Neuman Whitman, International and Interregional Payments Adjustment: A Synthetic View (Princeton, N.J.: Princeton University, International Finance Section, Department of Economics, 1967).

9. Larry Sjaastad, "Prices and Wages in Panama," mimeographed (Panama City: U.S. Agency for International Development, 1973), p. 6.

10. See John and Mavis Biesanz, The People of Panama (New York: Columbia University Press, 1955), chapters 2 and 3.

11. Joint Tax Program, Fiscal Survey of Panama: op. cit., chapters 1, 2, and 3.

12. A basic assumption in the model and projections presented in Chapter 13. A critique on this assumption and others associated with the so-called "two gap models" is given by Vijay Joshi, "Saving and Foreign Exchange Constraints," in Unfashionable Economics—Essays in Honour of Thomas Blough, ed. Paul Streeten (London: Weidenfeld and Nicolson, 1970).

13. As elaborated upon by Jaroslav Vanek in his Estimating Foreign Resource Needs for Economic Development (New York: McGraw-Hill, 1967), chapter 6.

14. For a similar approach see Luis Landau, "Saving Functions for Latin America," in Studies in Development Planning, ed. Hollis Chenery (Cambridge, Mass.: Harvard University Press, 1971), chapter 13.

15. See M. A. Rahman, "Foreign Capital and Domestic Savings: A Test of Haavelmo's Hypothesis with Cross Country Data," Review of Economics and Statistics, no.1 (February 1968) 137-38; and K. B. Griffin and J. L. Enos, "Foreign Assistance: Objectives and Consequences," Economic Development and Cultural Change 18, no. 3 (April 1970): 313-27.

16. For an extreme form of "disequilibrium system," see J. Clark Leith, Foreign Trade Regimes & Economic Development: Ghana (New York: Columbia University Press, 1974). The theory is summarized in Charles P. Kindleberger, "Liberal Policies vs. Controls in the Foreign Trade of Developing Countries", mimeographed (Washington, D.C.: Agency for International Development, 1967).

3

ECONOMIC TRENDS
FROM 1955 TO
THE PRESENT

With the stimulus of the war and increased government expenditure, Panama's economic growth began to accelerate from an average annual rate of about 2 percent in the late 1940s and early 1950s (1945-56) to over 6.2 percent in the 1955-65 period, and to 8.2 between 1966 and 1973[1] (Table 3.1).

The major impetus to this growth was the signing, in 1955, of the Remon-Eisenhower Treaty.[2] The treaty included three major clauses that radically changed the economic relationship between the Canal Zone and the economy of Panama. The crucial changes were:

(1) A single minimum wage scale was adopted for both Panamanian and United States employees. Prior to 1955 there had been a dual wage scale, with Panamanians earning considerably less than did the Americans.

(2) Nonresidents (mostly Panamanians) of the Canal Zone were greatly restricted in their use of commissary and import privileges. Before 1955 virtually all Panamanian Canal Zone workers had purchased most of their consumer goods at the nonprofit commissaries in the Zone.

(3) The Canal Zone's manufacturing and processing activities were closed down. The Zone's commercial dairy, laundries, shops, and other agricultural and service activities were thus phased out.

Each of these factors contributed to the demand for Panamanian-produced goods.

TABLE 3.1

National Income Statistics, Selected Years, 1950-73
(in millions of 1960 balboas)

Income Source	1950	1955	1960	1965	1970	1973
GDP	259.2	314.7	415.8	617.3	894.5	1,101.2
	105.4	122.6	149.1	256.4	396.4	464.1
Net factor payments	-10.6	-17.3	-12.4	-15.8	-26.4	-40.3
	(4.3)	(5.8)	(3.1)	(2.6)	(3.0)	(3.8)
GNP	248.6	297.4	403.4	601.5	868.1	1,060.9
Government consumption	34.2	38.0	46.9	67.0	102.4	125.5
	(13.8)	(12.8)	(11.6)	(11.1)	(11.8)	(11.8)
Private consumption	179.5	238.8	322.9	470.5	621.8	765.0
	(72.2)	(80.3)	(80.0)	(78.2)	(71.6)	(72.1)
Total consumption	213.7	276.8	369.8	537.5	724.2	890.5
	(86.0)	(93.1)	(91.7)	(89.4)	(83.4)	(83.9)
Private investment	26.5	32.5	49.4	75.4	162.9	220.1
	(10.7)	(10.9)	(12.4)	(12.5)	(18.8)	(20.7)
Government investment	9.6	10.1	12.0	21.7	59.0	80.8
	(3.9)	(3.4)	(3.0)	(3.6)	(6.8)	(7.6)
Change in stocks	5.0	4.2	6.4	15.7	20.3	22.3
	(2.0)	(1.4)	(1.6)	(2.6)	(2.3)	(2.1)
Total investment	41.1	46.8	67.8	112.8	242.2	323.2
	(16.5)	(15.7)	(16.8)	(18.8)	(27.9)	(30.5)
Import surplus (goods and nonfactor services)	-4.4	8.9	21.8	33.0	71.9	112.5
	(1.8)	(3.0)	(5.4)	(5.5)	(4.6)	(10.6)
Net import surplus	-15.0	-8.4	9.4	17.2	45.5	72.2
	(6.0)	(2.8)	(2.3)	(2.9)	(8.3)	(6.8)
Savings	34.9	20.6	33.6	64.0	143.9	170.4
	(14.0)	(6.9)	(8.3)	(10.6)	(16.6)	(16.1)
Savings-investment (external savings)	-6.2	-26.2	-34.2	-48.8	-98.3	-152.8
	(2.5)	(8.8)	(8.5)	(8.1)	(11.3)	(14.4)

Note: Figures in parentheses indicate percentage of GNP.
Source: Computed from Contraloria General de la Republica, Direccion de Estadistica y Censo, Ingreso Nacional, various issues.

THE 1955-56 PERIOD

One of the most remarkable features of this period of economic expansion was that it was accompanied by practically no inflation. Both government and private business had played key positive roles in the expansion: private business mainly through heavy reinvestment of profits in expanded productive capacity, and government through the building of social overhead capital—schools, an improved transport system, and a better communications network.

As was the case between 1945 and 1956, this period's growth was constrained by the foreign sector. An estimation of equations, using single stage least squares method of estimation,

$$S_t = a_1 + b_1 Y_t + b_2 F_t \tag{3.1}$$

and

$$M_t = a_2 + b_3 Y_t + b_4 F_t \tag{3.2}$$

indicates that the country could grow no faster than its ability to import capital equipment necessary for expanding the nation's productive capacity (see Appendix A for a description of the model and symbols).

$$S_t = -10.9507 + 0.2124 \, Y_t - 1.0257 \, F_t \tag{3.3}$$
$$(10.8230) \quad (3.3861)$$
$$r^2 = 0.96 \qquad DW = 2.2$$

$$M_t = -32.6686 + 0.4242 \, Y_t + 0.6144 \, F_t \tag{3.4}$$
$$(13.0238) \quad (1.2725)$$
$$r^2 = 0.82 \qquad DW = 1.7$$

Since the trade gap was binding[3] during this period, actual imports were the same as desired imports or

$$M_t = -17.9497 + 0.4415 \tag{3.5}$$
$$(23.7621) \quad (11.8763)$$
$$r^2 = .96 \qquad DW = 1.3$$

Thus the country's growth between 1955 and 1965 was still
(as between 1945 and 1956) dependent on foreign capital imports. Despite
this fact the increase in capital formation was still imperative. Panama was able, in large part, to grow rapidly during this period by
receiving high inflows of foreign aid, thus enabling the country to
maintain steady increases in investment (Appendix C).

Panama's expenditure pattern was at that time still dominated
by the private sector. During the late 1950s private consumption and
investment constituted about 85 percent of the country's GNP, whereas
government investment amounted to about 3 percent. The structural
changes in the country's internal demand after 1955 were therefore
mainly due to variations in the composition of private expenditure.
Private investment increased rapidly, averaging about 10 percent of
GNP in the 1950s, and increasing to about 15 percent by the mid-1960s.
At the same time savings of the private sector managed to grow fast
enough to more than finance the higher levels of capital formation.
The expanding banking system, high interest rates (competitive with
those prevailing in international capital markets), and the relative
affluence of the terminal cities (Panama City and Colon) all encouraged
high levels of savings.

While the government played a somewhat increasing role in
the economy during this period, through expanding its expenditures
(in absolute terms), its approach to the country's development up to
the early 1960s was never defined. Its first real development plan was
for the years 1962-66.[4] Prior to this plan, the government had never
adopted a development program covering a period of more than one or
two years. Ad hoc projects and annual appropriations were the prevailing pattern of public participation in economic development. Even
the five-year plan, formally adopted in 1963, was neither properly
funded nor rigorously administered, serving merely as a somewhat
vague guideline for the government's development expenditures.
Yet from occasional official declarations, from the pattern of public
expenditures during this period, from the government's conduct of
monetary and fiscal policy, and from the tenor of legislation, one
can easily infer that the dominant philosophy of the government's
economic policy during most of the postwar period was one of
favoring the promotion of trade and services, leaning heavily toward
assuring the private sector the greatest degree of freedom in its
internal and external economic relations.[5]

In addition the government kept out of many spheres that,
in other countries, were becoming legitimate public domain, even
in the advanced market-oriented countries in Western Europe. Many
public utilities were privately owned and run. Apart from its general
policy of ensuring freedom for private enterprise, the government

contributed directly to economic development through legislation
and the establishment of public (autonomous) agencies and departments
designed to serve some economic and social developmental purposes.
Government activity came essentially in the form of individual,
often uncoordinated, public works programs: that is, public sector
investments were not selected on the basis of their contribution to a
set of objectives contained in a long-run development plan.

Still the economy boomed. In 1961, for example, the gross
domestic product increased by about 7.5 percent. In the same year
the increase in domestic product exceeded the annual average growth
rate of 3.3 percent for the preceding 16 years, the average growth of
5.3 percent from 1951 to 1961, and even the very substantial increase
for 1960 of 6.4 percent. With an estimated yearly population increase
of 2.8 percent at that time, the net increase in per capita gross
domestic product in 1961 was 4.6 percent. Considering that the goal
of the Alliance for Progress[6] was an average annual increase in per
capita income of 2.5 percent in Latin America, Panama quite
obviously was ahead of schedule under the Alliance.

Despite these favorable trends in the aggregate GNP and
per capita income, it was difficult to find anything else that could
produce a feeling of satisfaction. Stating the domestic product in
terms of a per capita average obscured the fact that the unequal
distribution of income in Panama in the early 1960s resulted in a
part of the population being no better off than if they had lived in the
poorest and most stagnant economy in Latin America. While in 1960
the average family income was approximately B/2,000, about 16
percent of the family units had an income of less than B/1,000. A
hundred individuals or companies owned one-third of the agricultural
land, and 34,000 operated the remaining two-thirds. Sixteen percent
of the families at the lower end of the income scale received 6 percent
of the national income in 1960, while 13 percent of the families at the
higher end of the scale received 32 percent.[7]

THE 1966-73 PERIOD

Several features characterize the 1965-73 period.[8] First,
in terms of investment, only a small proportion of the country's
increase in investment resulted from increases in stocks. In 1968,
for example, the increase in stocks amounted to only 10.3 percent of
gross domestic investment. This indicates that aggregate demand
was keeping pace with aggregate supply. Second, since 1965, the
rate of total investment (particularly since 1968) has risen constantly
so that by 1973 it accounted for over 30 percent of GNP, whereas in

1960 it accounted for only 17 percent. This gave Panama one of the highest rates of capital formation in Latin America. *

One reason for the increase in investment stemmed from the fact that after 1965 the trade gap was no longer binding; that is, estimations of equations 3.1 and 3.2 yielded:

$$S_t = -66.0003 + 0.2699 \, Y_t - 0.2538 \, F_t \tag{3.5}$$
$$(2.0855) \qquad (0.5599)$$

$$r^2 = 0.92 \qquad DW = 2.1$$

$$M_t = -85.7811 + 0.4804 \, Y_t + 0.9880 \, F_t \tag{3.6}$$
$$(3.3549) \qquad (1.9696)$$

$$r^2 = 0.83 \qquad DW = 1.2$$

Since the coefficient of F_t in equation 3.5 is not statistically different from zero, and the coefficient of F_t in equation 3.6 is significantly positive, one could reasonably conclude that domestic savings (or the savings-investment gap) was binding during this period[9]. The replacement of domestic savings for imports as the main constraint on growth could have occurred for several reasons:

(1) Some goods and services that were potentially exportable began to be consumed domestically, thereby reducing savings.

(2) Some imports required for producing those exports were employed in the production of goods for the internal market.

(3) An increase in the level of private consumption was caused by shifting demand toward nontraded (domestically produced) goods. In part this last effect could be measured by an increase in the ratio of the consumption price index to the price index of total expenditures.

To test this hypothesis the price level is given by total expenditure in current prices divided by total available resources in the economy measured in constant (1960) prices, or

---

*See Appendix C for a comparison with other high-growth countries.

$$P = \frac{E}{Y + M - X} \qquad (3.7)$$

where P = general price level, E = total money expenditure of current prices, Y = GDP at constant prices, M = imports (including net factor payments at constant prices), and X = exports at constant prices. P is measured as GDP at current prices minus (value added by government minus depreciation allowances). The realized savings is then:

$$XS = S - (CS - C) \qquad (3.8)$$

where S = potential saving, CS - actual consumption, XS = actual savings, and C = desired consumption. The rise in the consumption price index, as defined above, will indicate the inflationary pressure due to inadequate potential savings.

The level of potential savings was determined when the trade gap was completely binding—the period 1955-65, and is given by equation 3.3. This indicates that the level of potential savings

$$S_t = -10.9463 + .2124\ Y_t \qquad (3.9)$$

is equal to the required investment for the associated level of income. Given the relatively high aid strategy followed by Panama during this period, it is reasonable to assume that there was enough foreign capital flowing in to fill the trade gap $(M - X)$. Since the actual value of the savings and trade gaps must be equal, there must have been a fall in savings below the potential value, an increase in investment, or both. Since private foreign investment (mainly in bananas and the oil refinery) and aid were unlikely to compete with local entrepreneurs for investment opportunities, it is assumed that the realized investment in Panama during the 1955-65 period was always equal to the potential level—that is, the minimum required for the attained level of income. Therefore all the adjustment was done by savings. This being the case, the actual savings fell short of the potential levels by an amount equal to F: foreign capital inflows were a complete substitute for savings.

Using equation 3.1 with F_t = O to estimate the potential level of savings for the 1955-65 period and subtracting each year's investment, it is clear that from 1955 to 1965 (particularly 1960-65) the country was in a position to have easily financed the required level of investment from domestic funds (Table 3.2).

TABLE 3.2

Sources of Excess Consumption Demand, 1960–72
(in millions of 1960 balboas)

Year	E	P	PC	PC/P	XS	S	XS-I	S-I
1960	375.4	0.8342	0.7414	0.8888	33.6	74.4	-34.2	6.9
1961	417.5	0.8470	0.8575	0.9227	54.1	84.7	-32.0	-1.4
1962	454.1	0.8617	0.8122	0.9426	68.9	93.1	-28.1	3.9
1963	493.4	0.8455	0.7814	0.9242	66.9	102.0	-42.1	-6.8
1964	532.5	0.8864	0.8084	0.9116	64.2	108.0	-35.2	13.6
1965	586.0	0.8797	0.7932	0.9017	64.0	116.8	-48.8	-4.0
1966	645.0	0.8994	0.8511	0.9463	97.1	126.6	-53.1	-23.6
1967	721.6	0.9277	0.8721	0.9401	101.6	137.4	-56.9	-48.1
1968	788.9	0.9618	0.9353	0.9724	130.5	145.7	-49.0	-32.0
1969	786.0	0.9590	0.9128	0.9518	128.4	161.3	-77.1	-44.2
1970	947.6	0.9545	0.9156	0.9592	143.9	173.4	-98.3	-68.8
1971	1,036.1	0.9423	0.9974	0.9497	149.1	189.0	-126.9	-87.1
1972	1,145.1	0.9722	0.9580	0.9844	187.2	201.9	-144.1	-131.4

Note: See equations 3.7 and 3.8 in the text for identification of symbols.

Source: Compiled by author.

A sharp change took place in 1966, however, as the country's growth was apparently becoming more constrained by its inability to mobilize domestic savings. This is evidenced by the increasing gap between not only actual, but potential savings. The rise in the calculated consumer price index (Table 3.2) indicates that inflationary pressures were also beginning to increase as a result of inadequate potential savings.

For several years after 1968 the government was able to maintain the growth rates of the 1960s. But since 1972, the development of world inflation and increasing domestic inflationary pressures have resulted in some deterioration of the country's economic performance. In 1974, Panama's economic growth dropped to the lowest rate experienced in recent years, to an estimated 3.5 percent compared with 6.5 percent in 1973. Contributing to this relative deterioration in economic activity was the continuing slack in agriculture, a slowdown in the manufacturing sector, and after a construction boom in the early 1970s, a rapid decline in the rate of growth of the construction industry. The current economic downturn after years of boom has evoked expressions of gloom from many local businessmen.

With an open economy closely geared to international trade, Panama has, in the last few years, been considerably affected by foreign inflation. As long as inflation in the United States and Panama's other trading partners was low, the economy did not experience any marked rise in its domestic price level. During the 1960s and through 1971, Panama's consumer price index rose at an annual rate of about 1.5 percent. Domestic inflation did not increase until 1970, two years after the start of inflation in the United States. By 1972 consumer prices were rising by 6.7 percent. This trend continued in 1973 with the December 1973 consumer price index up by 18.7 percent for the same period. Indexes of import prices and general wholesale prices both rose by about 26 percent during 1974, while the local consumer price index registered a 17 percent increase.[*]

Admittedly, the poor performance in recent years is by no means entirely of Panama's own making. Adverse weather conditions reduced the export of bananas, its main crop. The price of oil and other imports increased and the government could do little about it. In addition, the Zone has not helped pick up the slack in the economy by expanding its demand for Panamanian products. For example, between 1960 and 1971 the Panamanian work force in the Zone grew

---

*Preliminary data supplied by the Ministerio de Planificacion y Politica Economica.

at an annual rate of only 2.7 percent. Since 1968 the value added
from the Zone has dropped from 8.5 percent of GDP to 6.5 percent
(1973). Canal operations have expanded slowly, no new workers are
being hired, and the number of U.S. residents in the Zone and their
purchases of goods and services in Panama have not grown. Given
the government's new development priorities—the alleviation of ine-
quality, and growth with economic independence—the authorities
feel that they can not expect the canal to play a major economic role
in the country's future unless the treaty relationships between the
United States and Panama are changed.

Because of the downturn in economic activity, local political
leaders, particularly since 1970, have made an issue of U.S. control
of the Canal Zone; most of the resentment stems from the fact that
the Panamanians consider their country entirely dependent on the
United States—"A country within a country".* There is no question
that ties with the United States have dominated Panamanian foreign
relations, and within the last few years, there has been increasing
concern over those economic ties. Many Panamanians feel that the
treaties with the United States have created an environment in which,
given the presence of the Zone, Panamanian fortunes are dependent
on policies established in Washington and on market forces of which
the republic has had only limited control.

This situation has led to growing Panamanian dissatisfaction
with the treaty and its amendments. Since June 1971, the representatives of the two countries have been engaged in negotiations over a
new agreement concerning the use and control of the Canal Zone.
The main stumbling block to agreement involves the timing of the
U.S. relinquishment of its sovereignty over the canal and the Canal
Zone, both of which, in the early 1970s, still continue to influence
the development of Panama in three major ways: direct, fiscal, and
institutional (clauses in the treaties restricting Panamanian
economic policies).

---

*It may well be that the timing of the granting of sovereignty
is a secondary issue to the one of whether sovereignty should be
granted at all. Recently 37 United States senators co-sponsored a
resolution that "The government of the United States should maintain
and protect its sovereign rights and jurisdiction over the canal and
zone, and should in no way cede, dilute, forfeit, negotiate, or transfer any of these sovereign rights...." See U.S. Senate Resolution
301, 93rd Congress, 2nd Session, March 29, 1974.

The Canal Zone's Influence on the Economy

Approximately 47,500 people live in the Canal Zone; of these, about 39,000 are U.S. citizens; the remainder are mostly Panamanians. Of the total population, about 26,500 are military or civilian personnel of the U.S. armed forces and their families; 10,400 are employees of the Panama Canal Company and the Canal Zone government, together with their families. Of the 11,000 non-U.S. citizens employed by the company and the government, less than 2,000 (including their families) live in the Zone;[10] the remainder live in the Republic of Panama. As noted, the demand for goods and services by the residents and workers in the Zone was one of the major stimuli to Panama's growth in the 1960s. In addition, each year the United States pays Panama approximately $2 million for the use of the canal—a form of compensation established by the 1903 treaty and increased (from $250,000) to its present level over the intervening years.

In quantitative terms about one-third of Panama's GNP is directly or indirectly attributable to the canal activity and the Zone's military bases. Receipts from the export of goods and services to the Zone account for about 45 percent of the country's foreign exchange receipts.

Nearly one-third of the Panamanian labor force is directly or indirectly engaged in activities related to the presence of the Zone. In fact, within 30 miles of the Zone, more than two-thirds of the country's employment is canal-oriented largely as a result of these activities. The presence of the Zone has therefore contributed significantly to Panama's per capita annual income of nearly $800 (1974) which is the highest in Central America and more than twice the average for Central America. It is the fourth highest in Latin America as a whole, exceeded only by that of Argentina, Venezuela, and Uruguay.

The Canal Zone has had a marked influence on the country's sectoral composition of output. Only three sectors account for the major part of the GNP—agriculture, manufacturing, and services (including commerce, finance, and Canal Zone services). These three sectors accounted for over 67 percent of total GDP or B/788.6 million (1960 prices) in 1973 (Table 3.4).

TABLE 3.3

Sectoral Production, 1950-73

(in millions of 1960 balboas)

Sector	1950	1955	1960	1965	1970	1973
Agriculture	74.5	86.0	95.2	132.2	161.1	178.5
	(28.7)	(27.3)	(23.0)	(21.4)	(18.0)	(16.2)
Mining	0.6	0.9	1.1	1.7	2.3	2.8
	(-)	(-)	(-)	(-)	(-)	(-)
Manufacturing	23.5	33.2	54.5	98.1	153.6	185.6
	(9.1)	(10.6)	(15.5)	(15.9)	(17.2)	(16.9)
Construction	10.6	13.5	22.9	34.9	54.0	78.3
	(4.1)	(4.3)	(5.5)	(5.7)	(6.0)	(7.1)
Utilities	3.2	4.5	8.4	14.5	26.0	42.7
	(1.2)	(1.4)	(2.0)	(2.3)	(2.9)	(3.9)
Transport and communication	10.0	13.4	19.3	32.9	59.6	79.4
	(3.9)	(4.3)	(4.6)	(5.3)	(6.7)	(7.2)
Commerce	34.9	40.2	57.9	85.8	126.6	155.2
	(13.5)	(12.8)	(13.9)	(13.9)	(14.2)	(14.1)
Finance	4.5	6.2	10.3	17.6	34.8	49.2
	(1.7)	(2.0)	(2.5)	(2.9)	(3.9)	(4.5)
Housing	23.3	27.2	34.5	43.4	60.1	80.5
	(9.0)	(8.6)	(8.3)	(7.0)	(6.7)	(7.3)
Public administration	6.7	7.3	11.4	15.7	23.4	28.8
	(2.6)	(2.3)	(2.7)	(2.5)	(2.6)	(2.6)
Other services	43.1	58.5	69.4	89.1	122.7	148.8
	(16.6)	(18.6)	(16.7)	(14.4)	(13.7)	(13.5)
Canal Zone services	22.3	23.8	30.4	51.14	70.3	71.4
	(8.6)	(7.6)	(7.3)	(8.3)	(7.9)	(6.5)
GDP	259.2	314.7	415.8	664.1	894.5	1,101.2

Note: Figures in parentheses indicate percentage of GDP.
Source: Contraloria General de la Republica, Direccion de Estadistica y Censo, Ingreso Nacional, various issues.

INCOME DISTRIBUTION

Income is quite concentrated in Panama, both geographically and in certain income groups. Over 40 percent of the country's population live in the narrow urbanized belt around the Canal Zone, yet this area covers only about 7 percent of the country's land mass. Some 75 percent of the national income is generated within this area. The incomes in the remainder of the country vary from the relatively wealthy agricultural province of Chiriqui to Bocas del Toro (a province inaccessible by road and almost totally dependent on the banana company), the group of rather poor agricultural provinces in the central region, and finally the subsistence areas of the Darien and San Blas Islands.

Not only are there extreme disparities in income among the regions but also within them. Chiriqui and Veraguas have the most extreme concentration of income;[11] in Veraguas nearly a third of the province's income is earned by only one percent (or 337) of the families. Half of the province's income is earned by the highest 5 percent of the income recipients. Income distributions of this nature have led to much smaller local consumer markets than would be implied by the total provincial income. As a result of the income patterns in these areas, a profile of demand has been established in which the wealthier groups purchase most of their goods from Panama Province (because this is where the consumer durable goods are either produced or imported) rather than locally.

For example, the provinces of Cocle, Herrera, Los Santos, and Veraguas generate about 13 percent of the national income, and the percentage of the market for most products (particularly those that might be provided locally) is substantially less. The relatively small size of most local consumer markets has resulted in difficulties in attracting even small-scale industries to the provinces.

As long as real incomes were accelerating during the 1960s, most Panamanians (before 1968) did not mind the growing disparities in the income distribution. Recently, however, the slowdown in the country's rate of growth and the broadened social participation of a number of rural groups in the process of development (as a result of the 1968 revolution) have produced a rising middle class that is better educated and better prepared to participate in the political process. These groups also will not tolerate any further deterioration in the income distribution.

Now the lower (and some middle) income groups, less willing to accept a growing gap in income and wealth between themselves and the urban elite, are pressuring the government for further social programs and an increase in the pace of agrarian

reform.[12] At the same time, those areas of the country that have
lagged in income growth are challenging the regional distribution of
public expenditure, while other areas such as Panama City and Colon
are attempting to better their already favorable position by arguing
that the rate of return on investment in the existing urban areas is
higher and that the economy would grow faster and more efficiently
if some of the surplus generated there could be taxed, then redistribut-
ed to the less fortunate regions.

CONCLUSIONS

In 1970 it seemed that Panama had finally entered a period
of sustained growth. For nearly two decades its national product per
capita had increased at an accelerating pace. The level of investment
and the expansion of education and health services gave promise that
the economy would be able to continue at this rate of growth. But
inflation, a slowing industrial production, and a deterioration in the
income distribution has resulted in slackening growth.

The treaties in their present form worked well before world
inflation, and when economic growth, rather than social concern with
income and wealth inequalities, was the major preoccupation of the
state. The post-1968 government has, however, placed emphasis on
social issues. On coming to power, its leaders immediately began a
strong effort to reduce the regional and personal disparities of
income that had been created by previous growth. It increased public
outlays in order to raise the incomes of rural families; and it
expanded infrastructure projects and projects to support the growth
of urban activities. It further initiated an integrated agrarian reform,
increased the number of schools, and invested in directly productive
activities on the assumption that a continued expansion of output,
but on a more equitable basis, was possible in Panama.

Panama probably cannot expect a growth dividend from the
Zone in the future unless the present canal relationships between
the United States and Panama are changed. Negotiations over a new
treaty began in 1971.[13] The last public U.S. position (1975) included:
(1) an increase in the present $2 million annuity paid the government
of Panama to about $25 million, with annual increases thereafter
depending on the growth of canal traffic; (2) the gradually phased
return of about 50 square miles of land in the Canal Zone to full
Panamanian control; and (3) the establishment of a date for expiration
of a new treaty.

The present situation is uncertain, and few Panamanian or
U.S. authorities expect quick agreement on a new treaty. Because

of the necessity of a new sea-level canal (the existing facilities cannot handle supertankers and large battleships) and Panama's possession of the most favorable site for the new canal, the country's place in world commerce seems assured, and its longer term prospects of increasing the direct benefits stemming from interoceanic traffic are equally favorable. Until a new treaty is negotiated, however, the additional income and employment generated by the Canal Zone will be negligible.

In the meantime it is clear that Panama has numerous opportunities for future economic growth; it is one of the more politically stable countries in Latin America, and is already a financial center. The availability of large volumes of foreign exchange associated with the country's role in international finance is, however, unlikely to be sufficient to bring about economic development on a self-sustained basis. Instead there are three conditions necessary for this development: first, a more equal distribution of income in order to increase the domestic market for domestically produced goods; second, the reorganization of agriculture to provide a stimulus for further expansion of the industrial sector; and finally, the establishment of a policy of upgrading the skills of the labor force.

It is possible that a coordinated development plan for the country as a whole might allow Panama to achieve in the next decade, rates of growth similar to the levels of the 1960s. In this regard, it should be pointed out that the Ministry of Economic Policy and Planning (MPPE) has said that "a frontal attack on the problem of poverty by channeling a large volume of efforts and resources into integral development of the less advantaged groups in the country requires in turn that those sectors with an established production capacity continue to produce and invest."[14] This indicates that the MPPE considers social progress to hold the highest priority for the government. Social progress, however, is to be closely tied to the recovery of past growth rates which in turn requires reactivation of the agricultural and industrial sectors and of exports, and particularly more dynamic private investment and an imporvement in the status of public finance indebtedness. In short, effective progress in social development calls for joint advances in the economic and public finance sectors.

NOTES

1. Unless otherwise stated, the data used in this study have been obtained from the official publications of the Contraloria General de la Republica, Direccion de Estadistica y Censo. Because of space

limitations the data for each have not been presented. This information
can be provided by the Department of Economics, University of Santa
Clara, upon request.

2. See note 4 of Chapter 1 for references to treaties.

3. There are several alternative ways of statistically identifying the binding constraint. See Constantine Michalopoulos,
"Imports, Foreign Exchange, and Economic Development: The Greek
Experience," in Peter Kennen and Roger Lawrence, The Open
Economy (New York: Columbia University Press, 1968). The approach
used by Michalopoulos could not be applied in Panama, because some
of the required data was not available. Another approach used by
Michalopoulos could not be applied in Panama, because some of the
required data was not available. Another approach has been developed
by T.E. Weisskopf in his "The Impact of Foreign Capital Inflow on
Domestic Savings in Underdeveloped Countries," Journal of International Economics 2, no.1 (February 1972): 25-38; and "An Econometric Test of Alternative Constraints on the Growth of Underdeveloped Countries," Review of Economics and Statistics 54, no.1
(February 1972): 67-78. Weisskopf's analysis indicates that during
the period 1960-66 (using his approach) there was no identifiable constraint on Panamanian growth. The limitations of Weisskopf's
analysis are spelled out in Young Ki Hahn, "The Effect of Foreign
Resources on Domestic Savings," South African Journal of Economics
42, no.1 (March 1974): 85-94.

4. During the 1950s a number of sector plans were drawn up,
but no comprehensive framework for their integration into a national
plan was established. A typical example was: Comision de Caminos,
Aeropuertos y Muelles, "A Four-Year Program for Administrative
Reorganization, Personnel Training Rehabilitation and Maintenance
of Public Highways," mimeographed (Panama City: Republic of
Panama, 1955).

5. United Nations Economic Commission for Latin America,
Analysis y Proyecciones del Desarrollo Economico, VII, el Desarrollo
de Panama (Panama City: United Nations Economic and Social
Council, 1959), chapter 1.

6. U.S. House of Representatives, Committee on Government
Operations, A Review of Alliance for Progress Goals (Washington,
D.C.: Government Printing Office, 1969), chapters 3-5; Simon G.
Hanson, Five Years of The Alliance for Progress: An Appraisal
(Washington, D.C.: Inter-American Affairs Press, 1967),pp. 12-13.

7. Joint tax program of the OAS/IDB, Fiscal Survey of
Panama: Problems and Proposals for Reform (Baltimore: Johns
Hopkins Press, 1964), p. 2.

8. Several unpublished surveys of the 1960s are available and cover a number of points not discussed here. See for example: Arnold C. Harberger, "The Past Growth and Future Prospects of the Panamanian Economy," mimeographed (Panama City: U.S. Agency for International Development, 1972); Larry Sjaastad, "Prospects for Economic Growth in the 1970s: Panama," mimeographed (Panama City: U.S. Agency for International Development, 1972); Jarilaos Stavrou, "Macro de Referencia Macroeconomico," mimeographed (Panama City: Direccion General de Planificacion y Administracion, 1972); and James Christian, "A Macro-Sectoral Survey of the Economy of Panama," mimeographed (Panama City, Ministerio de Planificacion y Politica Economica, 1970).

9. This conclusion is derived from purely a statistical analysis. Given the underlying economic structure of the economy— lack of a capital goods industry, reliance on exports that were not consumed domestically—it might be argued that the trade gap was still the dominant constraint during this period. For a nonanalytical discussion along these lines see Markos J. Mamalakis, "The Export Sector, Stages of Economic Development, and the Saving-Investment Process in Latin America," Economia Internazionale 21, no.1 (February 1968): 56-62.

10. As estimated in Direccion de Estadistica y Censo: Estadistica Panamena serie "0" (Panama City: Contraloria General de la Republica, 1971), Table 3.

11. As estimated in Gain S. Sahota, "Public Expenditure and Income Distribution in Panama," mimeographed (Panama City: U.S. Agency for International Development, 1972) pp. 106-11.

12. For a description of the nature and pace of agrarian reform in Panama see the various publications of the Confederation of Asentamientos (Panama City, annually).

13. As of January 1976, no substantive agreements have been reached other than a list of "Eight Principles" agreed upon between the United States and Panama. These principles, however, are only areas in which discussions concerning a new treaty will be focused. See Stephen S. Rosenfeld, "The Panama Negotiations—A Close Run Thing," Foreign Affairs 54, no. 1 (October 1975): 1-13.

14. Nicolas Ardito Barletta, Que Presenta a la Asamblea Nacional De Representantes de Corregimentos (Panama City: Ministerio De Planificacion y Politica Economica, October 1973).

4

DEMOGRAPHIC
CHARACTERISTICS
AND THEIR
IMPLICATIONS

One of the significant factors affecting the economy of Panama is the change in the demographic pattern that has taken place since World War II. This, together with a number of social changes, has had a profound effect on the economic structure of the country. Several of the changes can be attributed to the presence of the Canal Zone; others, to the rapid rate of population growth. Together, they have created serious problems:

(1) Population has increased in certain regions, especially in the area surrounding the Canal Zone, drawn there by the hope of higher wages and the move facilitated by the improvement in the country's transportation network.

(2) Cultivated acreage in the provinces has passed its economic limits, thus forcing new workers to seek employment outside the agricultural sector.

(3) High wages paid in the Canal Zone have attracted many rural workers to the country's urban centers, especially to Panama City, resulting in serious overcrowding.

(4) The level of employment in the Canal Zone has stabilized and other activities have not created new jobs sufficiently fast to absorb the increase in the working population.

Because of their effect on the future economic performance of the country, serious attention must be directed toward the resolution of these problems.

POPULATION

The population of Panama at the present time is over 1.5 million, an increase in the past ten years of something over half a million. This represents a growth rate of over 3 percent annually, one of the highest growth rates in the world. At this rate, by 1980 the population will reach 2 million, and in 22 years it will double. This increase is due partly to the country's rather high birth rate and partly to improved sanitary conditions and medical services in some areas of the country which have resulted in a decline in overall death rates and particularly in infant mortality.

The implications of this growth are obvious: the small size of the country, the decreasing ability of the farmland to support its people, the lack of industry, the exodus from the rural areas to the cities by those seeking jobs or higher wages, and the consequent overcrowding in those cities, make the situation extremely serious.

An additional problem lies in the fact that approximately 44 percent of the population is 14 years of age or younger[1] and this places a very heavy burden on the adult population (15 years of age and older) to raise, support, and educate them. In the future, when those now in the under-14 age group begin to bear children the situation will become insupportable.

GEOGRAPHIC DISTRIBUTION OF THE POPULATION

Geographically, the population is largely concentrated in the three provinces of Panama, Chiriqui, and Veraguas, which in 1971 contained 68 percent of the population (Table 4.1). Panama alone accounted for 41 percent. During the 1960s the rate of growth in those provinces was 3.4 percent annually, and in the rest of the country, 1.9 percent. A further demographic change was the increase in the number of people living in the urban areas.* In 1971, there were 710,600 residing in such areas, in contrast to 287,800 in 1950 and 438,100 in 1960. The culmination of these trends in population growth and migration has given Panama a highly urbanized society—over 40 percent of the country's population lives in a narrow strip bordering the Canal Zone, an area comprising only 7 percent of the country's land area.

---

*Defined by the Panamanian Census as communities of over 1,500 with such modern services as paved streets, piped water and sewage, electricity, and secondary-level schools.

TABLE 4.1

Population Distribution and Selected Socioeconomic Indicators,
by Province, 1960 and 1970

	Bocas del Toro	Cocle	Colon	Chiriqui	Darien	Herrera	Los Santos	Panama	Veraguas
Income per family, 1970 (balboas)	1,572	1,159	2,013	1,543	965	1,191	1,087	2,413	954
Income per capita, 1970 (balboas)	402	295	794	373	145	314	290	881	212
Percent of total population, 1970	3.1	8.3	9.4	16.5	1.6	5.1	5.1	40.4	10.6
Percent of economically active population in agriculture, 1970	76.0	59.0	26.0	57.0	82.0	56.0	63.0	11.1	77.0
Percent of population 10 years and over illiterate,									
1960	47.4	22.5	19.5	33.0	43.6	37.8	34.5	8.5	52.8
1970	40.4	19.8	18.9	28.4	47.3	30.7	29.1	8.2	44.0
Percent of population aged 7-15 primary school enrolled,									
1960	47.1	73.3	71.4	61.6	72.0	64.3	69.7	86.4	51.4
1970	56.5	85.4	83.0	76.6	60.6	83.3	86.6	90.3	75.5

Sources: G. S. Sahota, "Public Expenditure and Income Distribution in Panama," mimeographed (Panama City: U.S. Agency for International Development, 1972); Direccion de Estadistica y Censo (DEC), Educacion Ano 1970, Serie "M"; DEC, Demografia Anos 1964, 1965, Serie "A"; DEC, Censos Nacionales de 1970, Vol. I, Lugares Poblados de la Republica; DEC, Censos Nacionales de 1960, Vol. II, Caracteristicas Educativas (Cuadro 18); Vol. IX, Poblacion Indigena (Cuadro 7 y 10) y Vol. IX, Caracteristicas Generales (Cuadro 28); DEC, Panama en Cifras 1960-64 y 1966-70; DEC, Estadisticas Vitales, Ano 1960; DEC, Estadisticas Vitales Ano 1970; DEC, Segundo Censo de Vivienda (1960), Caracteristicas de la Vivienda, y Tercer Censo de Vivienda (1970), Lugares Poblados de la Republica.

A number of problems commonly associated with urbanization have resulted: for example, congestion, slums, and increasing costs to the economy entailed in the provision of social services such as adequate sanitation and health facilities. In addition, marked differences continue to exist in the level of public facilities in the various provinces. The result has been a perpetuation of low health and educational standards in many areas of the country.

Several studies have shown a marked lack of animal protein and fruits and vegetables in the largely starch daily diet of much of the population. This condition is particularly prevalent in the rural areas. The malnutrition manifests itself primarily in figures for school children who are considerably under the normal weight and height for their age. In this regard, in 1967 60 percent of all children under age five suffered from some grade of protein/calorie malnutrition.[2]

To a considerable extent, Panama's future economic performance depends on the mix, size, and geographical distribution of its population. In particular, these factors will have an increasing influence on the level and structure of consumption and investment, and on the labor supply.

DETERMINANTS OF THE EXISTING SIZE
DISTRIBUTION OF POPULATION

Changes in the size distribution of the population in Panama are a result of movements over time of factors such as death, birth, fertility rates, migration, and social mobility (particularly of women).

Before projecting the country's population, it is therefore necessary to survey in some detail the main demographic characteristics of the country. Generally speaking, Panamanian population growth depends ultimately on the country's level and pace of economic development, the spread of urbanization, level of education, and the increasing emancipation of women. A not unexpected phenomenon has been noted since World War II: the higher the level of per capita income, and the wider the spread of education and urbanization, the lower the rate of population growth.

DEATH RATE

The death rate has declined continuously since the end of World War II. By 1960-62 the death rate had fallen to 7.9 per 1,000

persons; by 1968-70 it had fallen further to 7 per 1,000 or a drop of
12 percent. The major factor responsible for this drop was the rapid
decrease in child mortality. This rate was 52.1 per 1,000 births in
1960-62, and had declined to only 39.6 per 1,000 births in 1968-70,
a decrease of almost 24 percent.[3] Life expectancy has risen from
60 years in 1960 to 66 years in 1970 and is expected to average 69
years by the late 1970s.[4]

     The death rate is considerably higher in the rural areas.
In 1970, for example, the death rate was 5.5 percent per 1,000 inhabitants in the urban areas, but 8.4 percent in rural areas. Moreover, while 96 percent of all urban deaths were certified by medical
personnel in attendance, it is estimated[5] that 70 percent of all rural
deaths took place without the presence of any medical personnel.
This has given rise to increased government efforts to improve the
levels of preventive medicine in the more remote areas of the country.
In attempting to do so, however, the government is encountering a
number of serious obstacles.

     Historically there have been a number of reasons for the
relative deficiency in health care in the rural areas, the most important of which has been the lack of medical personnel and facilities.
Very few people have been trained in medicine. This situation exists
in part, because of expensive and overly lengthy medical training
programs in Panama, and partly because most of the provinces (in
contrast to Panama City) offer few attractions in terms of pay, work
facilities, accessibility, and physical comfort. In 1970, Panama City
had 14 doctors, 2.3 dentists, 19.4 graduate nurses, and 21.8 trained
nurses' aides per 10,000 inhabitants. Other areas of the country
with less than 20,000 population had from four to eighteen times
fewer personnel in each category.[6]

     Because of the rural area's sparse and uneven settlement
pattern, it is virtually impossible for the government to place a hospital within easy access of those living in towns of 500 or less. Yet
nearly 40 percent of the country's population resides in or near villages of this size. Therefore, as late as 1970 three quarters of the
nation's hospital beds were found in cities of 20,000 or more, while
the rest of the population obtained only very limited health care. In
large part this care was provided by 92 small health centers, each
providing only outpatient care.

     Another factor perpetuating the relatively high death rates
in rural areas is the inadequate level of water and waste-disposal
facilities. In 1971, 100 percent of the urban population had piped
water, over 92 percent had access to sewers, septic tanks or la-
trines. This not only met but surpassed the goals set by the Alliance
for Progress.[7] Yet in rural areas less than 50 percent had easy

access to pure water. Sanitary facilities were, however, somewhat
better, with 68.3 percent of the population served.

BIRTH RATE

During the 1960s the birth rate in Panama, while still high,
showed a significant decrease, from around 40.5 per 1,000 inhabitants
in 1960-62 to 37.6 per thousand in 1968-70, and the decline appears to
be accelerating. By 1970 the rate had dropped to 36 per thousand.[8]
Since the decline has been continuous since 1960, it cannot be considered to be simply a temporary phenomenon.

Three factors account for this decline: (1) the percentage of
females in the population, (2) the age composition of the female population, and (3) the fertility rate of each age group.

Panama is characterized by several unusual demographic
patterns. There are not only more men than women (unusual because
women usually live longer), but the ratio has increased from 102.8
in 1960 to 103.0 in 1970. Though this is an interesting statistic, it is
highly unlikely that this factor had any significant influence on birth
rates during this period.

The second factor affecting fertility rates is the age composition of the population. The proportion of women of childbearing
age, that is, between 15 and 49 years, dropped slightly between 1960
and 1970 and the proportion of women over 50 years, and thus out
of the childbearing group, increased. Using the age compositional
changes of the female population between 1960 and 1970, an estimate
of the effect of factor (2) can be made. For example, if the proportion
of women in childbearing age groups in 1970 was the same as in 1960
(given the fertility rates of 1970), there would have been 52,800 births,
or a birth rate of 37 per thousand. In 1970, however, the actual
number of births was slightly less than 52,000, giving a birth rate
of 36 per thousand.[9] The change in birth rates produced by the
changing age structure of the female population, therefore, had only
a minor role in explaining the drop in births between 1960 and 1970.

Of importance for estimation of factor (3) is the fact that
the distribution of women in the most reproductive age groups (20-
29) increased between 1960 and 1970. This factor, however, had only
a slight impact on the number of births; that is, if these women had
the same fertility rates as in 1960, there would have been 51,293
births instead of the actual figure of 52,802. It is unlikely, however,
that this factor can account for much of the decline since, over all,
the proportion of women in the reproductive age groups declined;

that is, with the age structure of 1960, the number of women of reproductive age in 1970 would have been 4,200 greater than the actual
number.

The effect of the final factor on birth rates, the fertility rate
by age group, indicates that there would have been 57,293 births in
1970, or a birth rate of 40 per thousand (if the fertility rate had not
changed between 1960 and 1970). Since the actual birth rate was much
lower (36 per 1,000), it is clear that the change in the fertility rate
by age group was the major factor in the drop of the birth rates in
Panama during the 1960s.[10]

Significantly, the fertility rate dropped the most for women
in the 20-29, 15-19, and 30-39 age groups. Two explanations of this
reduction are possible: a drop in the number of marriages, or a
marked change in the attitude toward family size. Marriages in the
1960s actually increased. It is evident, therefore, that the leading
factor in the decline in birth rates has been a change in Panamanian
attitudes toward family size. The degree of the drop in the fertility
rate also suggests that there was, even in a Catholic country, widespread response to the introduction of contraceptives and the family
planning programs sponsored by the government. *

SOCIOECONOMIC CHARACTERISTICS OF THE POPULATION

Education

Panama has traditionally had relatively low levels of illiteracy
by international standards. Education has been a prime concern of
the authorities. By 1950, only 28 percent of the residents in the two
terminal cities were illiterate. In the same year 62.7 percent of the
republic's primary-school-age children were in school—a proportion
that is even higher than that existing today in many Latin American
countries. During the 1950s and 1960s about 30 percent of the
government's current expenditures went for education. As a result,

---

*The Ministry of Health has been particularly active in this
area. It offers advice on family planning and assistance in better
birth control. In July 1972, for example, its objective of enrolling
32,500 persons in family planning courses was being achieved. The
only problem with the program conducted by the ministry is that the
supply of contraceptive pills that the ministry receives (largely
through international donations) is not sufficient to meet the demand.

the primary school system was expanded to many of the rural areas, and by 1968 most small villages had two- and three-room primary schools. For the country as a whole, the proportion of primary-school age students actually in school had reached 86 percent, and for secondary schools, 30 percent.

Panama's educational achievements have been particularly impressive, but rather expensive at the lower levels. In 1968, for example, 25.7 percent of the government's total expenditures were for primary and secondary education. The direct cost per primary and secondary student—B/100 per year—was high by Latin American standards. An additional 5.0 percent of the government's budget was spent on subsidizing the operations of the university and other educational facilities. The public outlays on education were 4.1 percent of GDP. The post-1968 government thus faced an expanding and costly public educational system.

The response of the new government to this situation was threefold. First, it decided to increase the coverage of the educational system by lowering the entering age of primary students from 7 to 6 years. Second, the government developed a program to: (a) expand primary and secondary education in rural areas, (b) revise the curriculum of the rural schools, and (c) introduce a new general cycle—the "basic cycle"—into public vocational schools. The basic cycle was designed to attract those students who desired academic preparation before completing their vocational studies. In 1972 the Ministry of Education began to establish "farm schools"—primary schools in agricultural communities in which half the student's time is spent on practical farming lessons.* These schools are ultimately expected to be financed by the communities themselves and from sale of the students' products.

The expansion in education has been impressive (Table 4.2). The post-1968 government has clearly improved the educational opportunities of all Panamanians. Since middle-class Panamanians already had access to a full spectrum of schooling in 1968, most of the increased primary and secondary enrollments came from poorer groups.

---

*These programs were rapidly expanded by the Instituto Para la Formacion y Aprovechamento de Recursos Humanos (IFARHU). Beginning in 1973, the functions of vocational training were transferred from IFARHU to the Ministry of Labor, and placement of the graduates is the responsibility of the unemployment service of that ministry.

TABLE 4.2

Public Education Indicators, 1950-71

	1950	Annual Average Growth (percent)	1960	Annual Average Growth (percent)	1968	Annual Average Growth (percent)	1971
Primary schools							
Govt. current expenditures for primary schools (balboas, thousands)	3,969.5	6.3	7,316.0	10.9	16,770.9	11.2	23,068.7
Primary students	103,932.0	3.8	150,892.0	4.1	208,817.0	9.4	273,324.0
Cost per student (balboas)	38.2	2.4	48.5	6.5	80.3	1.7	84.4
Cost per student/per capita national income (percent)	14.4	—	15.3	—	15.6	—	13.5
Students/teacher	32.4	—	30.0	—	29.7	—	28.6
Secondary schools							
Govt. current expenditures for secondary schools (balboas, thousands)	1,838.5	6.0	3,278.0	11.7	7,952.9	14.4	11,915.8
Secondary students	14,722.0	4.7	23,249.0	7.5	41,370.0	13.3	60,150.0
Cost per student (balboas)	124.9	1.2	141.0	3.9	192.2	1.0	198.1
Cost per student/per capita national income (percent)	47.2	—	44.5	—	37.3	—	31.7
Students/teacher	21.6	—	23.2	—	21.6	—	19.9
Total education indicators							
Appropriate age group enrolled as percent of appropriate age group:							
primary	n.a.		85.4		85.9		93.0
secondary	n.a.		24.2		30.9		36.0
Public current expenditures on education/public current expenditures (percent)	27.6*		26.0		26.4		24.5

*Central Government only; after 1950 includes current expenditures of Ministry of Education, University of Panama, IFARHU, and other public educational entities.

Sources: Ministry of Education, Statistics for the Analysis of the Education Sector, Panama (Panama City, 1973): 57.

The fiscal cost of this expansion has continued to be considerable and has been rapidly increasing. By 1972 the public expenditures
on education had risen to 4.7 percent of GDP, and 23.3 percent of
all the increase in public outlays. This rapid expansion will be difficult
to continue; the lack of trained teachers and administrators suggests
that a consolidation period is needed.

Education and Income Levels

The labor force in the nonagricultural sector is in general
well educated. For example, in 1970 only 4 percent of its employees
had no schooling, 54 percent some primary training, 34 percent some
secondary schooling, and 8 percent some university credits. The
agricultural sector in contrast has a high proportion of illerate workers, particularly those in older age groups. Many workers over 40
in this sector have had no schooling or other form of training.

Salaried workers in the metropolitan area* have a much
higher level of education than the average for the population as a
whole. In 1970, 41 percent had some secondary and 12 percent some
university education.[11] Less than 2 percent had no education. Most
of those with no formal education were employed as domestic servants and in construction. The sectors that required the highest
educational level were public utilities, commerce, transportation
and communication, and government. In those sectors over 50 percent
of the workers had high school or college training. In contrast, the
majority of workers in mining, manufacturing, construction, and the
Canal Zone had only several years of primary schooling.

The Labor Force

The labor force in 1973 was 550,000, or roughly 65 percent
of the population over 15. Nearly one-half of the working population
is employed in the metropolitan area (Panama City/Colon); the rest
is scattered throughout the rest of the country. Since 1960 the total
labor force has been growing faster than has the population—3.4 percent per year compared to 3.1 for the total population.

Men comprise approximately 70 percent of the work force,
although women are beginning to participate in increasing numbers.

---

*The metropolitan area, unless otherwise specified, con-
sists of the provinces of Panama and Colon.

By 1970, 35 percent were either employed or seeking work, in contrast to 25 percent in 1960.[12] Further, not only are more women
entering the work force but they are staying longer, particularly
those over 25. The overall participation rate for women increased
from 24.7 to 35.4 between 1960 and 1970. Traditionally women in
Panama have left jobs in their early 20s to have families, but this
is no longer a common pattern, particularly for women working in
urban areas. Women in the labor force are largely an urban phenomenon, particularly in the metropolitan area. In 1970, there were
92,000 women workers in that area; in contrast only 43,400 worked
in the rest of the country. This is reflected in the number of women
in the labor force in the two areas. In the metropolitan area nearly
45 percent of the women between the ages of 20 and 39 were in the
labor force; in contrast, only 24 percent of women outside the
metropolitan area and in this age group were in the labor force.[13]

        Women in the metropolitan area work generally for the cen-
tral government and the various government agencies, 56 percent in
the service sector, 18 percent in business, and 13 percent in manufacturing. Significantly, a large number of women have risen to high
administrative posts in government service—50 percent of those
employed in the professions and as technicians, managers, and
office workers are women.

SOCIOECONOMIC DETERMINANTS OF POPULATION GROWTH

        Birth rates for Panama, though declining, are still quite
high. The development prospects for the country are likely to depend to a significant extent on the future rate of decline. Influencing
the number of children that parents have, therefore, may become
one of the major policy tools available to the government in its attempt
to improve the country's standard of living. If the government were
to design a policy to modify fertility rates in the country, however,
it would have to have a clear understanding of the major determinants
of fertility at the family level. At present there have been no invest-
igations of this sort.[14] However, several tentative conclusions can
be made about those features of the environment in Panama that are
likely to influence the number of children parents want: child labor
and schooling, employment of women, and the incidence of child
mortality.

Child Labor and Schooling

High rates of fertility exist in Panama because children are a cheap source of farm labor. In rural areas, although not as commonly as a decade ago, it is still usual for children 6 to 10 to be working in the fields at least during seasonal peaks. Obviously the burden of childhood dependence is lessened because of this type of employment. On the other hand, spread of education (reducing the availability for work), the declining numbers of rural families, the difficulty of employing children in urban areas have resulted in an increased burden of childhood dependence. These two trends, the reduction of work opportunities in agriculture, and the increase in education should be major factors in causing further decline in the birth rate.

Employment of Women

A significant part of the costs of bearing and rearing children is the value of a mother's time devoted to these pursuits. When her most productive activities are easily combined with child rearing in the home, the opportunity cost (earnings foregone by not being in the labor force) of her time spent in caring for the children is small and a large family no great inconvenience. However, the household activities traditionally performed in Panama by women (weaving, processing family food, caring for livestock, and handicrafts) have tended to be displaced gradually by modern food processing, and textile and other light manufacturing. Women cannot profitably carry out these activities in the home. On the other hand, the service sector has become the largest employer of women in Panama. Work in this sector, however, particularly in the highly remunerative government jobs, entails working outside the home. Thus it is becoming increasingly difficult for women to find opportunities that combine salaried work with child raising. This is especially the case in the specialized economic environment of the metropolitan area. A large family therefore is increasingly becoming a limitation on a mother's opportunity to work, and this entails a substantial loss in potential family earnings. Urbanization and the associated rising value of women's time will probably induce more parents to be content with smaller families. Urban women in Panama already have a significantly lower fertility rate than rural women. For the periods 1962-63, 1966-67, and 1971 the fertility rate for urban women declined from 119.6 to 115.1 and 115.7 per thousand respectively. The corresponding values for rural women were 163.5, 157.3 and 148.1 per thousand respectively.

Interestingly, the index of change in the fertility rate declined
more for rural women than for urban women during the 1960s. This
does not refute an education-urbanization theory of fertility. The
patterns of urban-rural fertility in the 1960s can be explained by the
fact that Panama City and Colon had a high percentage of migrants
from rural areas during the 1960s.[15] At the same time, the standard
of family living in these two cities rose more than in other parts of
the country (inducing migration),[16] but much of the increase in
income came from male employment. Given the low educational
levels of most rural women, their migration to the metropolitan
area may not have improved their earning potential to a significant
degree, and at the same time their higher family income may have
facilitated the raising of more children. This hypothesis is substan-
tiated by two factors: (1) the rising rates of female participation in
the labor force are far more an urban than a rural phenomenon,
particularly of the Panama City/Colon area; and (2) the median weekly
salaries of women employees are related to their level of education;
that is, a major jump in earnings occurs between those with some
primary- and those with some secondary-level education. Women
with the higher level of education have more than three times as much
income as those without. Another major jump occurs between the
secondary and higher levels of education, with women with some
university education receiving almost twice as much as those having
attended only secondary schools (Table 4.3). It is clear, therefore,
that falling fertility rates are associated with those women with
higher than average levels of education and thus greater potential
earning power. The large drops in fertility occurred for women in the
20-24 and 25-29 age groups, which tends to further substantiate the
hypothesis developed above.[17]

Incidence of Child Mortality

It is reasonable to assume that parents in Panama frame
their reproductive goals in terms of their preferences for a particular
number of surviving children (or sons). Thus, parents are likely to
seek to regulate their fertility upon reaching or exceeding their
traditionally desired family size. In most countries, birth rates
have fallen only after the chances for child survival have improved
for an extended period. In this connection there are two unanswered
questions: (1) how long will a lag separate the decline in death rates
in Panama from the onset of the decline in birth rates (1960); and
(2) is there a threshold below which child death rates must fall to
trigger the desired reduction in birth rates? On the basis of only

TABLE 4.3

Average Weekly Salaries of Employees, by Education Level, Sex, and Area, 1970

(in balboas)

	Metropolitan Area		Rest of Republic	
	Male	Female	Male	Female
No education	27.11 (1.6)*	7.60 (2.0)	16.96 (6.3)	7.76 (5.0)
Primary	31.49 (46.7)	11.13 (43.2)	19.85 (66.9)	9.35 (55.2)
Secondary	39.65 (39.9)	33.81 (41.2)	30.65 (22.9)	29.79 (34.0)
University	70.72 (11.8)	53.18 (13.6)	71.05 (3.9)	40.20 (5.8)

*Figures in parentheses are the percentage of total "employees" covered at each educational level.

Note: In addition to the usual exclusion of the indigenous population and those living in institutions, hotels, pensions, etc., the data exclude the economically active in agriculture and those whose earnings are in the form of tips, commissions, payment in kind, or for piece work.

Source: Direccion de Estadistica y Censo, Estadistica Panamena, serie "O" (Estadisticas del Trabajo) (Panama City, 1970), Table 15, p. 24.

the trends of the 1960s it is too early to identify either factor in Panama. Still it is clear that the above factors—schooling, women's employment, and so on—are moving in a direction to lower the birth rate; that is, actual births are a function of the number of births that parents desire, which in turn is a function of the level of child mortality, the costs of rearing children, and women's foregone income as a result of having additional children.

To implement any policies in this area, however, the government will have to quantify these (and possibly other) relationships more precisely. It should begin by compiling data on fertility by various areas, educational levels of women, and family income groups.

FORECASTS OF PANAMA'S POPULATION
AND LABOR FORCE

Given the demographic characteristics of the population, the following sequence of events is likely to occur. First, because of the changes in the death rate, the postwar child population is growing more rapidly than is the adult population. This is creating a dependency burden on the older generation, one that is largely borne by parents supporting additional surviving children, but one that will be increasingly transferred to the state, which must provide additional education, job training, and child health services. Panama was in this first phase of population change in the 1960s and is currently in the process of completion of this phase.

In the latter 1970s, Panama will probably enter a second phase of population change, when the large surviving groups of those born in the 1950s and early 1960s will be entering the labor force. The dependency burden will show its ascent in this phase. The growth of the adult population will add increasingly to the needs for savings and investment to employ the growing flow of these new entrants into the labor force.

Because there are signs of declining birth rates, a third phase will occur in which the dependency burden will decline. This is likely to occur only after a two-decade lag or in the early 1980s. At that time growth of the labor force will diminish. This will release resources from child raising and make the resources available for either current adult consumption or other investment activities.

On the basis of the current age composition of the population and likely patterns of mortality and fertility rates, the dependency ratio (those under 14 to those over 14) should not change significantly until at least 1980. By 1980 the 0-14 age group is likely to account

for 44.6 percent of the country's population; the 15 to 29 age group is
likely to have grown more rapidly and thus attain 26.1 percent of the
total (in contrast to 25.4 percent in 1960).

Given the available data, it is impossible to estimate the
exact magnitude of the cost incurred by the rising child dependency
in the first phase and compare it with the cost due to the additional
savings required to maintain employment and income levels incurred
in the second phase. If we assume (as is reasonable) that in Panama
the cost in the first phase outweighs the second, the net social costs
of the demographic trends occurring today may be greater in the
early years than in the latter, as is evidenced by the rather high
interest rate in Panama.

Some quantification of these costs is possible. Simply sustain
the existing amount of capital per person, a more rapidly growing
labor force will require the country to generate a higher savings rate.
The magnitude of this effort is immense. The country's capital-
output ratio (the increment in output resulting from a one-unit increase
in capital) is likely to be about three to one in the next two decades.
This means that it will take three dollars of capital, on the average,
to create one dollar of income. If the capital output ratio remains at
this level, then a net savings rate from output of 9 percent will be
required simply to employ the 3 percent annual increase in the labor
force.

Panama's leaders, however, have continually stated that
they view the country's development process as more than simple
duplication of past efforts, products, methods and techniques of
production. They view development as a process in which an increasing
share of the population is allowed to engage in new and more productive
activities.[18] These modern economic activities, however, are likely
to require more capital and other modern inputs (skilled labor, for
example) per worker than were associated with the production
methods in common use during the 1960s.

The rate, therefore, at which labor will be absorbed into
this modern sector in Panama will be restrained and the development
process prolonged by the country's continued rapid population growth,
unless the already high levels of savings and investment are increased.

RECOMMENDATIONS

Panama would benefit from a lower rate of population growth.
The government should: (1) subsidize the provision of birth control
information, services, and supplies, and (2) influence the family's
desired family size. Until recently, only a small proportion of the

population understood the feasibility of limiting births or wanted to
do so. Surveys in most regions of the country[19] have found parents
in growing numbers expressing interest in modern methods of birth
control, but as yet few of the rural less educated have obtained access
to this information. It appears that in Panama private diffusion of
information on contraception is slow, even when apparently in great
demand.

In terms of a population policy, therefore, the government
could play a large role in accelerating the dissemination of information
about family planning. But there is no reason why policy should stop
there. It is also possible for the government to influence the birth
rate by influencing the number of children that people want to have.
Further extension of primary and secondary schooling to rural and
urban segments of the population, particularly women, could be
viewed not only as a cultural advance and an economic investment,
but also as a contribution to mitigating the population problem.
Assigning greater priority to achieving universal basic education than
to expanding further higher education might then appear a sound
development strategy. At the minimum, the interactions between
education and population policies should be emphasized more frequently and explicitly in the country's development planning than
in the past.

Obviously population control is only one of a number of means
available to the government for enabling Panama to achieve rising
living standards over time. The relevant question facing the government, however, is whether resources invested in population control
are liable to yield a rate of return to society that justifies their
being used for this purpose rather than for investment in other areas
in the economy—roads, schools, and so on. One economist who
believes that the social return to population control is very high is
Stephen Enke. Enke calculates that for a "typical" less developed
country the present value of a birth prevented is $263 (at a discount
rate of 15 percent). Further, he claims that for a major national
program stressing a reasonable mix of methods the cost per birth
prevented is probably $5. The scheme would apparently be socially
justified in Panama, although Enke's calculations are based on a
number of assumptions that may not be relevant for the country.[20]

Finally, child and maternal health care could be expanded
in conjunction with the provision of family-planning services and
supplies through the existing network of rural and urban combined
service centers in Panama. Low-cost tetanus inoculations, nutritional
supplements for pregnant women, and protein additives for young
children could drastically cut down death rates. Such a program would
require a new ordering of priorities, as well as some outside

financial assistance. But by its impact on child mortality and maternal health, the government could establish the preconditions for increased demand for birth control in the 1970s and a subsequent fall in birth and population growth rates, thus giving good prospects for accelerated development in the 1980s.

CONCLUSIONS

With almost half the total population under 15 years of age, the rate of growth of the labor force should increase substantially in the future. The expansion of the number of workers together with high rates of rural-urban migration, and a possibility for higher participation of women in the labor force, will create a great need for new employment opportunities in coming years. Unless substantial modifications in the existing productive structure are adopted, the country will not be able to meet these challenges. The scope for government action in this area is somewhat limited, however, since the country's rather unique balance-of-payments structure limits, to a large extent, the type of activities the country can engage in. Expanded growth in exports is, however, crucial if the country is to have any hope of preventing increased unemployment and declining economic growth.

NOTES

1. Unless otherwise specified, the data on population used in this chapter come from the census conducted by the Contraloria General de la Republica. For example: Direccion de Estadistica y Censo: Sexto Censo de Poblacion y Segundo de Vivienda (Panama, February 1965); Septimo Censo de Poblacion y Tercero de Vivienda (Panama, November 1971); and Estadistica Panamena, serie "0", published annually by the Contraloria.

2. Ministerio de Salud, "Proyecciones Cuadrienales de Salud," mimeographed (Panama City, 1972).

3. Contraloria General, op. cit., serie "0", various issues.

4. Situacion y perspectivas del empleo en Panama (Ginebra: Oficina Internacional del Trabajo, 1974), pp. 23-27.

5. Ibid. p. 31.

6. Ministerio de Salud, "La Participacion de la Comunidad en las Programas de Salud," mimeographed (Panama City, 1972).

7. Departamento de Planificacion, "Informe Economico", mimeographed (Panama City, 1972).

8. Direccion de Estadistica y Censo, Estadistica Panamena, boletin 417 (Panama City: June 21, 1971).

9. This is a relatively standard technique for estimating factors involved in changing population patterns. The pioneering study in this area was Ansley Coale and Edgar M. Hoover, Population Growth and Economic Development in Low-Income Countries (Princeton, N.J.: Princeton University Press, 1958), Appendix B.

10. For an in-depth analysis of the factors determining fertility in Panama see Situacion y perspectivas del empleo en panama, op. cit., part I and the references cited therein.

11. Ministry of Education, Statistics for the Analysis of the Education System (Panama City: Controller General, 1973), p. 43.

12. For a detailed analysis of the changing role of women in the labor force in Panama, see Situacion y perspectivas del empleo en Panama, op. cit., part V.

13. Ibid.

14. Concern for lack of information in this area was expressed in Lineamientos del Plan Nacional de Desarrollo, 1974-1978 (Panama City: Ministerio de Planificacion y Politica Economica, 1973).

15. An in depth analysis of migration during the 1960s has not been made. For the 1950s, however, there were several clear patterns of female migration. During the 1950s all provinces other than the province of Panama experienced net out-migration of single women. Net immigration of married women occured in Bocas del Toro, Chiriqui, Darien and Panama, while the other five provinces experienced a net out-migration of married women. Veraguas was the only province experiencing a net immigration of divorced women. The net out-migration of single females of younger ages for all provinces except that of Panama is consistent with the hypothesis that women in younger age groups move to get married or to find a higher paying job. The patterns of female migration during the 1950s indicates that the probability of women getting married in the later ages is nil, while younger women migrants are changing from single status to married. Also, apparently single women in the older age groups are returning to their place of birth or location of relatives because they have a low probability of getting married in Panama City. Movement of married women may be accounted for simply by the movement of their husbands. Out-migration of widows of all age groups may be due to the fact that they are willing to get remarried or to return to their province of birth after their widowhood. See Bali Ram, "Net Internal Migration by Marital Status for Panama: Females, 1950-1960, Social and Economic Studies 20, no. 3 (September 1971), pp. 326-30.

16. The reasons for this migration are dealt with in Arnold C. Harberger, "On Measuring the Social Opportunity Cost of Labor," in Benefit Cost Analysis, ed. Arnold C. Harberger et al. (Chicago: Aldine, 1972).

17. As developed in detail by T. Paul Schultz, Population Growth: Investigation of a Hypothesis (Santa Monica, California: The Rand Corporation, 1969). In this document the education-urbanization theory of fertility was developed in depth for Colombia.

18. See particularly the documents Lineamientos del Plan Nacional de Desarrollo, 1974-1978, op. cit., and Nicolas Barletta, Que Presenta a la Asamblea Nacional de Representantes de Corregimentos (Panama City: Ministerio de Planificacion y Politica Economica, 1973).

19. See Plan Trienal de Vivienda de Interes Social and Plan de Trabajo para el ano de 1974 (Panama City: Ministry of Housing, 1973).

20. Stephen Enke, "The Economic Aspects of Slowing Population Growth," Economic Journal 76, no. 1 (March 1966): 44-56.

5

BALANCE OF PAYMENTS

Development in a small open economy such as Panama's is dominated by its balance of payments, which comprises (1) the inflow of direct private foreign investment, (2) the export of goods and services, primarily to the Canal Zone, and (3) the export of primary products.[1] Historically, development policies in Panama have been centered in foreign trade, in the government's effort to increase exports on the one hand, and to expand the production of import replacements at home on the other. An examination of the country's balance of payments, therefore, should provide a useful insight into the country's economic structure and its stage of development.

Perhaps the most serious economic problem facing Panama is the excessive reliance of the economy on the provision of services, such as finance, and the fact that a large proportion of these services are sold to nonresidents. Most prominent are the services to the Canal Zone, tourism, and financial services. The market for these, particularly tourism and financial services, is highly volatile and the provision of services to the Canal Zone, while historically stable, is likely to be affected more and more by domestic and regional political tensions. For example, the banking sector is becoming increasingly dependent on international financial and monetary conditions; that is, large amounts of highly mobile funds held by the commercial banks in Panama constitute a growing potential threat to the stability of the economy. In fact, the main constraint on growth since World War II has been the volume and pattern of Panama's international transactions, a fact that poses numerous problems for present and future policymakers. The continued significance of the foreign sector's constraint on growth

TABLE 5.1

Balance of Payments, Selected Years, 1960-73
(in millions of balboas)

Goods and Services	Current Account Imports				Current Account Exports				Net Balance-of-Payments Position			
	1960	1965	1970	1973	1960	1965	1970	1973	1960	1965	1970	1973
Merchandise f.o.b.	108.5	192.1	330.1	455.2	39.0	92.6	130.3	159.5	-77.6	-99.5	-199.8	-295.7
Trade with Canal Zone	(11.1)	(2.6)	(3.8)	(4.3)	(8.9)	(17.4)	(22.1)	(24.9)	(-2.2)	(14.8)	(18.3)	(20.6)
Trade with rest of world	(97.4)	(189.5)	(326.3)	(450.9)	(30.1)	(75.2)	(108.2)	(134.6)	(-67.3)	(-114.3)	(-218.1)	(-146.9)
Nonmonetary gold	0.2	0.4	0.9	0.6	0.0	0.0	0.0	0.0	-0.2	-0.4	-0.9	-0.6
Freight and insurance	13.4	19.6	32.1	50.3	0.0	0.0	0.1	0.1	-13.4	-19.6	-32.0	-50.2
Other transportation	3.7	5.7	13.7	17.4	6.4	14.6	35.9	68.2	2.7	8.9	22.2	50.8
Canal Zone	(0.2)	(0.1)	(0.2)	(0.2)	(0.0)	(0.0)	(0.0)	(0.0)	(-0.2)	(-0.1)	(-0.2)	(-0.2)
Rest of world	(3.5)	(5.6)	(13.5)	(17.2)	(6.4)	(14.6)	(35.9)	(68.2)	(2.9)	(9.0)	(22.4)	(51.0)
Travel	7.1	10.0	22.7	26.1	25.1	38.3	78.2	91.0	18.0	28.3	55.5	64.9
Canal Zone	(0.0)	(0.0)	(0.0)	(0.0)	(13.3)	(21.4)	(37.3)	(39.0)	(13.3)	(21.4)	(37.3)	(39.0)
Rest of world	(7.1)	(10.0)	(22.7)	(26.1)	(11.8)	(16.9)	(40.9)	(52.0)	(4.7)	(6.9)	(18.2)	(25.9)
Investment income	12.5	17.7	41.0	97.6	2.2	2.5	12.6	52.8	-10.4	-15.2	-28.4	-44.8
Direct investment	(11.4)	(14.2)	(18.9)	(10.0)	(0.0)	(0.0)	(0.0)	(0.0)	(-11.5)	(-14.2)	(-18.9)	(-10.0)
Other	(1.1)	(3.5)	(22.1)	(87.6)	(2.2)	(2.5)	(12.6)	(52.8)	(1.1)	(-1.0)	(-9.5)	(-34.8)
Government, m.i.e.	2.8	5.7	7.4	8.8	4.3	7.9	12.3	13.3	1.5	2.2	4.9	4.5
Canal Zone	(0.0)	(0.0)	(0.0)	(0.0)	(2.6)	(5.1)	(7.6)	(6.9)	(2.6)	(5.1)	(7.6)	(6.9)
Rest of world	(2.8)	(5.7)	(7.4)	(8.8)	(1.7)	(2.8)	(4.7)	(6.4)	(-1.1)	(-2.9)	(-2.7)	(-2.4)
Other services	8.8	6.8	15.6	23.1	47.7	72.2	126.4	166.7	38.9	65.4	110.8	143.6
Net transactions of Colon Free Zone	(0.0)	(0.0)	(0.0)	(0.0)	(6.0)	(8.9)	(29.7)	(45.9)	(6.0)	(8.9)	(29.7)	(45.9)
Other transactions of Canal Zone Net	(0.0)	(0.0)	(0.0)	(0.0)	(36.7)	(51.6)	(76.3)	(90.9)	(36.7)	(51.6)	(76.3)	(90.9)
Other services	(8.8)	(6.8)	(15.6)	(23.1)	(5.0)	(11.7)	(20.4)	(29.9)	(5.0)	(4.9)	(4.8)	(6.8)

Note: Minus sign indicates deficit.

Parentheses are subcomponents of the item above.

Source: International Monetary Fund, Balance of Payments Yearbook, various issues.

and the government's response to alleviate that constraint will be
one of the major deterrents of Panamanian development in the next
decade.

Panama's balance of payments is extremely complicated and
there is no consensus on the best way of measuring the country's
international trade position. To avoid any ambiguity, the terms relating to Panama's balance of payments are as follows:[2] a balance of
payments disequilibrium in Panama is the deficit or surplus in the
balance of unrestricted trade and transfers. This deficit must be
matched by accommodating finance. In a broader sense, the "actual"
balance-of-payments deficit in Panama is defined as the actual amount
of accommodating finance used in any period of time, and a "potential"
balance-of-payments deficit is the amount of accommodating finance
that it would have been necessary to provide in any period to avoid
any depreciation in the exchange rate without the employment of
exchange controls, import restrictions, or other government measures
especially devised to restrict the demand for foreign currency. Here
the important distinction is between reliable and continuing capital
receipts on the one hand, and a temporary inflow, which may be
suddenly reversed, on the other. The most basic measure of balance-
of-payments disequilibrium in Panama is the country's surplus or
deficit of potential and continuing payments for autonomous (unrestricted) trade and transfers. Using these concepts, Panama's balance of payments can be examined through the International Monetary
Fund's (IMF) standard presentation. (Tables 5.1, 5.2) Trade balance
in the IMF classification represents the balance of transfer payments
and forms the balance of autonomous export and imports of goods and
services. This balance, plus that of unrequited transfers, forms the
balance of autonomous trade and transfers. In contrast to nearly all
other countries, Panama's merchandise exports do not even come
close to equaling her merchandise imports. The difference between
the country's merchandise exports and imports is made up by exports
of services to the Canal Zone. The balance of goods and services and
transfer payments must be equal to capital movements, which represent the extent to which the country's net creditor position that is,
assets minus liabilities) vis-a-vis the outside world has worsened
or improved in the period in question. Finally, using the IMF's
standard balance-of-payments presentation, the basic balance is
the total of the balance of goods and services, transfer payments and
capital movements and is, by definition, equal to the movement in
the monetary reserves held by the authorities. The difference between the basic balance and changes in monetary reserves represents
net errors and omissions. Exports to the Canal Zone present several

conceptual problems in terms of their classification in the country's balance-of-payments and national income accounts.

TABLE 5.2

Net Balance-of-Payments Summary, 1960-73
(in millions of balboas)

	1960	1965	1970	1973
Goods and services	-32.4	-29.8	-67.7	-127.3
Trade balance	-69.7	-99.9	-200.7	-296.3
Net services	37.3	70.1	-122.4	169.0
Net transfer payments	0.8	3.7	4.0	0.4
Goods, services				
and transfer payments	-31.6	-26.1	-63.7	126.9
Capital and monetary gold	29.3	23.0	136.6	206.8
Nonmonetary sectors	22.8	17.9	94.9	-504.3
Monetary sectors	6.5	5.1	40.7	711.1
Net errors and ommissions	2.3	3.1	-71.9	-79.9
Capital account	31.6	26.1	63.7	126.9

Source: International Monetary Fund, Balance of Payments Yearbook, various issues.

There are a number of technicalities in the Panamanian national income accounting that should be mentioned. Since several items in Panama's balance of payments and national income are treated by the Panamanian authorities somewhat differently than in the conventional manner, the reader should familiarize himself with these pecularities before attempting any empirical work or in-depth interpretation of the country's economic trends. The first convention of importance is that rises in the balboa value of imports caused by rises in import prices, and changes in the balboa value of exports caused by changes in export prices, are reflected automatically in the Panamanian national accounts when valued in current prices. However, when the national accounts are expressed in terms of balboas of 1960, changes in the prices of exports and imports are not reflected. The methodology of national income accounting used in Panama in principle follows the quantities, not the prices, of export and import items. Thus if the number of kilos of shrimp exported increased by 10 percent between 1960 and 1970, while the price doubled, the national accounts expressed in terms of balboas of 1960 would reflect an increase from, say 100 to 110, not from 100 to 220.

The doubling of shrimp export prices would be reflected in the rubric "Efecto Relacion Intercambio," which is not a part of the GDP expressed in real terms. Thus if one were trying to explain movements in the latter concept, it would be incorrect to say that some of those movements in the latter concept, it would be incorrect to say that some of those movements stem from changes in export and import prices, since the effects of such changes are not reflected in the GDP accounts expressed in real terms. Obviously Panama benefited from the rise in shrimp prices over the decade of the 1960s, but the benefit that Panama received from this source is simply not counted when the change in GDP (in balboas of 1960 purchasing power) is increased. Hence, if one were to attempt to explain changes in GDP at constant prices, it would be a mistake to say that the rise in shrimp prices contributed to the measured growth over the decade of the 1960s, since this rise does not appear in the change in GDP as measured.

A second point of importance is that wages and salaries earned by Panamanians working in the Canal Zone are treated a bit differently in the national accounts than items such as shrimp. When dealing with these wages and salaries, and in order to obtain the contribution of these items to GDP, measured in 1960 balboas, the actual amount of wages and salaries received by the workers in question is recorded and this amount is in turn deflated by the cost-of-living index for Panama (1960 = 100). As a consequence, if wage rates in the Canal Zone double, with employment remaining the same, and with the price index in Panama remaining constant, the result will be an increase in GDP in real terms equal to the rise in wages times the number of workers employed in the Zone. Thus, this factor should be included as one of the forces explaining the change in real GDP between any two time periods. [3]

Panama's balance of payments is characterized by several unique patterns. Exports of services to the Canal Zone during the 1960s were equal to half of the country's imports of goods and services. In addition to enabling the country to run a chronic deficit in its merchandise account, the Canal Zone provides Panama with a stable source of foreign exchange. In part, this stability results from the diversity of exports to the Zone. In 1966 (a typical year for the 1960s), for example, 20,000 Panamanian workers were employed in the Zone, and exports to the Zone amounted to $102 million. About 30 percent of these export earnings came from sales of Panamanian goods to civil and military institutions, contractors, and private organizations located in the Zone; 50 percent came from wages to workers and employees resident in Panama; and the remaining 20 percent were from purchases in Panama by Canal Zone residents. On the average, two-thirds of the export earnings from the Canal Zone come from the operation of the Canal and one-third from the Zone's military bases.

Each of these components is determined by different factors: (1) the wages of Panamanian workers employed in operating and maintaining the Canal Zone depend on shipping; (2) purchases and wages paid by contractors in the Zone are determined by public works programs; and (3) expenditures in Panama by Canal Zone residents vary according to the wage policy adopted by the Canal Company and the United States government agencies in the Zone. U.S. residents in the Zone are an important source of foreign exchange for Panama; during the 1960s they spent between 15 and 20 percent of their income in Panama.

Panama's other exports fall largely into two categories: (1) export of goods, and (2) transit trade, tourism, and other services. During the 1960s, these averaged around 30 and 20 percent, respectively. The Canal Zone therefore accounts for nearly half of Panama's exports.

BALANCE-OF-PAYMENTS PERFORMANCE
AND ECONOMIC GROWTH IN PANAMA

A great deal of controversy is currently taking place in Panama over the relationship between balance of payments, economic growth, and the social objectives of the country—the question of whether all of these can be achieved simultaneously at levels considered desirable or acceptable by the government. Virtually all of this discussion, however, has been based on a priori reasoning. Two opposing views have been advanced. * The first claims that a good balance-of-payments performance in Panama can be achieved, as a rule, only through pursuing deflationary domestic policies to reduce the country's rate of inflation and thus make the country's exports more competitive. The other school of thought maintains that expansion of domestic policies can actually have a favorable impact on the country's balance of payments through fuller utilization of the

---

*Basically there is no formal debate. One view is that espoused by the numerous consultants from the University of Chicago, and the second, that of the economists associated with the United Nations Economic Commission for Latin America. It is, however, misleading to categorize the two viewpoints as diametrically opposed.

country's resources. This study analyzes both of these opposing
views. Our analysis indicates a positive relationship between changes
in the balance of payments and GNP. To summarize our findings:
growth in Panama has usually been associated with a strong balance-
of-payments performance, particularly when such a performance
has been the result of a rapid expansion in exports.* Imports have
also accelerated in these circumstances, but their expansion has
usually lagged behind that of exports. Sustained rises in the inflow
of foreign capital have also had a favorable effect on growth. On the
other hand, it appears that the country's periods of weak growth performance, which were associated with a good balance of payments,
took place when foreign reserve gains were attained by restricting
imports through trade controls.

The behavior of the balance of payments in Panama during
the last decade permits the identification of two periods. The first
extends from 1965 to 1970, during which trade in goods and services
left a small but positive balance, the annual average of which was
U.S. $1.8 million. The second period, from 1971 to the present, has
resulted in a significant negative balance on the same account: the
average annual deficit totaled $37 billion between 1971 and 1972. The
deficit continued to increase in 1974 and 1975.

BALANCE OF PAYMENTS
AND THE CAPACITY TO IMPORT

One of the major reasons for Panama's rapid growth during
the 1965-70 period was its growing capacity to import. That capacity
encompasses all balance-of-payments receipts and payments over
which the Panamanian authorities are assumed to have only limited
control; that is, it represents the sum of all balance-of-payments
flows with the exceptions of (1) the part of merchandise import payments that reflects a variation in the import volume, (2) short-term
capital movements (including errors and omissions), and (3) international reserve changes. The country's capacity to import in the
late 1960s can be quantified by examining the trends of these underlying determinants, that is, by measuring changes in export volume,
in the terms of trade, in the service and transfer account, and in
long-term and medium-term capital flows.[4]

---

*See the Keynesian model developed in Chapter 11.

In terms of an analysis of the interrelationships among government policy, the capacity to import, and rate of economic growth, the period from 1965 to 1970 is particularly instructive. During that time the country sustained a high rate of economic growth and simultaneously a good balance-of-payments performance with little government interference. The country added to its reserves in each year except 1969; in 1970 it had $17 million in reserves. In contrast, the 1965-70 average was $6.1 million. At the same time, the net official international reserve position of the country averaged 15 percent of GDP.

MEASUREMENT OF PANAMA'S CAPACITY TO IMPORT

Panama experienced a marked growth of export volume, particularly in 1968 and 1969, which was the most important factor by far in the country's rather impressive gain of capacity to import. In absolute terms, the country's annual exports at 1965 prices between 1966 and 1970 averaged $19.8 million or 2.7 times the $7.1 million figure of 1965. The rise in exports was progressive, reaching more than $31 million in 1970.

The terms of trade did not favor Panama between 1965 and 1970. A small initial improvement in 1966 and again in 1968 was followed by sharp reversals in 1969 and 1970. The changes in the terms of trade cost the country $23 million during the latter 1960s or an average of $4.7 million per year. (It was the progressive rise in import prices, and not a drop in export prices, that was responsible for the adverse trend in the country's terms of trade. The rise in import prices cost the country an average of $17.8 annually, with a progressive deterioration reaching $33.5 million in 1970.)

During the 1965-70 period, the service and transfer account had a small positive impact on the country's capacity to import merchandise. The gain in this account amounted to $23.2 million over the period, but there was no discernible pattern in the year-to-year fluctuations. Since the service and transfer account includes receipts from the Canal Zone and tourism in the country, these would seem to be the major sources of this improvement.

Long-term and medium-term capital flows were a distinctly positive factor in the country's balance-of-payments performance during the 1965-70 period. The improvement in this account in relation to 1965 netted the country $30.5 million over the five years, with a markedly progressive improvement beginning in 1969.

The combined balance-of-payments effects of these four areas of change—in export volume, in the terms of trade, in the service and transfer account, and in long-term and medium-term capital flows—resulted, during this period, in a gain in import capacity in relation to 1965 of over $260.5 million. Except for 1967, this gain was progressive, rising from $27.4 million to $94.9 million in 1970—an increase of nearly 250 percent.

UTILIZATION OF THE CAPACITY TO IMPORT

To determine how the country utilized its increased capacity to import,[5] it is necessary to compare the calculated import capacities with actual import levels—that is, the demand for imports to the actual rates of import capacity utilization. Changes in import prices over the period under revies (1965-70) have been incorporated in the data used for calculating the changes in the terms of trade—one of the more significant factors affecting the capacity to import. Therefore the demand for imports is defined here in terms of 1965 prices.

During the years 1965-70, the country's import demand increased very rapidly from year to year, particularly from 1968 to 1970. In absolute terms, the annual import volume in this period was $52.1 million, or more than 25 percent of its 1965 level. The increase reached almost $95 million in 1970.

More relevant to the present analysis is the country's change in import demand in relation to change in capacity to import, that is, the degree of underutilization or overutilization of import capacity. A constant rate of utilization of the capacity to import in relation to 1965 would imply that the country's policies—in the fields of import taxation, import and exchange restrictions, credit policy and exchange rate policy—had a net impact on import demand equal to the change in the capacity to import. A positive change would signify that the country overimported while a negative change would indicate that it did not fully use the change in its import capacity. For Panama, there does not appear to be a discernible trend. The average of 1965-70 was 100 percent, indicating that over the period as a whole, the country kept its import capacity and imports fairly closely balanced.

In assessing this result, it is important to bear in mind that a 100 percent rate of utilization of import capacity, by definition, precludes any international reserve gain, save for inflows of short-term funds and allocations of special drawing rights. While there was, on the average, little difference between the rate of utilization of import capacity and the level of import capacity, it is possible that several of the factors determining the country's import utilization may have been active during the 1965-70 period, although only to offset each other. These factors include import taxation, import restrictions, and credit policy. Other policy variable changes in the exchange rate were of course precluded, since the United States did not devalue the dollar during this time.

The weight of import taxation in Panama in terms of annual ratios of import tax revenues to cost-insurance-freight (c.i.f.) import values did not change significantly between 1965 and 1970. The average was 9.2 for the country. One has to conclude, therefore, that changes in import taxation probably did not contribute significantly to changes in intensity of utilization of import capacity.

An extensive system of exchange control, tariffs, and non-tariff import restrictions designed to control the level of imports has not been introduced in Panama. The country does have a system of restrictive import quotas and prohibitions, but these devices have been used mainly to protect local industry, and in any case did not change significantly between 1965 and 1970.

Domestic financial policy has the potential for being a powerful tool of balance-of-payments management in Panama. Financial policy is carried out by the country's commercial banks and these are not under direct government control. The banks have, however, in the past been rather responsive to the changing needs for funds of both the public and private sectors, and hence reflect the government's fiscal policies. To this extent the government's financial policies are represented by changes in the volume of commercial bank credit. The amount of credit extended by the country's commercial banking system has become a major factor in determining the level of the country's imports. However, a measurement of the effects on import demand of a given credit policy is made difficult by the fact that this policy—and the financial policy mix for which it is a proxy—influences not only the country's balance-of-payments performance but also the nation's domestic prices. *

Any problem involving financial considerations in Panama is difficult to analyze because there are no reliable estimates of the money supply. The money supply in countries with national currencies is conventionally defined as currency in circulation plus demand deposits, or as currency in circulation plus demand and time deposits. The absence of such data for Panama poses difficult but not insurmountable problems for the analysis of the role of money in the economy. Data on bank deposits do exist, and given other information about the Panamanian economy, reasonable inferences based, for example, on country comparisons can be made

---

*This is elaborated upon in detail in Chapter 11.

about the relationship between money, inflation, and balance of
payments in the economy over time.[6]

It is assumed here that the impact of credit policies on the
capacity to import in Panama operates through a mechanism whereby
changes in the stock of bank credit must equal changes in the country's
stock of savings (in the form of claims on the banking system, generated by real income changes plus or minus changes in the community's preference for such savings) in order to be consistent with
the country's balance-of-payments equilibrium and domestic price
stability. For example, if domestic prices in Panama are to follow
the price level in the rest of the world rather than remain absolutely
stable, then the changes in the stock of bank credit will also have to
reflect the movement of foreign prices. The change in prices is
simply a result of the fact that credit policy is incapable of influ-
output in Panama in the short run; given some of the country's rigidities in production(for example, deficient transport system), the
structure of production could not be easily altered in a short period
of time. Any departures in Panama from balance-of-payments
equilibrium and disparities between domestic and foreign price
movements are therefore an indication that the observed change in
the stock of bank credit differs from the equilibrium stock.

For example, during the 1960-68 period (selected because
this was prior to the rapid development of commercial banks in
Panama), bank deposits in Panama, defined as demand, time, and
adjusted interbank deposits, grew at an average annual rate of 14.9
percent. Assuming that currency in circulation was a constant
proportion of total bank deposits, this rate of monetary expansion,
being almost twice as large as the rate of expansion of real GDP,
almost certainly would not have been consistent with the observed
price stability during this time period. Although a more detailed
analysis is required to reconcile these figures, it is reasonable to
conclude that a substantial reduction in the ratio of currency in
circulation to the money supply occurred during this period. If
this were the case, expansion of the money supply would have pro-
ceeded at a lower rate than that of deposit expansion, say, at a
rate about one and a half times as large as the growth of real GDP.
Such a crude estimate appears to be consistent with the observed
behavior of income velocity, taken in the special case of Panama as
the ratio of money GDP to bank deposits. With this definition of
velocity, the country's velocity ($V = PT/M$, where V = velocity,
PT = money GDP, and M = money as defined here) for 1960-68
displayed a rather definite negative trend, falling from 3.43 in 1960
to 2.43 in 1968. With the exceptions of 1961 and 1964, when velocity
rose to 3.70 and 3.74, respectively, the decline in velocity through

the period was relatively steady. The extent of the decline, however, was quite substantial, much more than would ordinarily be expected over a relatively short period of time. [7]

If currency in circulation declined as a proportion of the money supply, however, the decline in velocity would not have been so sharp. For example, money GDP rose by 7.6 percent between 1967 and 1968 while bank deposits rose by 17.0 percent. If one makes the reasonable assumption (based on the experience in other countries) that the income elasticity of demand for money was 1.5, it would follow that currency in circulation would have had to decline by about 5.6 percent to maintain monetary equilibrium and price stability. [8]

Credit policy, however, can be judged only in terms of its combined effect on the two variables, bank credit stock and equilibrium stock, and this raises the technical problem of devising a combined measurement of balance-of-payments performance and price movements. The methodology followed here satisfies the need to bring to a common denominator annual balance-of-payments performance and annual price changes. The former is defined in terms of net international reserve movements; the latter as changes in domestic price levels—levels of consumer prices—deflated by changes in import prices.

Using these relationships and definitions, international reserve movements and changes in domestic prices relative to those in the rest of the world can both be related to changes in the country's stock of money (demand deposits) and quasi-money (demand deposits, time and savings deposits, and other restricted deposits). The effect of international reserve movements on changes in the stock money and quasi-money in Panama is calculated by using a straight-forward one-to-one conversion. [9] The price effect was calculated by applying the percentage change of domestic prices relative to import prices during the year to the stock of money and quasi-money at the beginning of the year. The two calculated effects were then added or netted, and this sum or difference was taken to represent domestic bank credit expansions or contractions in excess or short of those that would have been consistent with external and internal equilibrium. These credit excesses or shortages were then related to the observed annual changes in bank credit. Changes in bank credit were calculated to indicate when credit expansion was in excess or short of that which would have been consistent with absolute balance-of-payments equilibrium and absolute domestic price stability relative to prices in the rest of the world.

The results of these calculations for Panama indicate that (during 1965-70) the country had a relatively low rate of credit expansion (93.7 percent) on the basis of the definition used here. [10]

For the period as a whole, the change in short-term capital movements (securities that mature in less than a year) was not large. However, in 1970 short-run inflows of capital totaled $20.2 million in contrast to a $0.6 million average for the period as a whole. The question regarding short-term capital movements most relevant to the present analysis is the extent to which they were or were not induced by national policies. Such a judgment is relevant here because to the extent that short-term capital movements are policy induced, they should be treated in the context of the present analysis as explaining rates of utilization of import capacity; and to the extent that they are judged to be spontaneous, they should be treated as explaining import capacity.

But a judgment of motivation[11] is at most hazardous, and the fact that short-term capital movements are lumped together with errors and omissions—some of which must be ascribed to other balance-of-payments flows—detracts even more from such evidence as is available. Given the country's liberal banking policies, it is clear that the inflow of sizable short-term funds into Panama in 1970 was at least partly induced by the country's authorities.

To summarize, changes in the weight of import taxation and in the level of restrictiveness of nontariff import and exchange restrictions do not seem to have played major roles in import demand management in Panama during the period under review. Also Panama, by observing restraint in its domestic financial policies, moderated its demand for imports.

After 1970, a marked change in government policies toward the foreign sector seems to have taken place (in comparison with 1965-70 period), but because of the preliminary nature of the data, only general conclusions can be drawn. In general, indications are that the authorities appear to be following a more restrictive set of policies vis-a-vis the external sector. For example, in the early 1970s the government increased trade restrictions on imports, particularly quantitative restrictions, in order to stimulate import replacement industrialization.

It is too early to assess the total impact of the government's increased restrictions on the foreign sector after 1970. Trends in the components of the country's balance of payments indicate, however, a rapid deterioration in the country's external position.

RECENT DEVELOPMENTS IN THE
BALANCE OF PAYMENTS

In 1972 the combined transactions in goods and services and unrequited transfers resulted in a deficit of $115 million, or seven times that for 1968. The net inflow in the capital account, which was about $37 million higher than for 1971, was more than sufficient to finance the current account deficit. Export earnings in 1972 declined by over 2 percent after an increase of 6 percent in 1971, was more than sufficient to finance the current account deficit. Export earnings in 1972 declined by over 2 percent after an increase of 6 percent in 1971, while imports increased by 2 percent in 1972 and 10 percent in 1971. The trade deficit, which amounted to $129 million in 1968, rose steadily after that year, reaching $225 million in 1971 and $258 million in 1972. Net receipts from invisible transactions with the Canal Zone continued to give strength to the balance of payments, and in 1971 were responsible for financing roughly one-half of the trade deficit. The public sector's growing debt burden was reflected in 1972 by a 20 percent increase in net outflows of investment income.

The total value of merchandise exports has demonstrated a sluggish rate of growth in recent years and there has been practically no evidence of diversification. The average annual rate of 3.7 percent for 1968-72 was substantially below the real rate of growth of GDP during the same period. As a result, the percentage of total exports to GDP measured in current prices has declined steadily from 14 percent in 1968 to 10 percent in 1972.[12]

In 1972 there was a total deficit of almost $97 million in the current account. In the capital account this deficit was financed by net inflows of external funds (chiefly of private origin) of almost $40 million to the national government and $38 million to the government's autonomous institutions, and by net external private investment of $19 million. At the same time, the banking system contributed net inflows of almost $60 million. Whether on the basis of an "actual" or a "potential" deficit,[13] it is clear that by the early 1970s Panama was experiencing a fundamental disequilibrium in its balance of payments.

SUMMARY

The balance of payments is the major determinant of the pace of economic development in Panama. Yet the government has had little control over the foreign sector, particularly in terms of reducing a deficit. As a result, the level of aggregate demand and the pace of economic growth in the economy as a whole have had spillover effects on the balance of payments; that is, although ad hoc modification through tariff changes and direct controls has been used as a substitute for changes in the effective exchange rate, it has not been effective in controlling the level of imports and exports.

The limited flexibility of the latter (due to the constant peg to the dollar) imposes a real constraint on domestic economic policy.

A more fundamental linkage between domestic economic performance and the balance of payments also exists in Panama. The country's current account deficits, however financed, represent a transfer of real resources from the rest of the world to the domestic economy. For Panama, this transfer is particularly important, in part because the current development effort is resulting in a constant push against the country's limited resources, but also because foreign resources extend the range of goods available to a relatively far greater degree than do domestic resources. Imports often incorporate the latest technology. For this reason, the ability of the country to finance a high level of imports—and optimally a large current account deficit—has become a major factor in its economic growth and welfare.

Balance-of-payments financing in Panama has two aspects: magnitude and permissiveness. The magnitude determines how large a deficit the country can support; permissiveness, how much domestic effort is needed to increase the magnitude of financing. Permissiveness is important even if it is temporary. The post-1968 government's economic philosophy has been built up around the notion of a concentrated and major acceleration in investment. One of the components of this policy is a temporary period of maximum balance-of-payments permissiveness. The government's assumption is that increased foreign exchange availability will be instrumental in promoting rapid economic growth and that a permissive balance-of-payments position will thus facilitate rapid capital expansion without a heavy load on domestic savings or in taxation.

The government's strategy appears sound. However, its strategic balance-of-payments permissiveness can be only temporary. Sooner or later the country will have to pay more of its own way. For this reason exports are beginning to assume critical importance, as are the classic development problems of import replacement and exchange regimes. For Panama, it appears that the margin of permissiveness will be less generous in the future than formerly. Continuation of former levels of balance-of-payments financing is uncertain, let alone additional financing of balance-of-payments deficits. And reducing payments deficits to levels that can be supported largely by the country's own resources and productivity is an even harder problem. More and more, however, the country should be prepared for the day when it may have to base its economic development mainly on its own resources and efforts.

In the early 1970s, rapidly increasing import requirements, resulting in part from the government's expanded expenditure program, coupled with stagnating trends in major exports including revenues from the Canal Zone, have resulted in rising current account deficits. These have required expanded external borrowing by the government, and are threatening to impair its creditworthiness.

CONCLUSIONS

Panama's balance-of-payments position is crucial to the country's development strategy. A shortage of foreign exchange could force the government to cut back on a number of its key programs. The role of the canal and associated treaties is particularly important in influencing the movements of the country's balance of payments. In evaluating the country's performance in this area and in relating it on the one hand to government policies and, on the other, to factors partially or entirely beyond the control of the government, it will be of particular interest, as negotiations proceed, to have a clear idea of the effect that minor changes in the treaties might have on the economy through their impact on the foreign sector.

NATIONAL INCOME AND THE
BALANCE OF PAYMENTS

Panama's balance-of-payments disequilibrium is reflected in the country's national income accounts (Table 5.3) as an increasing trade deficit. The deficit between imports (including net factor payments) and exports is equal (due to national income accounting conventions) to the difference between domestic savings and investment. The deficit in the balance of payments can also be looked at in terms of the growing deficit between domestic supply and demand. *

---

*Aggregate demand consists of private consumption, private investment, public consumption, public investment and the capacity to import. Aggregate supply consists of gross domestic product and imports. In 1960 aggregate supply was greater than aggregate demand by 6.8 million (1960) balboas. By 1964 aggregate demand had become greater than aggregate supply by 0.9 million (1960) balboas. The difference between aggregate demand and supply steadily increased so that by 1969 aggregate demand exceeded aggregate supply by 39.0 million (1960) balboas. By 1971 aggregate demand was still 32.4 million (1960) balboas in excess of aggregate supply. Detailed estimates of the supply-and-demand balances for Panama are available from the author upon request.

TABLE 5.3

The Foreign Resource Gap, 1950-73
(in millions of 1960 balboas)

	1950	1955	1960	1965	1970	1973
Exports of goods and nonfactor services	109.8	113.7	127.3	223.4	324.5	351.6
	(44.2)	(38.2)	(31.6)	(37.1)	(37.4)	(31.9)
Imports of goods and nonfactor services	105.4	122.6	149.1	256.4	396.4	464.1
	(42.4)	(41.2)	(37.0)	(42.6)	(45.7)	(43.7)
Net factor payments	-10.6	-17.3	-12.4	-15.8	-26.4	-40.3
	(4.3)	(5.8)	(3.1)	(2.6)	(3.0)	(3.8)
(Exports – Imports) Goods and nonfactor services	4.4	-8.9	-21.8	-33.0	-71.9	-112.5
	(1.8)	(3.0)	(5.4)	(5.5)	(8.3)	(10.6)
(Exports – Imports) Total	-6.2	-26.2	-34.2	-48.8	-98.3	-152.8
	(2.5)	(8.8)	(8.5)	(8.1)	(11.3)	(14.4)

Note: Figures in parentheses indicate percentage of GNP.

Source: Computed from Contraloria General de la Republica, Direccion Estadistica y Censo, Ingreso Nacional, various issues.

The causes of the country's balance-of-payments disequilibrium can therefore be analyzed in terms of the movements in the different accounts presented in the IMF standard presentation, the domestic gap between savings and investment, or the difference between aggregate demand and supply.[14]

Panama's balance-of-payments disequilibrium could result from two broad causes. The first is the low competitiveness of domestic production in world markets, and the second the substantial expansion since 1968 in domestic expenditure. Both factors are interrelated and as a result identification of the relative importance of each is extremely difficult to quantify. Combining information gained from different facets of the economy, however, it is possible to piece together a fairly clear picture of the underlying mechanisms responsible for the country's increasing foreign account deficit. An examination of the country's monetary system and the determinants of the country's money supply, for example, would show how changes in the country's financial structure and money supply have created the disequilibrium through their influence on aggregate demand and supply. A purely monetary approach, however, does not provide detailed data on demand and supply and, hence, demand and supply analysis is a necessary supplement.

While an analysis of the major elements of demand and supply (particularly for Panama's main exports and imports) is superior to the analysis of monetary factors (because the quantity of money in Panama is very difficult to determine), neither approach taken by itself is sufficient to identify the policies needed to be undertaken by the authorities to solve the country's external imbalance and at the same time achieve long-run objectives.

NOTES

1. The balance-of-payments accounts for Panama are published in the International Monetary Fund Yearbook (Washington, D.C.: International Monetary Fund) and are derived from data supplied to the Fund by the Direccion de Estadistica y Censo, which publishes the country's official balance of payments statistics in greater detail in Estadistica Panamena, serie "D" (Balanza de Pagos).

2. As defined in J.E. Meade, The Theory of International Economic Policy, Volume I, The Balance of Payments (London: Oxford University Press, 1951), p. 15.

3. See Arnold C. Harberger, "The Past Growth and Future Prospects of the Panamanian Economy," mimeographed (Panama

City: Agency for International Development, 1972), pp. 8-10, for a
more detailed discussion of these points. Other conventions such as
the treatment of wages and salaries earned by Panamanians working
in the Canal Zone are discussed in Balance of Payments Yearbook
(Washington, D.C.: International Monetary Fund, 1975), vol. 26,
bound edition.

   4. The concept of the "capacity to import" has been defined
in a number of different ways in the literature. It should be noted
that the text has been consistent in the measurement of Panama's
capacity to import. Somewhat different results would of course
have been obtained from other measures. It is particularly important
to note that the capacity to import is not being defined in the manner
usually done by the United Nations Economic Commission for Latin
America. See their Analysis and Projections of Economic Development, VII, The Economic Development of Panama (Panama City:
United Nations Economic and Social Council, 1959).

   5. All data in these calculations are from the International
Monetary Fund Yearbook, op. cit., various issues.

   6. Of particular interest is the work of Arnold C. Harberger.
See his "Reflections on the Monetary System of Panama," in
Chicago Essays in Economic Development, ed. David Wall (Chicago:
University of Chicago Press, 1972), pp. 158-73.

   7. See Milton Friedman, Money and Economic Development:
The Horowitz Lectures of 1972 (New York: Praeger Publishers, 1973)
for a theoretical explanation of the stability of velocity under circumstances similar to that existing in Panama during most of the 1960s.

   8. See James Christian, "A Macro-Sectoral Survey of the
Economy of Panama," mimeographed (Panama City: Ministerio de
Planificacion y Politica Economica, 1970): 8-9.

   9. Admittedly this is an arbitrary procedure, yet one
usually accepted in the literature. See for example Harry Johnson,
"Panama as a Regional Financial Center: A Preliminary Analysis
of Development Contribution," Economic Development and Cultural
Change 24, no. 2 (January 1976): 270-76.

   10. These conclusions, while differing in magnitude from
other studies, are consistent with them. For example, in an excellent study Alvaro E. Larravide identified a clear-cut trend in a
number of financial variables during the 1960s. He concludes that
factors such as interest rates in line with those prevailing in free
markets abroad, and a high degree of confidence in the currency,
fostered savings habits in Panama and promoted strong increases
in financial savings. He estimates that claims of the private sector
against the banking system doubled from 1964 ($107.5 million) to
December 1969 ($220.3 million). In turn, this rapid growth made

possible an equivalent expansion (according to his estimates) in
domestic credit from $128.0 million in 1964 to $283.2 million in
September 1969. At the same time, however, he feels that the monetary effects of external developments automatically generated cor-
rections at the source of demand pressures—the total stock of money
and quasi-money—and this in turn led to a pattern of relative domestic
price stability with yearly price increases averaging 1 percent during
this period. Alvaro E. Larravide, "Monetary Discipline and Growth—
The Case of Panama," Finance and Development 7, no. 2 (1970),
pp. 49-50.

11. See in particular Fritz Machlup, "Three Concepts of the
Balance of Payments and the So-called Dollar Shortage," Economic
Journal 60, no.1 (March 1950): 46-68, for a description of some of
the pitfalls involved in interpreting the balance-of-payments
statements of a country.

12. Contraloria General Direccion de Estadistica y Censo,
serie "C" Ingreso Nacional, various issues.

13. Again following Meade, op. cit., p. 16.

14. According to the quantity-theory approach, the condition
under which the economy is balanced is that the quantity of money
increases in the same proportion as GNP at constant prices. The
quantity-theory approach is, however, identical to the demand-
and-supply approach only if the income velocity of money is equal
to the marginal capital output ratio—a condition that could occur
only by chance. Only in proportional equilibrium growth could
this condition be achieved. In any case, it is highly unlikely that
the country has planned for proportional growth, or that it will do
so in the future. Bent Hansen, Long- and Short-Term Planning in
Underdeveloped Countries, Professor Dr. F. de Vries Lectures
(Amsterdam: North-Holland Publishing Company, 1967), pp. 46-47.

While the major causes underlying the deterioration in Panama's balance of payments are easy to identify, the mechanisms responsible for the observed trends are extremely complex and warrant a detailed analysis. Many export items of goods and services need to be identified by their basic determinants, for each major category is determined by separate forces. Registered exports[1] of goods, for example, are determined by the import pattern of the country's major trading partners—especially the United States. In addition, Panama's strategic geographical position results in numerous activities connected with the traffic in goods and persons through the Isthmus: the entreport trade, sales to ships and aircraft in transit, sales of goods and services to tourists and transients, and also activities of the Colon Free Zone, which facilitate international commerce.

Panama's balance of trade and particularly the composition of its exports differ from those of most small country economies[2] as a result of three major factors: (1) the presence of the Panama Canal and other facilities operated by the United States in the Canal Zone; (2) the absence of a central bank, a feature that precludes Panama from engaging in an independent monetary policy, and (3) the existence of a free zone—the Colon Free Zone which has developed since World War II into a major distribution center for Latin America. Each of these characteristics has significantly affected the past trends and current composition of Panamanian exports.[3]

TRENDS IN EXPORTS TO THE CANAL ZONE

The major exports from Panama to the Canal Zone consist of (1) wages paid to Panamanians working in the Zone, and (2) purchases in Panama of goods and services by residents of the Zone. Traditionally these items have represented the country's single most important credit in its balance-of-payments account. These flows are registered in the Panamanian national income account statistics as current account activities (Table 6.1). However, unlike most items traditionally included in the current account, these revenues are unresponsive to domestic economic policy or economic activity. Sales of Panamanian goods to the Zone, for example, are a function of the size of the United States military presence in the Zone, the number of dependents in each military family, the volume of new construction on the canal, and so on. Obviously, most activity in the Canal Zone is undertaken by the United States without consultation with the Panamanian authorities. In any case, these activities could not be influenced by Panamanian monetary and fiscal policies. Therefore, activities in the Zone influence rather than reflect Panama's economic performance. After peaking at $85 million in 1943, when they represented over 90 percent of Panama's current account earnings from abroad, net receipts from the Zone fell to $41 million in 1947 and remained at that level throughout the 1950s. Nevertheless, they still represented over 50 percent of current account receipts. Their importance to Panama was reflected in the depression and deflation set off by their decline in the late 1940s and early 1950s.

The provisions of the Remon-Eisenhower Treaty of 1955 strongly affected Panama's net receipts from the Zone, and their impact on the Panamanian economy between 1956 and 1965. During that period, earnings from the Panama Canal Zone rose to over 13 percent per year.[4] The economy became more dependent on the Zone as a source of exports needed to cover the country's chronic deficit with the rest of the world. By 1968, these exports covered 80 percent of this current account deficit, in contrast to 1950 when they covered only 65 percent. However, since 1968 net receipts from the Zone have increased at the rate of only 4 percent yearly. As a result, by the early 1970s their coverage of the current account deficit with the rest of the world has continued to decline.

Purchases of goods and services from Panamanian enterprises and individuals by the agencies and individuals of the Canal Zone produced an average of $55 million per year in the 1960s. They more than doubled between 1960 and 1970 (from $33 million to $74 million). The high rates of expansion registered are mainly

TABLE 6.1

Balance-of-Payments Current Account to the Canal Zone, Selected Years, 1950-72
(current prices, in millions of balboas)

	1950	1955	1960	1965	1970	1972
Exports						
Merchandise	6.6	8.6	8.9	17.4	22.1	24.2
	(13.9)	(17.2)	(14.0)	(17.7)	(14.5)	(14.8)
Travel	24.5	24.5	13.2	21.4	37.3	39.7
	(51.7)	(48.9)	(20.7)	(21.8)	(24.6)	(24.2)
Government services	0.4	0.5	0.7	3.2	7.6	5.5
	(0.8)	(1.0)	(1.1)	(3.3)	(5.0)	(3.4)
Other services	15.3	14.6	38.1	52.8	77.6	84.2
	(32.3)	(29.1)	(59.7)	(53.7)	(51.1)	(51.3)
Private transfers	0.6	1.9	2.9	3.5	7.3	10.4
	(1.3)	(3.8)	(4.5)	(3.6)	(4.8)	(6.3)
Total	47.4	50.1	63.8	98.3	151.9	164.0
Imports						
Merchandise	4.3	8.0	11.0	2.6	3.8	4.6
	(79.6)	(87.9)	(78.0)	(55.3)	(62.3)	(65.7)
Freight	0.7	0.6	1.6	0.6	0.8	0.9
	(13.0)	(6.6)	(11.3)	(12.8)	(13.1)	(12.9)
Other transport	0.2	0.2	0.2	0.1	0.2	0.2
	(3.7)	(2.2)	(1.4)	(2.1)	(3.3)	(2.9)
Government services	—	—	—	—	—	—
Other services	0.2	0.3	1.3	1.4	1.3	1.3
	(3.7)	(3.3)	(9.2)	(29.8)	(21.3)	(18.6)
Total	5.4	9.1	14.1	4.7	6.1	7.0
Current account balance	42.0	41.0	49.7	93.6	145.8	157.0

Note: Figures in parentheses indicate percent of total.
Source: Contraloria General de la Republica, Direccion de Estadistica y Censo, serie "C" Engreso Nacional, various issues.

attributable to increased purchases by the official agencies and non-Panamanians living in the Canal Zone (rates of 9.8 and 11.9 percent, respectively). As a result, their contribution to the country's export earnings from the Zone increased from 29 to 36 percent during the 1960s.

The canal annuity, the wages and salaries of Panamanian employees (including pensions and retirement benefits), and purchases of goods and services amounted on the average to $115 million in the 1960s. This represented 43 percent of the exports of goods and services and other foreign exchange income earned by Panama. Earnings also increased very rapidly (8.7 percent per year). They rose from $70.2 million in 1960 to $161.5 million in 1970, thus supplementing the even higher rates of growth of exports to the rest of the world, which increased at 13.6 percent a year during this period.

This favorable trend in export earnings from the Zone in the 1960s is in sharp contrast to that of the 1950s. In the 1960s the average rate of increase was 8.8 percent as compared with 2.3 percent in the 1950s. The increase in the 1960s was due to the following factors: (1) military establishments employed larger numbers of civilians; (2) the average wage rates of persons employed by official agencies increased; and (3) the demand for manufactured goods or services originating in Panama rose.

Panama's exports to the Canal Zone have therefore permitted the country to enjoy a large and chronic deficit in her commercial transactions with the rest of the world (here "rest of the world" includes transactions with countries or areas other than the Zone).

The major reason for Panama's large trade surplus with the Canal Zone is its competitiveness. To a large degree the Zone is a captive market for Panama, in the sense that Panama can deliver its goods and services to the Canal Zone with very low transport costs. Also, the wage structure in the Canal Zone for Panamanian workers has been adjusted to that of United States workers.[5] This is considerably higher than that which these workers would obtain in the Panamanian sector. Thus, those factors (labor and capital) trading with the Canal Zone receive a greater remuneration than would be possible if they had to produce exports for world markets. Consequently, Panama receives a benefit from the Canal that is partly in the nature of a transfer (the United States minimum wage laws) and partly a result of comparative advantage (location).[6]

Because of price changes in world markets, purchasing power of exports to the Canal Zone have declined since 1950. In

1950 revenues received by Panama from exports to the Zone accounted for 62.4 percent of the country's ability to purchase imports. By 1970 this figure had fallen to 39.6 percent.

There is little reason to believe the favorable conditions created by the Canal Zone will continue through the 1970s, since the numbers of military personnel necessary to meet the strategic needs of the United States have reached their maximum. If anything, there will be a decline in military forces located in the Canal Zone (for jungle training purposes) and military traffic through the Canal Zone (as a result of the ending of hostility in Southeast Asia). Also, the rate of wage increases of Panamanians working in the Zone should decline since wages have nearly attained a level comparable to those prevailing in the United States Civil Service. The Canal Company's (the U.S. agency responsible for maintaining the canal) programs for increasing the productivity of Panamanian workers may also level off, as a new sea-level canal will probably be in operation by 1985; few improvements are being made on the existing canal in anticipation of the construction of a new interoceanic route. [7]

In short, it appears that the canal and the Canal Zone are unlikely to continue their role of the 1960s as the driving force of the Panamanian economy. It is possible that the Zone could resume its stimulating impact on the economy if a new treaty established a new set of relationships between the Zone and the republic. For example, a reasonable and equitable increase in the canal annuity received by the government (the United States pays Panama about $2 million yearly for the use of the canal while it gives Spain $25 million for the use of several isolated airfields) might give the country the means and a period of time to correct the economy's existing structural balances. If some sort of new economic arrangement between the United States and Panama is not reached, the country's continued progress will become more precarious, and if maintained, would involve a considerably higher economic cost than was involved in the rapid economic expansion of the 1960s.

If Panama is given greater access to the markets of the Canal Zone and an appropriate share in the income or profits of the Canal Company and other suitable compensation, the government will acquire a freedom of action that, properly employed, will lead to a substantial rise in the rate of development of the country and to the initiation of economic and social programs of great significance for the country.

The Colon Free Zone

The Colon Free Zone, which was created by Decree Law No. 18 in 1948, [8] is unique in the Western Hemisphere as a distribution and processing center serving Latin America and the Caribbean. It was established to encourage the development of activities in the area in which Panama has a great comparative advantage: the provision of services to facilitate international commerce.

After the beginning of operations in 1953, it developed slowly during its early years, but grew quite rapidly in the 1960s, expanding from 14 to 100 acres of warehouses, manufacturing plants, and display centers. More than 600 companies involved in international marketing are at present using it for warehousing, processing, assembling and packing, increasing the volume of in-transit merchandise each year; goods brought to the Free Zone are later shipped abroad by sea, air, and land, free of all customs duties. Almost 170 firms carry on operations in the area (not including operations only).

The Free Zone has been an attractive area for investment because of the existence of the canal and the fact that Tocumen International Airport is a significant hub in the airline route system of the entire Western Hemisphere. It has also been encouraged by fiscal incentives; firms operating in the Zone receive an exemption equal to 90 percent of their income tax liabilities. [9]

The Free Zone contributes to the Panamanian economy in three ways: (1) by increasing the employment of labor; (2) by increasing exports leading to improvement in the balance of payments; and (3) through foreign firms in the Zone which introduce and expose Panamanian workers to advanced technology. At the same time, the legal conditions covering production in the Zone make resale of these goods in the Panamanian economy illegal. These arrangements make it possible for the country to take advantage of the benefits derived from the Zone while at the same time protecting its own domestic industries from the competition of foreign producers in the Zone.

In 1971, the Zone's labor force was estimated at close to 2,500 and operations in the area contributed approximately $39 million, on a gross value-added basis, to Panama's balance of payments. Net receipts after deducting profit remittances and other transactions of nonresident companies were $16 million. [10]

In 1973, chemicals, manufactures, and machinery constituted 96 percent of exports, most of which were air freighted to final destinations after having reached Panama by ship.

Two limitations stand in the way of possible expansion of the Colon Free Zone.[11] The first, and more important one, is the lack of space for new installations. The second relates to several new laws[12] concerning incentives for exports. This legislation extends some of the benefits granted to firms producing in the Zone to firms producing (only industrial products) in other parts of the country.

The Colon Free Zone is operating at peak capacity and, as it is situated on a peninsula surrounded by the Canal Zone, a shortage of land may eventually slow down its expansion. To avoid this, an 11-acre site near the city of Colon is being developed. In the longer run, it is possible that a 450-acre area including an air strip, which is currently part of the Canal Zone, can be utilized to expand the Free Zone's facilities. At present, plans are being studied for the development of an industrial park and a free zone at the new Tocumen Airport.[13]

Travel and Transportation

Export receipts from services such as travel and transportation (other than freight) are a major source of income to Panama. Gross receipts from tourism, excluding expenditure in Panama by Canal Zone residents, grew at an average annual rate of just under 12 percent from 1968 to 1972 and totaled $42 million in 1972. In that year the number of tourists entering the country increased by over 9 percent, largely as a result of the promotional activities carried out by the Panamanian Tourism Institute (IPAT). Moreover, Panama's central geographical location has resulted in the recent establishment of new air links with Europe. This should enhance the country's ability to attract tourists. In addition, the introduction recently of lower air fares between the United States and Panama should further boost receipts from tourism in the near future.

Fueled in part by two tourism investment incentive laws[14] enacted in 1967 and 1972, the construction of hotels and tourist-related activities, which involves investments of about B/46 million over the next four years, is under way. Under these two laws, investors in tourist-related activities are exempt from all import duties for 5 years, from real estate taxes for about 15 years, and from profit taxes for 13 years. The largest and most ambitious project being undertaken involves the construction of a convention center in Panama City at an estimated cost of B/8 million—including a 500-room hotel which will be partially financed with the proceeds of a U.S. Agency for International Development (AID) loan.

When completed in 1976, the center could increase foreign income
receipts from tourism by as much as 50 percent.

Transportation receipts amounted to an estimated $56 million
in 1972, and have more than doubled since 1968. This trend can be
explained by the new bunkering service introduced in 1967, resulting
in larger sales of bunker oil and lubricants to ships. These sales
have almost tripled since 1968, constituting 75 percent of total
transportation receipts.

The major limitation to receipts is the tonnage constraint
on the present canal, largely related to the new supertankers and a
number of larger battleships. Unless the present canal is expanded,
exports are likely to level off. One possibility being discussed for
maintaining the isthmus as an international route for supertankers
is the construction of an oil pipeline across the isthmus combined
with the addition of wider locks to accommodate the larger ships.
This alternative, which is only in the discussion stage in Panama
and neighboring countries, could render the present canal more
viable in the future. The implementation of this or any other alternative project concerning the canal must, however, await the outcome
of the current negotiations.

Merchandise Exports

Panama's remarkable export performance in the 1960s was
largely due to two factors—the major increases in both output and
price of bananas, and the installation of the oil refinery that began
producing for both the domestic and foreign markets in 1962.

The structure of Panamanian exports of goods (Table 6.2)
appears to have changed somewhat since the early 1960s; that is,
there has been a major decline in the relative importance of food
products. This shift, however, is merely a reflection of the introduction of the petroleum refinery in 1962. If petroleum exports are
substracted, it becomes clear that food exports showed only a slight
decline between 1960 and 1972 in their importance in merchandise
exports—from over 97 percent to over 95 percent. Exports of manufactured articles by the early 1970s accounted for only about 2.5
percent of merchandise exports. Panama's merchandise exports
are therefore highly specialized and hence dependent upon world
demand conditions for four products—sugar, bananas, shrimp,
and coffee.

The rate of growth of merchandise exports has begun to
slow in recent years, and, in addition, the average annual rate of
3.7 percent for 1968-72 was substantially below the real rate of

growth of GDP during the same period. As a result, the ratio of total exports to GDP measured in current prices has declined steadily from 14 percent in 1968 to 10 percent in 1972.

Bananas of course dominate the export picture, the volume of which exhibited a spectacular threefold increase from 1960 to 1968. By the early 1970s they accounted for about 50 percent of the total value of merchandise exports. By and large, bananas are both produced and exported by one foreign (U.S.) corporation—United Brands. Although banana exports displayed considerable dynamism during the early 1960s, in 1970 production was seriously affected by floods, and despite a small increase in unit value, exports declined by 1 percent. In 1971 and 1972, production recovered from the 1970 flood damage, and exports increased by 1.8 and 4.8 percent respectively, notwithstanding a significant decline in world prices. Expansion in 1974 and 1975 was constrained somewhat because of the government's imposition of a dollar-a-box tax on each crate of bananas exported. This was considerably higher than the export tax charged in other countries (Ecuador charges no tax). Negotiations over the tax between United Brands and the Panamanian government has eventually (January 1976) resulted in the government's purchase of United Brands' interests in Panama.

Panama's second most important export product, refined petroleum, declined in value from $24.1 million in 1969 to $21.5 million in 1970, but rebounded to $25.1 million in 1971 and $26.5 million in 1972. Since refining has been growing at a relatively stable rate, the uneven performance of refined petroleum exports may be explained for the most part by the changes in sales of bunker oil and lubricants to ships (which are recorded in Panama's external accounts as receipts from transportation activities).

Shrimp exports, which had remained virtually stagnant through 1970, increased in value by 18 percent in 1971 and 12 percent in 1972, despite a decline in volume.

Sugar exports, which amounted to 41,000 metric tons in 1971 and 36,000 metric tons in 1972, have been well below the U.S. sugar quota of 59,000 metric tons allocated to Panama. *

----

*With the completion of La Victoria sugar mill in 1975, the country should have no trouble in filling its quota. Uncertainty over the United States maintaining its policy on sugar imports, however, makes projections of exports in this area very difficult.

TABLE 6.2

Merchandise Exports, 1960–72
(in millions of balboas)

	1960	1961	1962	1963	1964	1965	1966	1967	1968	1969	1970	1971	1972
Sugar	0.4	0.8	0.5	1.6	2.5	2.1	1.6	3.9	4.6	5.4	5.0	6.3	6.7
	(1.5)	(2.8)	(1.5)	(4.4)	(5.7)	(3.9)	(1.8)	(5.5)	(5.8)	(6.2)	(5.8)	(7.1)	(6.9)
Bananas	18.2	20.1	20.1	25.1	29.1	39.6	44.5	49.6	56.5	63.4	61.8	62.9	65.9
	(68.7)	(70.3)	(62.0)	(69.5)	(66.6)	(72.8)	(70.7)	(70.3)	(71.0)	(73.0)	(72.0)	(70.7)	(68.2)
Cacao	1.2	0.5	0.8	0.8	0.4	0.4	0.4	0.5	0.4	0.4	-	-	-
	(4.5)	(2.1)	(2.5)	(2.2)	(0.9)	(0.7)	(0.6)	(0.7)	(0.5)	(0.5)	(-)	(-)	(-)
Coffee	1.1	0.3	1.4	0.4	1.4	0.7	0.6	1.4	0.6	1.1	1.7	0.9	2.0
	(4.2)	(1.0)	(4.3)	(1.1)	(3.2)	(1.3)	(1.0)	(2.0)	(0.8)	(1.3)	(2.0)	(1.0)	(2.1)
Shrimp	5.0	5.9	7.9	6.2	7.4	7.8	9.0	9.6	9.7	9.7	10.2	12.0	15.0
	(18.9)	(20.6)	(24.4)	(17.2)	(16.9)	(14.3)	(14.3)	(13.6)	(12.2)	(11.2)	(11.9)	(13.5)	(15.5)
Meat and fish products	0.1	0.1	0.9	0.7	0.8	0.7	0.7	1.4	1.7	1.3	2.2	3.3	2.2
	(0.4)	(0.4)	(2.8)	(1.9)	(1.8)	(1.3)	(1.1)	(2.0)	(2.1)	(1.5)	(2.6)	(2.6)	(2.3)
Petroleum products	-	-	13.8	23.6	25.0	23.7	25.9	22.9	18.9	24.1	21.5	25.1	26.5
Other	0.5	0.7	0.7	1.2	1.9	2.5	3.6	3.1	4.1	5.3	4.1	4.6	4.8
	(1.9)	(2.4)	(2.2)	(3.5)	(4.3)	(4.6)	(5.7)	(4.4)	(5.2)	(6.1)	(4.8)	(5.2)	(5.0)
Total merchandise	26.5	28.6	46.2	59.7	68.7	78.1	88.8	93.5	98.5	111.0	107.3	114.1	123.1
Total nonpetroleum	26.5	28.6	32.4	36.1	43.7	54.4	62.9	70.6	79.6	86.9	85.8	89.0	96.6

Note: Figures in parentheses indicate percentage of total nonpetroleum merchandise.
Source: Contraloria General, Direccion de Estadistica y Censo.

Beef exports in the late 1960s and early 1970s marked Panama's first successful attempt at diversifying her merchandise exports. However, these exports were temporarily prohibited as of November 1972 because of domestic shortages and the Panamanian government's desire to stem the rise in domestic prices of beef products.

The possibilities for additional export diversification are good. The proposed construction of a fishing and container port and the development of a major copper deposit in the Colon region could pick up much of the slack in export earnings caused by the decline of Panama's more traditional exports. In addition, the modified industrial incentives law enacted in August 1971[*]provides for fiscal incentives aimed at the promotion of export-oriented industries.

To summarize, the only significant change in the pattern of Panamanian exports over the decade of the 1960s has come about because of the oil refinery. The refinery can hardly be regarded as introducing any significant diversification into the export picture, however, since very little value added is produced by Panamanian workers. Thus, while Panama appears to remain in the dangerous position of having her exports highly dependent on world prices of a very few products, her overall foreign exchange supply situation is much less precarious. This results from the size and stability of the foreign exchange proceeds from the Canal Zone as well as the Free Zone of Colon, which together contribute a substantially larger amount to the balance of payments than to the exports of merchandise. Indeed, despite the high degree of specialization in her merchandise exports, it is nevertheless true that Panama faces less instability in her foreign exchange earnings than nearly all other countries of a similar size.

IMPORTS

Panamanian imports show a high degree of stability in their composition (Table 6.3). As in the case of merchandise exports, the introduction of the oil refinery in 1962 blurs this picture. If oil imports are assumed to have expanded at the same rate as that prevailing prior to the introduction of the refinery, the only item exhibiting a significant decline in relative importance would be food products. These patterns reflect the fact that the government's

---

*A critique of the law is given in Chapter 11.

TABLE 6.3

Merchandise Imports, 1960–72
(in millions of balboas)

	1960	1961	1962	1963	1964	1965	1966	1967	1968	1969	1970	1971	1972
Food products	13.3	15.1	14.7	15.9	18.3	17.1	18.7	18.8	19.9	20.9	24.8	34.2	33.8
Beverages and tobacco	2.8	2.8	3.8	1.5	1.4	1.8	1.9	2.2	2.4	2.9	3.1	3.5	2.9
Fuels and lubricants	11.8	11.0	27.1	37.8	35.4	40.3	47.6	47.3	53.0	60.6	62.1	66.2	68.1
Chemical products	11.4	13.3	13.8	15.2	16.8	18.1	19.4	21.2	24.0	26.8	29.2	31.9	40.4
Manufactured items	39.1	46.1	49.1	50.1	52.2	62.8	72.9	80.4	85.9	100.4	126.8	132.2	154.0
Machinery and transport equipment	24.1	30.3	31.8	31.3	32.1	39.9	49.7	54.2	58.5	68.1	89.9	90.4	112.8
Other merchandise imports, errors, and omissions	6.7	5.7	4.9	11.0	9.1	9.6	4.4	5.2	-0.3	-1.0	-9.4	0.6	-12.7
Total imports	109.2	124.3	145.2	162.8	165.3	189.6	214.6	229.3	243.4	278.7	326.5	359.0	399.3

Source: Contraloria General, Direccion de Estadistica y Censo.

import replacement policy (based mainly on quotas of manufactured
goods) has had its principal impact on the food industry.

Between 1960 and 1972, manufactured articles plus transport
equipment accounted for about 60 percent of Panamanian imports.
This is a direct result of the diminutive size of the Panamanian market which makes production of manufactured items, particularly
durable goods for the domestic market, very expensive. Moreover,
the government's import replacement policy of the 1960s did not
favor the production of such goods, except for apparel and some
minor construction materials.

In fact, imports reflected the openness and smallness of
the economy and its relative affluence. In spite of protective quotas,
most consumer durables, many luxury items, and all capital equipment were imported. As a result, merchandise imports remained
at about a quarter of its GDP during the 1960s.

On the average, nearly 60 percent of Panama's imports came
from two countries—the United States and Venezuela. Imports from
the latter consisted almost exclusively of crude petroleum. The
United States heavily dominated Panama's import trade, but that
dominance has been slowly but consistently declining over time.
The Free Zone of Colon has been gaining in importance (there are
no statistics on the true origin of Panamanian imports from the Free
Zone) at the expense, it would appear, of the Canal Zone, which
ceased to be a significant source of imports after 1962-63.

Apart from Costa Rica and Colombia, trade with nearby
countries is negligible. Trade with Japan is still small (only about
5 percent) but has been growing over time; it is the second most
important supplier of the Free Zone.

In general, when the oil refinery is taken into account,
there have been no major shifts of sources of Panamanian imports
since 1960. Those shifts that have occurred are a consequence of
bilateral trading agreements (with Nicaragua and Costa Rica),
changing institution arrangements (the Free Zone versus the Canal
Zone), and the growing competitiveness of certain countries (for
example, Japan and Italy).

Although Panama appears to have quite low import duties,
the total restrictions on trade are much more severe than the data
suggest. The reason for this is the establishment, primarily
since 1965, of a greatly expanded import quota system.[15] This
system has resulted in extraordinarily high rates of protection in
the food and clothing industries, and a great deal of subsequent
import replacement. The narrowness of the Panamanian market
results in inefficient production in many cases. It is probably in
Panama's interest to examine thoroughly its import replacement

program, and in many areas, reverse the import replacement trends begun in the 1960s. An economy such as Panama's cannot expect to long experience rapid growth of income without a corresponding rapid growth of imports (which in turn requires rapid growth of exports). Because of its small size, Panama can never hope to produce at home the types of consumption and investment goods that will be demanded as income grows.

The qualitative relationship of exports to the country's development can be easily outlined. * If for some reason the economy were prevented from increasing its foreign exchange earnings above current levels, the economy would continue to grow, but no additional resources would go into the export sector. The country's growth would, however, produce a continuing growth of the demand for imports. The result would be a deterioration in the country's balance-of-payments equilibrium which in turn would prevent any long-run increase in imports, except to the extent that the country received substantial amounts of capital inflows (borrowing aid, private invest-ment). Imports would then be financed by an outflow of dollars. This would, in turn, cause prices to fall in domestic industries (the excess demand for international goods would be reflected in excess supply of home goods), and hence incomes in those industries producing goods for the domestic market would increase more ra-pidly than otherwise would have been the case. In addition, import replacement would take place in response to the rise in the relative prices of international goods, leading to less and less efficient uses of the country's resources. The net effect of these relative price movements and trade outflows would be a slackening and eventual stagnation of the rate of growth of real income. [16]

THE INFLUENCE OF THE CANAL ZONE
ON PANAMA'S TRADE PATTERNS

The presence of the Canal Zone and its associated institutions has a number of implications for the Panamanian economy and par-ticularly for the country's pattern of foreign trade. Without the Canal, the Zone's military and other facilities, Panama's commercial rela-tions would, obviously, have to be conducted exclusively with the rest of the world. The Canal Zone has, in effect (mainly because it

---

*The author is grateful to Larry Sjaastad for pointing out this mechanism in Panama's balance of payments adjustment mech-anism.

is a captive market--because of location it is most effectively supplied by Panama) provided the country with a unique supply of foreign exchange not available to its neighbors. This, as seen above, has resulted in the country's exports (particularly of goods) to the rest of the world being much smaller than its imports.

Conceivably, for diversification, Panama in the near future might want to divert many of her exports from the Canal Zone to the rest of the world. Attempts to do this have been made, but without success.[17] The reason for this failure is simple. The country's exports to the Canal Zone are highly labor-intensive and workers are paid a wage higher than in other developing countries. Hence, the Canal Zone has given Panama a large source of foreign exchange but the same foreign exchange (through increasing the Panamanian cost structure) has prevented the country from developing manufactured goods that are competitive in world markets. The explanation of this pattern is as follows: the nature of the Panamanian monetary system (the use of the dollar as the nation's currency and the inability of the Panamanian authorities to control its volume) often results in rapid expansions in the domestic money supply. The construction boom in the early 1970s was a good example of this process. The increase in money caused by loans from commercial banks to construction creates additional demand for domestic goods, that is, those not traded. Since the prices of traded (international) goods are not likely to be affected by inflation in Panama (because it is such a small seller and buyer in international markets), any expansion in the domestic money supply, through credit expansion or export surpluses, therefore results in a rise in the price of home goods relative to international goods. Because of the domestic price increase relative to world prices, consumers in Panama tend to purchase foreign goods rather than those produced in the country. This increase in imports, in turn, results in a reduction of Panama's foreign exchange receipts (including those derived from the Canal Zone) over her foreign exchange expenditures. The source of the initial expansion in the money supply and the original position of the country's balance of payments is important in determining the final result. For example, if the country's balance of payments was initially in equilibrium and the country's money supply expanded because of an increase in exports, the process would stop when the trade deficit with the rest of the world just equaled the trade surplus with the Canal Zone; at that time the country's internal inflation would cease. The final result of this process, beginning with an initial export surplus, is a higher price even for goods produced in Panama, relative to international goods. The significant fact, however, is that this price level will be higher than that which would

have resulted in the absence of the Canal Zone. This result is modified
somewhat in the short run if the assumption of an initial balance in
the external sector is not met.[18] But the general conclusion holds—
one of the important consequences of the Canal Zone is to cause Panama to run a chronic trade deficit with the rest of the world. This
deficit over time is just sufficient to offset the trade surplus with
the Canal Zone. Capital flows will not alter this basic mechanism,
since these flows are most likely to be determined by factors other
than current account balances. Current account balances in Panama
tend to adjust to capital flows in the long run, rather than the other
way around; that is, they are not induced by domestic economic activity, but determined by a number of factors (such as banking laws,
foreign aid, and so on) not associated directly with existing economic
conditions.

The important point here is that the country has little control
over the structure of prices of goods produced in the country both for
domestic consumption and export. Yet this price structure will to
a large degree influence the economy's competitive position in international markets and thus its trade patterns.

The country's price structure is determined, of course, by
the relative costs of factor inputs, that is, land, labor and capital.
The structure of interest rates in Panama is largely determined by
world interest rates; again, since the country is small, its actions
have little effect on the international capital supply and demand. The
prices of labor and land, however, are free to change since they are
not traded internationally; only the products or services they provide
are exported.

As noted, any inflation in Panama will result in a balance-
of-payments deficit with the rest of the world, which will eventually
be balanced through an offsetting trade surplus with the Canal Zone.
In the process of adjustment, however, the demand for different
factors will change. Since Panama exports labor services to the
Zone, the demand for labor in Panama will increase relative to
capital and land, that is, wages in the country will move directly
with the relative price of domestically produced goods. This is not
a common pattern for most countries—few countries export services
to the extent Panama does. But Panama would not export services
if it were not for her geographical position vis-a-vis the Zone. The
presence of the Canal Zone therefore results in higher Panamanian
wages than would otherwise be the case.

Obviously, the substantial increases in the wages and salaries of persons recruited by the official agencies of the Zone have
had a very favorable impact on the country's level of living and
foreign exchange earnings. On the other hand, the Zone's tendency

to push up national wages has resulted in large amounts of unemployment due to a slowing down of Zone activity and the inability of large numbers of workers to produce manufactured goods for export.

Developments in Panamanian labor markets therefore account in large part for the country's observed trade patterns. For example, initial rise in Panama's exports over imports results in laborers being drawn out of sectors producing goods for the home market. They are attracted into the export sector by higher wages. Increasing export prices, however, cause consumers in Panama to choose imports over locally produced goods. If the increase in the demand for imports is less than the net increase in the production of exports, the trade surplus will cause inflation, since the money supply will expand as foreign consumers pay exporters in dollars.

Since only the price of goods produced locally can increase (Panama is too small to influence world market prices), the process will continue until the trade surplus has disappeared. During this period wages, in order to keep up with increases in the domestic cost of living, will also be rising. If the initial increase in the demand for imports is greater than the net increase in the production of exports, a trade deficit will occur. The deflation caused by lack of demand for locally produced goods will result in a fall in the relative price of home goods. These prices, however, cannot fall to the initial level at the beginning of the export boom. If they did, the output of domestically produced goods would have to be at its original level. This, however, implies that all the labor drawn into production for export came from the sectors already producing exports. But this is precluded by the fact that the associated rise in wages in that sector spread (through competition) to sectors producing goods for the home market. Hence, it necessarily follows that wages would be higher after an export boom in Panama than before.

The Canal Zone and associated institutions, therefore, have considerable influence in determining the international competitiveness of Panamanian exports (and the country's income distribution). One of the chief consequences of the Zone and the country's monetary system is that Panamanian wages are high in relation to the skill level of the labor force, higher than they would be without the Canal Zone, and just high enough to cause exports to be at the level required to bring about a long-run balance-of-payments equilibrium for the country.

The validity of this mechanism is confirmed by Panama's pattern of exports outlined above. The amount of manufactured exports not going to the Canal Zone is minute. The country has not been able to diversify its exports. They still consist mostly of agricultural and marine products. The presence of the Canal Zone and its related institutions can be held responsible for the fact that the country's exports are predominately nonmanufactured items. Panama cannot simultaneously have the benefits of the Canal Zone and an industrialized export sector.

CONCLUSIONS

The trade patterns in Panama are influenced by a number of the country's unique features including: (1) the presence of the Panama Canal and its impact on Panama's productive and wage structure; (2) the existence of the Colon Free Zone and the special problems as well as opportunities it poses for increased trade with neighboring countries; (3) Panama's traditional liberal attitude toward trade, with resultant low import and export duties; and (4) the more recent and, during the middle 1960s, rather widespread use of import quotas together with fiscal incentives to induce import replacement of certain consumer goods.

Any realistic policy for the foreign sector must take into account Panama's (1) high dependence on trade—about 60 cents out of every dollar is spent on imports; (2) its traditional role as a center for trade and commerce; (3) its reliance on inflow of foreign investment, foreign expertise and manpower—in 1971 foreign investment accounted for 70 percent of new capital formation in manufacturing; and (4) its goal of becoming a financial center.

The post-1968 revolutionary government is bringing about changes in the traditional approach to economic policy, yet seems to lack a number of traditional instruments for carrying out public action. This is particularly marked in the case of the external sector.

The country's trade patterns, particularly the extreme dependency on a single source of foreign exchange for development, have not been fortunate. The country depends on the rate of growth of the Canal Zone and on a series of agreements with the United States which have lasted for decades. Although these agreements have led to substantial achievements in the modernization of the economy, they have had a limiting effect on long-term efforts to meet the new requirements of development to improve the levels of living of the people.

NOTES

1. The term "registered exports" is adopted in Panama in order to distinguish exports of domestic products to other countries

from sales to the Canal Zone and to ships, aircraft, and persons in transit. United Nations Economic Commission for Latin America, Analysis and Projections of Economic Development, VII—The Economic Development of Panama (Panama City: United Nations Economic and Social Council, 1959), p. 18.

2. For an examination of trade patterns of "normal" small developing countries, see Peter J. Lloyd, International Trade Patterns of Small Nations (Durham, North Carolina: Duke University Press, 1968).

3. See Larry Sjaastad,"Possibilities for Panama's Participation in the Andean Common Market," mimeographed (Panama City: Agency for International Development, 1970) for an excellent discussion of these points.

4. Direccion de Estatistica y Censo, Balanza de Pagos, various issues.

5. Sjaastad, op. cit., pp. 43-57.

6. Ibid.

7. As discerned from the Panama Canal Company, Annual Report (Balboa Heights, Canal Zone), various issues. Trends in canal traffic together with projections for future revenues are given in two reports by Stanford Research Institute for the Panama Canal Company: A Review of World Shipbuilding and Merchant Ship Fleet Trends (Menlo Park, California: Stanford Research Institute, 1967). The possibilities of alternative sites for a new canal are contained in Robert B. Anderson, et al., Interoceanic Canal Studies, 1970 (Washington, D.C.: Atlantic-Pacific Interoceanic Canal Study Commission, 1970). An excellent study of the relationships between the Canal Zone and Panama is given in United Nations Economic Commission for Latin America, The Economy of Panama and the Canal Zone, Vols. 1, 2 (Mexico City: Economic Commission for Latin America, 1972). Unfortunately the contents of this study are classified and cannot be summarized here other than to say that there are numerous possibilities for Panama to increase her benefits from the Canal Zone through treaty moditications, and that it is highly unlikely that any of these changes in the treaty would be detrimental to the security or economy of the United States.

8. An excellent account of the Colon Free Zone's development is contained in Clapp and Mayne, Inc., Estudio sobre ZLC: Importancia Economica, Problemas que Enfrenta y Posibilidades de Expansion (San Juan, Puerto Rico: Clapp and Mayne, 1968).

9. "Colon Free Zone Serves the Region," IMF Survey 4, no. 3 (February 3, 1975), p.47.

10. Ibid.

11. The government's plans for expansion of the Free Zone, together with a detailed list of possible new industries for the Zone and surrounding area, are contained in a preliminary master plan: Nicolas Ardito Barletta, "Bases para el Desarrollo de la Region de Colon," mimeographed (Panama City: Ministerio de Planificacion y Politica Economica, 1974). (Informe Preliminar)

12. Particularly Decree 172 enacted in 1972.

13. See Arie Cohen,"Establishment of an Industrial Free Zone at the Tocumen International Airport," mimeographed (Vienna: United Nations Industrial Development Organization, 1973). (restricted)

14. For the country's long-run strategy in the area of tourism see Direccion General de Planificacion y Administracion de la Residencia Estudios Sectoriales: Potencial de la Industria de Turismo (Panama City: Instituto Panameno de Turismo, 1970)

15. Historically, quotas on imports have been much more prevalent than tariffs. An excellent critique of the limitations of a quota system is given in Arnold C. Harberger, "Memorandum sobre Incentivos Fiscales," in Estudios sobre Politica Arancelaria, Incentivos y Comercio Exterior (Panama City: Direccion General de Planificacion, 1970).

16. See Robert Baldwin, Foreign Trade Regimes & Economic Development: The Philippines (New York: Columbia University Press, 1975) for an interesting account of this process in another country.

17. It is unlikely that joining a regional common market such as the Andean Common Market or the Central American Common Market would enable Panama to increase her exports of manufactures significantly. See Larry Sjaastad, "Possibilities for Panama's Participation in the Central American Common Market," mimeographed (Panama City: U.S. Agency for International Development, 1970).

18. Ibid., p. 36.

7

MONETARY POLICY

It was not until 1968 that foreign capital flows into Panama's commercial banking system were of substantial volume. Up to that time, private direct foreign investment and foreign aid represented the largest sources of external capital; in contrast, public investments, financed by the government's foreign medium-and long-term government borrowing, averaged less than $3 million per year in the 1950s and about $4 million yearly from 1961 to 1968. Together, they averaged only about 20 percent of the country's current account balance-of-payments deficit.

Since 1968, the role of foreign capital has changed dramatically. Medium-and long-term borrowing, principally by the central government and autonomous public agencies, has averaged close to $50 million yearly. Moreover, the banking sector, which before 1968 was largely limited to domestic operations, developed into a booming regional financial center. Net inflows of short-term funds, that had averaged less than $5 million in the 1951-68 period, rose to an average of $50 million in 1969-74.

Several principal reasons account for Panama's attempts to become a regional financial center. [1] Since the country is very small, relatively few transactions take place in the domestic capital and in money markets compared to larger countries, even those with much lower per capita incomes. Money and capital markets in a country of Panama's size, if confined exclusively to domestic transactions, could never become as highly developed as in a larger country, unless indeed it became the Switzerland or New York of its geographic area; and this limitation on the development of capital markets would greatly compound the country's problem of mobilizing

and investing locally potential available savings. It was the absence
of a highly developed money and capital market in Panama that caused
(in the 1960s) a number of local institutions and individuals to place
their money abroad. [2]

So far as the creation of the country as a financial center is
concerned, it should be noted that the country may well sacrifice the
effective mobilization of domestic savings in the hope of getting an
inflow of foreign capital, and in fact the country might end up with
the worst of both worlds; the location of U.S. and European banks in
Panama make not only capital inflow into the country easier, but also
make the outflow of domestic funds easier.

More important questions arise concerning the adequacy
with which the foreign-owned and -controlled banking system meets
the wider needs of the Panamanian economy at its present stage of
development. A great deal of private foreign capital has gone into
Panama in recent years, associated with the development of the
country as a regional financial center. [3] The contribution of the
center to Panama's growth must be evaluated in terms of those
activities and sectors of the economy into which these funds have
flowed. If the banking system has not channeled much credit into
areas given a high priority by the government, then it is difficult to
see how the attraction of foreign short-term funds into the country
through the commercial banking system as it now exists could play
a significant role in the country's future development. [4]

To benefit most from the creation of Panama as a financial
center, the authorities must therefore evaluate its potential contribution in terms of the government's objectives of promoting
economic development, reducing unemployment, alleviating poverty,
and achieving a more equitable distribution of income. To justify
itself, the financial center must be able to provide benefits to the
country sufficient to offset the costs associated with its continued
development.

INSTITUTIONAL SETTING

The rapid development of Panama as an international
financial center began after the enactment of the banking law of
1970. [5] Before that law, Panama already possessed the characteristics
that would normally have attracted the establishment of banks for
the purpose of conducting international business; that is, it had (1) the
use of the U.S. dollar as legal tender, (2) complete freedom of
international payments and exchange transactions, (3) ease of communications, and (4) a favorable geographic location and growth of

other international services. In addition, the banking law offered
the following incentives : (1) it provided relatively easy requirements
for establishing a bank; (2) it permitted the establishment of banks
to carry out only overseas (foreign) operations; (3) it gave banks
with domestic operations clear and liberal regulations; and (4) it
made interest rates on domestic savings deposits subject to a limit,
with all other interest rates being determined by market forces.

Under the 1970 banking law, private commercial and mortgage banks were classified into three groups:* Class 1—domestic
and foreign banks conducting regular banking business in Panama;
Class 2—offshore banks (engaged primarily in foreign transactions)
set up in accordance with Panamanian law and with offices in Panama, but conducting business abroad only; and Class 3—foreign banks
with only representative offices in Panama.

Class 1 banks included (in 1972) 23 commercial banks and two
mortgage banks, the latter being required by law to place 75 percent
of their portfolio in mortgages five or more years to maturity. As
of June 1972, there were 25 banks registered in Class 1; 7 in Class 2;
and 3 in Class 3. Also under the same reform plan the Comision
Bancaria Nacional was established to regulate the banking system
and create conditions to promote Panama's development as an international financial center. The commission was also given the power
to change legal reserve requirements for local sight and time deposits within a range of 5 to 25 percent in response not only to the
needs of banking liquidity, but also to changing monetary conditions.
As the reserve requirements had previously been left unchanged,
this gave some flexibility in counteracting sudden capital outflows. [6]

Since 1970 the growth of deposits in the country's banks has
been extraordinary (Table 7.1). As of December 1971, total assets
for the banking system as a whole (Class 1 banks plus government-
owned institutions) were 1.13 billion balboas, compared with 345 million balboas on December 31, 1967, and 816 million on December 31,
1970. Total bank assets had risen (as of June 1972) to 1.45 billion
balboas. Of the 1.13 billion balboas at the end of December 1971,
962 million were accounted for by the private sector (Class 1 banks).
This growth is in part reflected both in the large number of new
banks that were established in Panama and in the expansion of the
existing banks. In 1969 the country had 33 banks. By early 1975

---

*Other divisions were included in the law, but are not
considered here.

TABLE 7.1

Panama's Banking System
(in millions of dollars)

		Deposits			Loans	
	Total	Local	Foreign	Total	Local	Foreign
Total all banks						
1967, December	300.2	195.1	105.1	263.2	233.2	30.0
1973	3,260.3	656.9	2,603.4	2,339.8	1,026.0	1,313.8
1974	6,044.9	795.9	5,249.0	4,528.9	1,367.1	3,161.8
1975, June	6,219.5	845.0	5,374.4	4,929.0	1,408.0	3,521.0
Panamanian banks						
1967	82.6	74.1	8.5	76.7	76.7	0.0
1973	288.9	255.9	33.0	263.4	262.0	1.4
1974	360.3	280.1	80.2	343.1	330.5	12.6
1975, June	371.3	288.7	82.6	350.7	336.1	14.6
Foreign banks						
1967	217.6	121.0	96.6	186.5	156.5	30.0
1973	2,971.4	401.0	2,510.4	2,076.4	364.0	1,312.4
1974	5,684.6	515.8	5,168.8	4,185.8	1,036.6	3,149.2
1975, June	5,848.1	556.3	5,291.8	4,578.3	1,071.9	3,506.4

Source: Banco Nacional de Panama.

there were nearly 60 banks actively operating in the country; many
had branches in some of the major provincial towns. *

WORKINGS OF THE BANKING SYSTEM

Because it has no currency of its own nor a central bank,
the government does not have a monetary policy in the traditional
sense; that is, it cannot use its monetary system as a means of
controlling domestic interest rates, nor can it alter the money
supply in circulation to prevent inflation or declining aggregate demand.[7] Instead, the government's decisions in the monetary field
are limited to the operations of the two government-owned banks:
the Savings Bank and the National Bank. The latter, in the absence
of a central bank, functions as the sole depository of national and
local government agency funds, as well as agent for the government
in the placement and service of government bonds.

The Banco Nacional de Panama's total assets have grown
107 percent from the end of 1968 to 162 million balboas on June 30,
1972. The bank not only performs the important ancillary central
bank functions of government deposit and fiscal agent; it also plays
an important role as a commercial and development banking institution. Utilizing the Panamanian government and public institutions,
as well as international development institutions, as sources of
funds, the Banco Nacional has extended credit for commercial,
industrial, housing, and agricultural activities. As of June 30, 1972,
94.4 million balboas were outstanding in loans for those purposes,
compared with 48.6 million on December 31, 1968. Other important
government institutions include the Caja de Ahorros, which accepts
savings deposits and invests in mortgages; the Instituto de Fomento
Economico, which obtains funds from domestic and international
sources for loans to the agricultural sector; the Instituto de Vivienda
y Urbanismo, which extends credit for and promotes private family
dwellings in urban areas; and the Caja de Seguro Social, which is
the social security administration.[8]

Under this system, Panama's foreign exchange reserve is
its own domestic money supply; that is, it consists of U.S. dollars

---

*This is somewhat unusual for a regional financial center.
The branch banks apparently indicate that rural areas in Panama
contain high levels of savings and that the country is benefitting by
this mobilization of funds.

held by the citizens and the government, and their claims on foreign
banks. These assets are neither easily measured nor easily mobilized
by the government. But although the government of Panama does not
control the nation's foreign exchange reserve in the usual sense,
except to the extent that it holds U.S. currency or has claims on
foreign commercial banks, there is no necessity for it to intervene
in a foreign exchange market to stabilize an external rate of exchange.

Normally a deficit in Panama's overseas transactions is
reflected in a decline in Panamanian claims on the foreign-owned
banks, usually in the form of a decline in their claims on their parent companies or affiliates abroad, or an increase in their borrowing
from them.

In countries that do have a national currency and a central
bank, the monetary authorities can offset these fluctuations in currency or assets by deliberately expanding or contracting domestic
money. This course of action is not open to the Panamanian government. The attitude of foreign banks is crucial; if they are willing
to make loans to the Panamanian government or to the private sector,
a decline in money supply arising from a deficit in international payments can be offset; if they are not willing to make the loans, the
payments deficit will result in a contraction in the country's money
supply. In making such loans the banks are acquiescing in the decline
in their net foreign-asset position, thereby financing the deficit in
Panama's balance of payments. The alternative course of action of
attempting to reinstate their foreign-asset position would imply a
reduction in loans to Panama's citizens or government, with further
consequences for economic activity. All this implies that the Panamanian government can exercise an independent monetary policy
only to the extent that it can exert political or other pressure on the
banks to conform. Moreover, since its currency is the U.S. dollar,
the government is unable to pursue an independent exchange-rate
policy.

The fact that the Panamanian currency is the U.S. dollar
and that banks in Panama are predominantly foreign owned obviously
has a bearing on the operation of the system, and also raises the
question whether the monetary system, as a whole, adequately meets
the needs of the Panamanian economy.* Looking at it from the purely banking point of view to begin with, the fact that the banks have

---

*Note that commercial banks are not considered to be
capital market institutions. They are, instead, primary partici-
pants in the money market—usually the market for debt issues with

close relationships with home offices or affiliates abroad, and have
ready access to funds from them, implies that the banks do not
have to be concerned about their cash position. For one thing,
there is no law in Panama or even a convention governing the cash
reserves of the banks. In addition no uniform ratio of reserves to
deposits is observed by them. Also there is no secondary reserve
ratio proper (deposits backed up by short-term assets), nor for
that matter are there any Panamanian assets which could properly
serve as secondary reserve assets.[9] However, there is no doubt
that the liquidity position (ability to honor withdrawals) of the banks
is secure, provided that the position of their home offices or affiliates abroad also remains so.

The ability of the banks to draw on their associates abroad
and to move U.S. currency in and out according to need implies that
the banking system plays an important part in financing deficits and
surpluses in the Panamanian balance of payments—in the same way,
for instance, as the U.S. banking system makes possible the money-
flow imbalances between the individual states. Panama is simply an
extension of the U.S. banking system. In this sense it is no different
vis-a-vis the U.S. banking system than, say, California; that is,
local money supply can be maintained in the face of a deficit in the
balance of payments, if the banks are willing to increase their net
lending to Panamanian residents on the basis of a decline in their
claims on their associates abroad or an increase in their borrowing
from them. The crucial matter is the state of business activity in
Panama and the availability of profitable and secure lending opportunities. Banks operating in Panama will have a vested interest in
maintaining and increasing their operations and it is this fact that
may well provide Panama with a very effective foreign exchange

---

maturities of less than one year. Some pains are taken here to make
this point, since all too frequently the distinction between money market institutions and capital market institutions is not made explicit in
discussions of development finance. Often commercial banks are
faulted for failing to devote a larger share of their loan and investment
portfolios to relatively risky, long-term debt issues. The nature of
commercial bank operations however will not permit them to engage
in substantial participation in the capital market; if there is an insufficient supply of long-term finance, it should be interpreted as the
result of a weak capital market rather than the result of poor economic performance on the part of the commercial banks.

reserve. Admittedly, the obverse of such action is the bank's build-up of debt with parent or affiliated institutions abroad, but the banks may be very willing to allow this if the return on their loans in Panama exceeds the cost to them of the overdraft facilities.

But while this close connection between banks operating in Panama and affiliates abroad carries advantages to Panama, there may also be some disadvantages. One disadvantage might be that the money and credit situation in Panama could be at the mercy of the money and credit situation in the countries where the parents or affiliates are located. A credit squeeze in the United States imposed by the U.S. Federal Reserve, because of the domestic situation in the United States, might cause a restriction of American-owned bank credit in Panama.[10] The resulting effects on the Panamanian economy might be out of all proportion to the impact of the credit squeeze in the United States. Also the confidence in a bank located in Panama might be shaken by events affecting profitability and liquidity of a partner or affiliate abroad. One small bank operating in Panama was in fact forced to stop operations because of the failure of its associate abroad, but such difficulties are unlikely to arise for the banks conducting the bulk of banking business in Panama. As to the effects of credit squeezes overseas, in principle this possibility cannot be denied. In practice, however, the size of operations of, for instance, the Bank of America branch in Panama is so trivial, compared with the scale of operations with the home office in the United States, as to make the Panamanian branch's existence insignificant in the total situation of the home office, and it can hardly be argued that lending in Panama would be affected by such events overseas.

Still, many of the newer banks entered Panama mainly to do foreign business and only secondarily to lend in Panama. Some are not fully aware of all the ramifications of their operations for the economy. Most have not experienced a temporary crisis. Because of this situation the government is restricting its permits to only major, well-known international banks. Panamanian authorities are now considering possible controls over the banks in order to create a more stable environment. * It may be difficult, however, to impose controls over such banking actions without threatening to lose the banks to another country offering more favorable treatment.

---

*Part of the function of the National Banking Commission is to look into these possibilities, although it is unlikely that much regulation over the banks could be imposed without impairing the country's growth as a financial center.

Because of this possibility the government is exploring voluntary measures in close consultations with bankers.

PANAMA'S CONTINUED ROLE AS
REGIONAL FINANCIAL CENTER

Panama's continued role as a regional financial center depends to a large extent on the influence of possible or probable changes in the external environment of the international monetary system. Thus far Panama has derived much of its comparative advantage as a regional financial center from the absolute fixity of the value of its currency in terms of U.S. dollars, and from the position of the U.S. dollar as the reserve currency and foundation of the international monetary system. [11] The international monetary crisis of 1971 led to a readjustment of exchange rates among the major currencies—specifically, a devaluation of the U.S. dollar in terms of other major currencies—and a restoration, at least temporarily, of the relatively fixed exchange-rate system. These developments (especially the relatively fixed exchange-rate system currently employed by most countries), if they can be maintained, will restore the status quo and leave Panama's position unchanged. But the question is whether the existing world monetary system can last, and if not, how this will affect Panama.

There is already a distinct possibility of the establishment of a new common European currency, the purpose of which would be to allow the European currencies as a group to float against the U.S. dollar. [12] So far, the plan involves only common flotation within the limits around parity values allowed by the post-Smithsonian [13] and IMF rules. But it might, if it worked successfully, lead to a European decision to float the European common currency, either freely or subject to management in relation to the dollar.

Such a move would create an environment composed of elements that would both enhance and at the same time jeopardize Panama's development as a regional financial center. On the one hand, Panama would probably cease to attract additional European and other non-dollar-area banks through the variability of the value of the balboa in terms of the currencies of their countries—though admittedly there is the possibility that foreign banks would prefer to set up regional self-contained subsidiaries which could balance their books in terms of the local currency, rather than to assure themselves against the risks of exchange rate changes.

On the other hand, flexibility of exchange rates between Europe and the United States would tend to accentuate the existing

trend toward polarization of the world into economic regional blocs.[14]
This would be beneficial to Panama as a regional financial center,
since such polarization would tend to enhance Panama's role; the
bulk of Latin American trade is with the United States and regional-
ization—which would involve close relations between Africa and Europe
on the one hand and Latin America and the United States on the other—
would tend to reinforce the trade and investment relationships between Latin America and the United States, on which Panama's role
as a regional financial center largely depends.

      As a result it seems likely that the evolution of future inter-
national monetary arrangements will not have any significant adverse
effect on the prospects for Panama as a regional financial center; on
the contrary, whatever happens is likely to be favorable. The country
need not have any fear, therefore, that any direct expenses involved
in promoting Panama as a regional financial center will be lost.

THE ROLE OF COMMERCIAL BANKS
IN PANAMA'S DEVELOPMENT

      The role of the banking system in helping to promote eco-
nomic development can be examined from two related points of view:
(1) the contribution that has been made and is being made by the
banks to the monetization of the economy, and (2) the contribution
being made by them to the wider development of the Panamanian
economy, through their lending policies.

Monetization

      The present stage of the monetization of the economy can
perhaps be judged by the amount of money being used in the Panamanian economy at the present time. Total bank deposits owned by the
private sector (residents) amounted (January-September 1972) to
about $393 million, $281.9 million of which was in the form of time and
saving deposits. There is, however, no reliable direct estimate
of the amount of currency in circulation. Obviously there can be no
information on the amount of currency that moves in and out of the
country as a result of the movement of residents in the Canal Zone
in and out of the country. The same, of course, applies to tourists.
One can attempt an estimate by referring to the ratios of currency to
GNP and to demand deposits in the banking system, typical of countries at roughly the same stage of development and with the same
level of real income per capita as Panama. Assuming the former

ratio to lie in the neighborhood of 0.05 percent and the latter to lie
close to 1 percent, the amount of currency circulating in Panama in
the early 1970s could be assessed at roughly $25 million at a minimum
and $50 million at a maximum. The importance of the financial sec-
tor may be seen from the fact that the ratio of liabilities of the financial sector to the GNP for Panama is relatively high at 61 percent.
This compares with a ratio of 51 percent for Mexico and 30 percent
for Argentina.

Further monetization of the economy must await the development of commercial farming in the subsistence sector of the economy,
and this obviously does not depend simply on the initiative of the commercial banks. Moreover, development of branch banking, while
rather extensive, is undoubtedly held back by poor communications
with and poor roads to many parts of the interior of the country.
Apart from these obstacles, the banks themselves are somewhat
reluctant to seek out the savings of the small cash farmer or individual
worker, since the administrative costs of handling small savings or
thrift accounts are rather high. At the same time the mobilization of
such savings and the direction of these funds into investments, considered vital by the government for the future development of Panama,
is unlikely to take place without some pressure from the government.[15]

Economic Benefits of the Commercial Banks

On balance, the financial system has had a positive effect on
employment and real growth in Panama. While employment in banking
rose rapidly from 889 in 1960 to 4,000 in 1972, it is only slightly over
1 percent of nonagricultural employment. Nevertheless, value added
in banking now represents 4 percent of GDP and the indirect effects
are large. Many business travelers come to Panama on banking
business. The construction industry has been particularly stimulated
by the need for bank offices, and the availability of banking services
provided by banks from exporting and importing countries has assisted
the growth of commerce. Hemispheric banking and services allied
to it are among the best urban growth prospects available to Panama.

The commercial banks have played little part in financing
the major economic developments in the Panamanian economy that
have taken place in recent years. The development of banana production and the expansion of the oil refinery have been financed by
the operating companies themselves by bringing in capital from
abroad. Commercial bank credit, however, did increase economic
activity in general. Commerce, consumer credit, and construction
were largely financed by commercial bank credit after 1968. During

1971-73 banks competed heavily to make loans; even some relatively
risky projects easily received short-term financing.

     In spite of the importance of commercial banks, Panama has
not yet benefited fully from its growth as a regional financial market.
While there is ample short-term credit, there is a lack of long-term
credit, especially for agriculture and the public sector.[16] Thus many
of the investments made by farmers have been financed with short-
term credit. This is not completely the fault of the banks, however.
The government, particularly the central government, has not offered
realistic interest rates or terms on its domestic borrowing. To take
full advantage of the presence of the foreign banks, public institutions
such as the agricultural bank must increase their creditworthiness.
This can occur only through the development of a competitive market
for government securities. And this will occur only when the government and the public agencies are willing to redeem their bonds at
par.*

     The short-term needs of the small-scale businessman operat-
ing in the towns are met to some extent by the commercial banks.
Usually, however, this accommodation has been provided in the form
of personal loans, but the experience of banks with this type of lending
has been such that they are now increasingly reluctant to continue
doing so. It is even more difficult, if not impossible, for the small
businessman to obtain substantial funds on a medium-term basis,
for such loans tend to be outside the banks' normal lending conventions,
and there is no other source of finance to which borrowers can turn.

     These difficulties met by agriculture and small-scale indi-
genous industry in obtaining finance for fixed-and working-capital
formation are typical of many less developed countries, and the
lending policies of the commercial banks come under fire in those
countries as well as in Panama. But the difficulties of the commercial
banks are equally real. In establishing the banking habit in underdeveloped countries, banks must ensure the confidence of the public in the
security and liquidity of their deposit liabilities, and in turn this
necessitates bank concern over the security and liquidity of their own
assets. While foreign-owned banks may often be strong enough to
bear the losses arising in lending to small business in countries like
Panama, they must first take into account the interests of their
shareholders. Foreign banks are not chartered to subsidize local
industry nor should they be expected to do so. These considerations

---

     *The reasons for the reluctance of the public to hold govern-
ment securities are discussed in Chapter 9.

imply that the government of Panama is obligated to a more creative role in the formation of indigenous bank and nonbank financial institutions, underwriting their security and liquidity in the early stages of operation so as to create and maintain the confidence of depositors, while at the same time stimulating investment in areas considered by the authorities to be essential for the country's development.

CONCLUSIONS

All things considered, Panama does not seem to have benefited significantly from the creation of Panama City as a regional financial center. Nor has the country been hurt by this development. It would seem that if the authorities are successful in establishing a number of development banks in the country, the growth of the foreign commercial banks might be a powerful agent in promoting Panamanian economic development. (A number of alternative monetary systems are considered in Appendix D).

NOTES

1. This is simply theory and does not necessarily imply that all of the following reasons were motivations for the government's policies toward the commercial banks. Apparently two factors, the rapid economic growth rate of the 1960s and the development of a regional financial center, led the Panamanian authorities to believe that Panama should attempt to develop an organized equities market. The Panamanian authorities felt that equities markets could play a significant role in (1) mobilizing new savings, especially the large deposits of foreign savers; and (2) efficiently allocating the savings to users in Panama's private sector. Their hypothesis concerning the desirability of increased financial intermediation was based on the assumption that (1) there was an unsatisfied demand for equity-financed capital on the part of Panamanian business firms; (2) Panamanian business firms were willing and able to sell common and preferred stock to the public; and (3) such stock sales would result in a competitive rate of return for buyers relative to the alternative forms of saving, such as savings accounts or foreign securities. See Nicholas J. de Grazia, "A Study of the Establishment of Organized Equities Markets in the Republic of Panama: Conclusions and Recommendations," mimeographed (Panama City: U.S. Agency for International Development, 1972), pp. 1-2.

2. A common problem when a country is tied to the currency of one of its major trading partners. For an interesting comparison see R. A. Sowelem, Towards Financial Independence in a Developing Economy: An Analysis of the Monetary Experience of the Federation of Rhodesia and Nyasaland, 1952-1963 (London: George Allen & Unwin, 1967).

3. See Harry Johnson, "Panama as a Regional Financial Center," Economic Development and Cultural Change 24, no. 2 (January 1976): 261-86.

4. The growth of financial institutions and the deposits in them were not natural outgrowths of the development of Panama. The development of the banking sector was not in response to shortage of capital funds in the private sector, nor was it in response to national size or the competency of national banks in international business. Rather, the financial institutions established operations in Panama because of liberal banking and tax laws, the absence of a central banking system, the absence of exchange controls, and the relative stability of the government. See Nicholas J. de Grazia, A Study of the Establishment of Organized Equities Markets, op.cit.,p.9.

5. Of course the country had begun its development long before 1970 by establishing a favorable climate for international banking. In this regard, it is interesting to note the comparison Harry Johnson draws between the different types of financial centers. According to Johnson a financial center of any kind is a city in which are concentrated financial activities—banking, insurance, and ancillary types of financial business—that cater to a region outside the city itself. An international financial center like London or New York, according to Johnson, caters to the financial requirements of a region extending beyond the boundaries of the nation within which the city is located to embrace the whole world or a substantial part of it. Such a center develops from a strong base as a national financial center in a large and powerful country with the natural market support of citizens of that country. Regional financial centers like Panama derive their role primarily from a combination of geographical proximity to the countries in which the customers operate, and the safety and ease of operation of subsidiaries, branches, and agencies of foreign banks whose head offices lie in the international financial centers, rather than in generating customers in other parts of the region through their own national size and international power and the competence of their own national banks in international financial business. See Harry Johnson, op. cit., p.261.

6. This is particularly important during periods of recession, and gives the government some protection against sudden deflation.

It is unlikely that this regulation would impair Panama's position as
a regional financial center, although Johnson, op.cit., seems to
feel it might.

7. The Panamanian monetary system is one of the few remaining examples of a purely automatic system. With the exception
of an insignificant number of coins minted by the authorities, there
is no monetary creation by the government or by an institution under
its influence, such as a central bank. The volume of the money supply is determined entirely by private bank credit and by the balance
of payments. Moreover, with the dollar in circulation there is no
possibility of altering the exchange rate and very little prospect of
carrying out an effective exchange control. In general the system is
somewhat similar to Cuba's prior to 1932. See Henry Wallich, Monetary Problems of an Export Economy—The Cuban Experience 1914-
1947 (Cambridge: Harvard University Press, 1950) for a detailed
discussion of the implications of this type of monetary arrangement.

8. A complete list of financial institutions is contained in a
special issue of The Banker on Panama. See The Banker 125, no.596
(October 1975): 1039-1072. Of special interest is Robin Pringle,
"Banking in the Land of Balboa," The Banker 125, no. 596 (October
1975): 1195-1201.

9. Many financial institutions such as banks and insurance
companies buy government bonds, but it appears that their motivation
is not to acquire a profitable financial asset. Rather the laws governing the operation of most financial institutions require the purchase
of government bonds as a fianza (a bond of surety). The empirical
data also indicate that the rate of return on government bonds as
well as corporate securities is below that of alternative forms of
savings, such as time deposits for individuals and loans for financial
institutions. Obviously there is little incentive for one of the commercial banks to buy a security that pays 5-6 percent before taxes
when it can earn 9.5 to 12.5 percent on loans made to domestic and
foreign borrowers. De Grazia, op. cit., p.7. The causes behind
the poor reputation of Panamanian government securities are discussed in Chapter 9.

10. See The Creation of a National Monetary System in
Panama (Washington, D.C.: Inter-American Committee on the
Alliance for Progress, 1966), p.6.

11. As Johnson notes, without the dollar Panama would be
just another small country with its own currency. Johnson, op.
cit., p. 286.

12. Some of the possible implications of this system are
discussed in John Makin, Capital Flows and Exchange-Rate Flexi-

bility in the Post-Bretton Woods Era (Princton, N.J.: Princeton
University Department of Economics, International Finance Section,
1974).

13. The idea of European monetary union and the floating of
that currency against the dollar are examined in Giovanni Magnifico,
European Monetary Unification for Balanced Growth: A New Approach
(Princeton, N.J.: Princeton University Department of Economics,
International Finance Section, 1971).

14. In terms of possible regional blocks in Latin America,
see Carlos F. Diaz-Alejandro, Less Developed Countries and the
Post-1971 International Financial System (Princeton, N.J.: Princeton
University Department of Economics, International Finance Section,
1975).

15. Part of the problem of finance in Panama is that while
the country has developed as an international or at least regional
financial center, its domestic capital markets remain underdeveloped.
See Peter Treadway, The Feasibility of Creating an Underwriting
Market-Making Fund in Panama (Washington, D.C.: Organization
of American States, 1974).

16. The agricultural credit situation is particularly critical
in the light of the government's efforts to stimulate production in
this area. For an excellent discussion of the problems of credit in
this sector, see William C. Merrill, et al., Panama's Economic
Development: The Role of Agriculture (Ames, Iowa: Iowa State
University Press, 1975) Chapter 6.

When the present government of Panama came to power in October 1968, it announced plans for a fundamental transformation of the pattern of development in the country: the excessive dominance of the canal and Canal Zone would be broken, the unequal distribution of wealth and income would be changed, and a genuine popular part-icipation in the national development would be promoted; new exports would be developed and as rapid an economic growth would be sought as would be compatible with government goals. To achieve this trans-formation, the role of the state in the government would be greatly expanded and for the first time in the country's history it would begin to play a major role in the economy. At the same time, private sectors would be actively influenced by government policies, and thus directed along a new path more compatible with the government's new development orientation—an orientation more toward providing social services and regional development than prior administrations.

This was indeed an ambitious goal. Previous Panamanian governments had been unable to reverse the social and economic disparities that had been built up over the years. Public investment for development purposes had traditionally been limited, usually averaging less than 3 percent of GDP. The major towns, Panama City and Colon, had been exposed to the cosmopolitan tastes of much richer countries, which had led to a demand in these cities for large quantities of imports and for increased social services. Previous governments had given higher priority to satisfying the demand in those cities than to extending public services to rural areas, or to the development of the country's other resources (basic agricultural crops, for example). Further, their policies had been based on the philosophy that the economy would best prosper through the development of relatively unregulated private activities such as services, commerce, and trade. Protection for domestic industry had been relatively limited, the labor market unregulated, foreign investment had been welcome on very liberal terms, and until the 1960s, public corporations in areas such as utilities had been of minor importance.

GOVERNMENT ECONOMIC POLICIES

The Panamanian government is now expanding its role in the country's economy by (a) participating directly in developing and exploiting the country's basic productive resources and in the marketing of some of its main export products (in early 1976, for example, it purchased United Brands' banana plantations); (b) carrying out structural reforms in the agricultural area, including a land reform that entails substantial changes in land ownership, farm organization, and management; and (c) stimulating economic growth in regions outside the Panama City-Colon area through the use of revenues obtained from economic activity centered in the metropolitan area.

In order to attain these objectives, the government is carrying out the following:[1]

(1) A greatly enlarged program of public investment projects designed to achieve specific objectives in the key socioeconomic areas of agriculture, exports, industry, education, and urban development.

(2) The encouragement of increased export of goods and services by means of a policy of export promotion, investment incentives to those firms engaged in export activity, and directly, or with the participation of the private sector, developing projects oriented toward exports, that is, pipelines, copper mining, mineral transportation, container and fishing ports, and tourism infrastructure.

(3) A program of public development expenditures, to provide required economic and social services to neglected regions.

(4) Reformation of the institutional structure of the government and public administration so as to increase efficiency of the expenditures made by the public sector and to eliminate bureaucratic obstacles to the smooth functioning of public policy.

(5) Promotion of a rapid increase in agricultural output while achieving substantial progress in rural development, thereby improving rural conditions, slowing migration, and thus easing the pressures of urban congestion and unemployment.

(6) Stimulation of the manufacturing sector through increased protection from foreign competition.

The growing complexity of the economic and administrative system and the need for stronger efforts to program, set priorities, and promote specific projects have made it necessary to expand and reorganize a number of public agencies. Most significant has been the transformation of the General Planning and Administration Bureau to the Ministry of Planning and Economic Policy (MPPE). This ministry's basic tasks are to prepare development plans (in cooperation with other government agencies), formulate economic and social policies, extend the coordination and planning function to the provincial and municipal levels, promote specific projects, negotiate foreign loans, and represent the country in international organizations.

The ministry discharges these functions through its bureaus for economic and social planning, regional planning and coordination, national budget, administrative and personnel administration, and through advisory units. The new ministry has undoubtedly contributed to the improvement of planning and the preparation of investment programs, and the planning process itself has been oriented to incorporate all segments of the population in the decision making process under the new Constitution. An assembly of local representatives was created to prepare plans based on a study of the problems facing each community. These plans, after they have been approved at several levels and with citizen participation, are synthesized, checked for overall consistency, and are then incorporated into the National Development Plan.

The MPPE is currently preparing and revising the National Development Plan which will set the orientation of the government's policies through 1979. The basic objectives of this plan are: (1) fuller utilization of domestic natural resources in order to reduce dependence on external economic forces; (2) faster economic growth and a reduction of the unemployment rate; and (3) achievement of the nation's socioeconomic integration and improvement of the living conditions and the income level of marginal groups throughout Panama.

On the basis of the goals of the plans, the public investment program has begun to develop a distinct policy for both the rural and urban areas. The government's urban policy[2] is designed to remove bottlenecks created in the rapidly growing terminal cities and their suburbs, responding to the increasing needs of those areas by stepping up its expenditures on electricity, transportation, water, and low-income housing, by encouraging their economic potential. For example, in Panama City the expansion of Tocumen International Airport and convention facilities is designed to strengthen Panama's position as an international financial center and also to stimulate tourism.

In the rural areas, the government has built its strategy around the goal of achieving rapid increases in output of basic food products. [3] To accomplish this the authorities are expanding rural investment, especially in smaller-sized projects such as feeder roads.

The acceleration in government expenditure after 1968 and the resulting problems encountered by the authorities indicate that the extent of the increase in public demand and the manner in which it is financed, will have significant direct and indirect influences on the country's economic development. This is particularly true with respect to the ability of the authorities to influence the distribution of income and wealth, and on their ability to combat inflation and the country's increasing balance-of-payments deficits.

PUBLIC EXPENDITURES

Because of the government's expanded programs in all areas, its total current expenditure has risen rapidly. In 1960 government expenditures were B/47,791; in 1968 they rose to B/158,448, and by 1973 to B/359,593 (Table 8.1). In part, this increase (particularly after 1968) was attributable to the emphasis on social sectors, where wages and salaries are an important component; for example, total employment in the public sector increased from 45,000 employees in 1968 to over 60,000 in 1975. The creation of new decentralized agencies dependent on transfers of funds from the central government for their revenues also contributed to current expenditure growth. By 1975, current and capital funds (transfers) received by these agencies from the central government had risen to B/56.5 million, from B/12.2 million in 1960 and B/30.5 million in 1968. In the early 1970s over 70 percent of public sector expenditures were made by the central government, either directly or indirectly, by transferring its funds to other agencies which in turn carried out the actual expenditure.

Until the last several years public expenditures in Panama have been characterized by little centralized control. The autonomous agencies acted and borrowed independently of the central government and of each other while increasing their dependence on central government transfers. Several ministries, especially Education and Public Works, consistently exceeded their budgets.

TABLE 8.1

Central Government Operations, 1960–73
(in millions of balboas)

	1960	1961	1962	1963	1964	1965	1966	1967	1968	1969	1970	1971	1972	1973
Current revenues	58.0	62.9	67.6	70.3	75.6	86.5	100.3	112.7	119.4	133.0	160.1	181.2	197.9	225.2
Current expenditures	47.8	48.4	50.4	58.6	59.4	62.7	72.6	83.8	89.3	101.6	117.8	134.2	163.8	177.3
Savings	10.2	14.4	17.2	11.7	16.2	23.9	27.7	28.9	30.1	31.5	42.4	47.0	34.1	47.9
Transfers	12.2	13.1	14.2	14.0	15.7	17.3	18.1	22.0	25.6	26.5	38.2	35.9	42.6	38.6
Savings after transfers	-2.0	1.3	3.0	-2.3	0.5	6.5	9.6	6.9	4.6	5.0	4.2	11.0	-8.5	9.3
Capital expenditure	8.3	12.7	11.4	28.1	11.2	14.5	17.9	27.1	25.3	54.3	58.0	45.6	70.7	93.9
Overall surplus (+) or deficit (-)	-10.3	-11.4	-8.4	-30.4	-10.7	-7.9	-8.3	-20.1	-20.7	-49.3	-52.8	-34.6	-79.3	-84.6
Net internal borrowing including social security	4.5	-5.2	2.0	9.7	3.9	-0.1	-0.2	6.8	14.4	10.9	6.3	-3.6	15.5	-3.1
Net social security borrowing + floating debt	-0.4	10.4	1.4	5.8	4.7	4.9	5.7	7.3	7.5	7.0	8.9	9.8	15.6	12.0
External borrowing net	7.3	2.6	4.6	15.4	0.8	3.4	6.1	3.0	-0.4	34.1	35.8	32.7	41.5	63.7
Change in assets (- increase)	-1.0	3.6	0.3	-0.6	1.3	-0.2	-3.3	3.1	-0.8	-2.7	1.9	-4.2	6.7	12.0
Total financing	10.3	11.4	8.4	30.4	10.7	7.9	8.3	20.1	20.7	49.3	52.8	34.6	79.3	84.6

Source: Controller General, Annual Reports, various years.

The level of public expenditure is important for creating sufficient aggregate demand for full employment. For stabilization purposes there is little need for concern over the composition of that expenditure. On the other hand, the composition of the government's expenditures may have a marked impact on the country's income distribution among citizens at various income levels.

In terms of income distribution, the government's expenditures have tended to fare better than have its tax measures. In 1970 for example, while public expenditures were concentrated in the high-income terminal cities rather than in the low-income rural areas, these expenditures were relatively less concentrated than was personal income, that is, the ratio of public expenditure incidence (or benefits bestowed) to income is much higher for the rest of the republic than for the terminal cities. The central government has used its direct expenditures or allocations, therefore, as a major policy tool to achieve its expressed goal of broad popular participation, particularly of low income rural groups in the economy.[4] More importantly, in 1970 capital expenditures for schools and health, for example, were much less concentrated in the terminal cities than were noncapital or current expenditures. In quantitative terms the effect of public expenditures in reducing the disparity of incomes between the terminal cities and the rest of the country can be measured by a disparity index, defined as the ratio of the terminal city income level to that in the rest of the country. In 1970 this index was 3.3, calculated with per capita personal income alone. It declined to 2.8 when calculated with per capita personal income augmented by public expenditures.[5] Admittedly, however, there was an increase in the absolute per capita disparity in personal incomes from B/616 to B/709 respectively, when calculated without the augmented public expenditure and with the augmented public expenditure. These two apparent conflicts in the data (the decrease in the index of disparity of income with the absolute increase in money income differentials) are easily reconciled. First, while the terminal cities received more per capita from the public sector than did those in other areas of the country, it was a smaller proportion of their income than of the incomes of individuals residing elsewhere. Second, in 1970, households in Panama City paid about B/183 in taxes to the central government and received back only B/102 in expenditures that could be attributed directly to government expenditures.[6]

In the rest of the republic, households paid only about B/27 per capita but received back B/78. Since about 80 percent of government revenues came from the area surrounding the terminal cities, but only 45 percent of its direct outlays were spent in that area (48

percent of current outlays and 39 percent of capital expenditures),
the regional income disparity ratio was reduced from 3.3 to 2.7 when
only the net transfer effect of government revenues and expenditures
is considered. The government therefore appears to have made a
good start in its regional distribution efforts.

By 1970 some key public services were already beginning
to be distributed in favor of the provinces rather than the terminal
cities, the most notable examples of which were primary education,
some public health services, and economic services for agriculture.

The government has not only increased the level of public
investment but has shifted its sectoral composition of expenditure.
While prior governments had concentrated three-quarters of public
investments in transport and social infrastructure, the new government reduced this proportion to less than two-thirds. There were
two major reasons for this shift: (1) a move to public ownership of
several directly productive activities (power), and (2) the emphasis
on expansion of public services in rural areas. Because of its goal
to improve equity and at the same time maintain a high rate of economic growth, the government's investment program has been concentrated in the agricultural, industrial, and tourism sectors. This
change in the government's expenditure pattern has increased the
proportionate share of fixed investment in these sectors from 6.6
percent in the mid-1960s to 16.9 percent during 1969-72.

PUBLIC SAVINGS

As a result of the step-up in government investment, the
internal gap (the difference between domestic savings and investment)
between gross investment and domestic savings widened appreciably
from 1968 to 1973. Admittedly the government has greatly expanded
its level of expenditures but it has been the failure of the authorities
to finance this expenditure through tax revenues that has caused the
gap between domestic savings and investment to expand. For example,
domestic savings financed less than 50 percent of gross investment
in 1973 (at 1960 prices) and the ratio of domestic savings to total
gross capital formation has been falling rapidly since the late 1960s.
In fact the gap between savings and investment has more than doubled
since 1969, reaching B/152.8 million in 1973 compared to B/34.2
million in 1960.

Public savings have decreased in relation to public investment faster than have private savings in relation to private investment.[7] To finance this deficit, the government has resorted to

external borrowing and deficit financing; by the early 1970s this had reached inflationary proportions. The almost continual decline of public savings as a percentage of both domestic savings and GDP demonstrates that the internal tax effort of the government has not been keeping pace with the growth of the Panamanian economy. In addition, inflows of foreign funds into the banking system have grown more rapidly than has commercial bank relending abroad, allowing more funds to become available for financing domestic private investment.

In the last several years the government however has been somewhat successful in improving its financial position. It held public expenditures to an increase of only 5.7 percent in 1972, at which time the central current operating budget was in balance for the first time since 1966. The government's efforts at fiscal reform were continued in 1974 and 1975, but with increasing difficulty.

Some of the government's current fiscal problems are related to the fact that the country's tax structure has not been able to expand revenues in line with GDP growth in order to finance its expanding investment program. The government has tended to borrow at relatively high interest rates, and the high cost of borrowing has imposed an ever-increasing debt service burden on the government's budget. In 1973, for example, the government's debt obligations were 30 percent of current revenues.

In order to continue its rate of expenditures the government will have to initiate a number of fiscal measures. These include (1) tax reforms designed to increase government savings by increasing its tax revenues, (2) a reform of the tax system, and (3) the creation of confidence in public domestic credit by the issuance of higher interest bonds.

THE TAX SYSTEM

The government of Panama has traditionally been constrained in its attempt to increase its revenues. In part, some of this limitation has come from the proximity of the Colon Free Zone and the Canal Zone (smuggling from these duty-free areas has been very difficult to stop). Until recently a major deterrent to increased revenues was that income of workers in the Canal Zone was, until the treaty revision of 1955, exempt from Panamanian taxation,[8] and as a result the country had to concentrate on corporate profits and indirect taxes. After World War II the country's tax system was characterized by the same tax rate on the incomes of both corporations and individuals. The schedules were progressive, so that a

number of companies were induced to search for ways of reducing
their obligations to the government. This was easily done by simply
dividing themselves into smaller entities (to take advantage of the
lower ratio for small firms). Another inducement derived from the
tax structure was to engage in activities such as commerce, banking,
and shipping, since the tax system affected only income earned in
Panama. Firms expanded therefore into the above areas where profits could easily be attributed to foreign operations.

        Because of the relative importance of progressive taxes on
personal incomes and corporate profits in Panama's tax system, the
revenues of the central government have followed a cyclical pattern
in relation to GDP; that is, the ratio of revenues, while varying from
about 12 to 14 percent of GDP, have usually increased at a substantially faster rate than has GDP during periods of rapid economic
growth. Similarly, at times of slower economic growth, government
revenues tend to rise more rapidly than does GDP. This pattern of
relation of revenues to GDP, while scarcely marked before 1955,
became much more pronounced subsequent to the treaty change in
that year; one of the major provisions in the 1955 treaty was the
granting to the Panamanian government of the power to tax the incomes of Panamanian workers in the Canal Zone.

                Patterns of Tax Revenues in Relation to GDP

        The quantitative relationships between changes in GDP and
the various sources of government revenues are quite marked.
For example, between 1950 and 1960 a 1 percent increase in GDP
yielded only 0.89 percent increase in additional receipts from import
duties (when increased rates during this period are excluded), although imports in this period remained a relatively constant share
of GDP; in contrast the percentage rate of growth of income taxes
to GDP was 1.98.[9]

        With respect to imports, only the special import surcharges
(which applied a fixed percentage tax on the value of imports independently of their type or quantity) showed a marked increase during
periods of increasing economic activity. These surcharges, however, were changed frequently. By 1957 the surcharge was 5 percent
on those goods for which there was a specific duty and 8 percent on
duty-free goods. The import surcharge was eliminated in 1957 but
reintroduced in 1959.[10] It increased from about 1 percent in 1959 to
about 3.5 percent in the early 1970s. In general, import duties
have grown slightly as a percentage of merchandise imports only

because of rate increases. When rate increases became less frequent
in the 1960s, import duties proportionately declined.

For some specific imports, revenues actually declined with
rate increases. An attempt to raise these taxes in 1962 by 40 percent
led to so much smuggling from the Canal Zone and Colon Free Zone
that receipts actually declined. Receipts rose slowly thereafter as
consumption increased, but a similar attempt to increase liquor
taxes in 1972 again resulted in an absolute decline in revenues.
Smuggling was mainly from the Colon Free Zone, since by 1972 the
Canal Zone's taxes on liquor were the same as those of Panama.

Another reason for the slow growth of nonincome tax revenues
was that industrial incentive laws enacted in 1950 and 1957 granted new
firms a number of exemptions from import duties, primarily on imports of capital and raw material goods.[11] The 1957 law not only re-
tained those exemptions but established 15 years as the period of
exemption from the duties. The loss in revenues from this source
was significant. The exemptions cost the government B/3.6 million
in 1962 alone; by 1968 the loss had increased to B/6.3 million. These
figures represented 17 and 70 percent of actual receipts from import
duties in 1962 and 1968, respectively.

During the 1950s and 1960s, a number of direct taxes also
showed a slow increase during periods of accelerating income growth.
A property tax was imposed, but its collection was hampered by the
absence of an adequate method of updating the valuation of properties.[12]
In addition, rural properties were arbitrarily valued at B/30 per
hectare and taxed according to a progressive schedule. In response
to this tax many of the large landowners partitioned their properties
so that the effective tax rate on rural land was very low.

Taxes on domestic production or transactions also made no
significant response to GDP growth. The number of products taxed
has always been limited, but by the latter half of the 1950s taxes on
domestic products had become increasingly concentrated on only a
few commodities (beer, liquor, cigarettes, and gasoline). By 1960
these commodities accounted for 91 percent of receipts from taxes
on domestic production; by the early 1970s they accounted for about
95 percent.

In contrast to other taxes, the average rate of growth of
income taxes compared to GDP growth was 1.98; that is, a 1 percent
increase in GDP in the 1950s resulted in a nearly 2 percent increase
in income tax revenues. As a result, in the early 1960s emphasis
was placed on improving even further the income tax system as a
source of government revenue. In 1961 income tax rates were increased from 15 to 20 percent and in 1962 an additional 10 percent.

Also, starting in 1962 a 40 percent surcharge was imposed on business profits and a 10 percent surcharge on personal incomes above B/1,800.[13]

A major reform of the income tax system was made in 1964 on the recommendations of a major study by an OAS/IDB tax mission.[14] The principal change in the system at this time was the adoption of different tax schedules for corporations and individuals. Rate increases were highest on corporate profits. The tax schedule for corporations was divided into seven brackets, with rates ranging from 5 percent on taxable income of B/5,000 to 26 percent on incomes of B/100,000. A tax on dividends was also introduced. The result of the 1964 reform was that the income tax replaced import duties as the principal source of the country's tax revenues.[15]

Still, because of lagging nonincome tax revenues, Panama's tax revenues did not perform particularly well in the 1960s from the point of view of generating additional revenue concurrent with economic growth. Between 1960 and 1968, for example, tax revenues rose by 9.4 percent annually compared with a GDP growth rate of 9.5 percent. During this period taxes on foreign trade increased by 3.8 percent annually, and nontax revenue rose by only 7.0 percent annually. This performance of import duties was due mainly to the negative effect of raising the import duty on liquor in 1962, to the exemptions under industrial incentive laws, and to the fact that import duties were set on a specific (fixed) basis rather than a percentage of the value of the goods. The result of these three factors was that although imports increased by 10.5 percent annually between 1960 and 1968, import duty receipts rose by only 1.2 percent annually.

In sum, the tax system inherited by the post-1968 government, while relatively progressive because of the high proportion of income taxes to total taxes, was not appropriate for the expansion of the central government's role in the economy. Since 1950, tax revenues had remained a constant share of GDP of about 10 percent, despite several rate increases. Nontax revenues remained at about 4 percent of GDP from 1960 to 1968; thus government current revenues were about 14 percent of GDP in both 1960 and 1968.

Recent Changes in the Tax Structure

Because of the current government's stepped-up level of expenditure a number of significant tax changes (mostly in 1970) have taken place. These include:

(1) an increase in both personal and corporate income tax rates in
      1970;
(2) an intensive effort in the administration of the income tax through
      increased audits of individual returns;
(3) an increase in the tax on dividends (corporate income tax sur-
      charge) in 1970;
(4) an increase in the rate of assessment on land, particularly in
      urban areas;
(5) an increase in rates for the business net-worth taxes in 1970;
(6) a near doubling of the ad valorem import surcharge rates (from
      3.5 to 6.0 percent).

     Of these tax and administrative changes in the system, the
most successful were those relating to the income tax. Because of the
reforms of 1964 and 1970 the income tax emerged as the single most
important revenue source and the primary element in revenue growth.
Even so, income tax receipts have not shown a significant response
to income changes in the last several years.
     In 1972, however, the emphasis of government revenue
efforts shifted from taxes on income and property to taxation of liquor, tobacco, and gasoline, and a tax package was issued consisting
of the following rate increases:[16]

- Imported liquor: from B/3.50 to B/7.00 per liter.
- Domestic liquor: from B/0.0267 to B/0.07 per percent of
      alcohol per liter.
- Beer: from B/0.10 to B/0.20 per liter.
- Cigarettes: From B/0.0375-0.10 per pack to B/0.06-0.135
      per pack.
- Gasoline: from B/0.12485 to B/0.22195 per gallon of regular
      and from B/0.12614 to B/0.22264 per gallon of
      premium.

     These measures were considerably more revenue oriented
than were those adopted in 1970 and there was less regard for equity.
The government estimated that the net effect of these tax changes
would produce B/19 million in new revenues; however, they produced
only B/5.6 million.[17] The poor results of the 1972 tax package led
to negative central government savings for the first year since 1963.
     The failure to the 1972 tax package was largely due to the
Panamanians' ability to respond rapidly to price rises by finding, as
in the past, alternative supplies. Further, the increased duties on
imported liquor led to smuggling from the Colon Free Zone. The
result was an absolute decrease in imported liquor revenues.

Similar results ensued from the rise of tax rates on beer and cigarettes. The only tax that was successful was the increase in the gasoline tax, since this commodity is not easily smuggled and its consumption is not as responsive to price increases as the other
commodities. In December 1972 the tax rates on imported and domestic liquors and beer were reduced to their previous levels.

Evaluation of the Tax System's
Ability to Generate Reserves

The low revenue increases obtained from the 1972 tax reform
call for a reevaluation both of the country's whole tax structure and of
the constraints involved in tax collection. This reevaluation is required if the government is to increase its revenues proportionately.
to GDP. In considering the changes, the following points are of
particular significance:

(1) Because of the past emphasis on corporate income taxation, the corporate sector is relatively efficiently taxed.

(2) The major area of income tax evasion is in personal income, which is not subject to withholding. This suggests that the
collection effort of the government may be usefully expanded into
checking the income of the many professionals, merchants, and other
self-employed individuals in the two terminal cities.

(3) Taxes on easily smuggled goods should be deemphasized.

(4) Corporate profits are taxed three times—by the Social
Security System, for education insurance, and by the central government. Since corporate income tax receipts are a large proportion of
government tax revenues, any changes in these taxes should be
carefully reviewed.

(5) Changes in the land tax system can now be made for increased revenues. A reevaluation of the fast growing terminal cities
has been completed, and rural land values have been assessed. A
tax on the failure to use land to its best potential could be justified on
the basis of equity as well as revenues.[18]

(6) The undesirability (for efficiency reasons) of increasing
tariffs on most imported goods indicates that this source of revenue
should not be seriously considered in any major tax reform.[19]

(7) Since the government is already tapping the terminal
cities heavily for revenue, taxes in these cities for the purpose of
expanding government investment in poorer regions have probably
reached their limit. Changing the structure of the taxes within the
urban classes, however, remains a matter for government concern.

(8) The progressiveness of taxes in Panama varies considerably from income bracket to income bracket. In the lowest brackets of income the system is progressive, but in the middle income groups it is proportional. At the highest income levels the tax incidence becomes even regressive. These patterns are a result of two major factors: (a) the relative unimportance of personal income taxes in Panama's tax revenue structure, and (b) some monopoly power in several areas of the domestic market that allows some firms to pass some of their corporate taxes and import duties on to consumers in the form of higher prices. In many cases these products are consumed primarily by the lower income groups.

(9) Since smuggling is a major problem in Panama, any change in import taxes must come from a restructuring of the existing level of duties. This could best be done by changing many of the existing rates from a specific to an ad valorem basis, that is, a percentage of the sales prices.

REFORM OF THE TAX SYSTEM

Any tax reform in Panama must be undertaken with the sole purpose of enabling the government to achieve more efficiently its stated socioeconomic goals. Thus reforms in this area must cover the areas of: (1) the level of taxation and the tax structure, and (2) the level and distribution of government expenditures made possible by these taxes.

In terms of the level of taxation the main requirement of reform is to prevent the gap between government expenditures and taxes from becoming excessive. In terms of equity, the main requirement of reform is to prevent distributive inequialties resulting from the deficiencies in the structure of the existing tax system.

Panama's tax system has, over time, relied more and more on the income tax as a major source of revenue. Yet because of the variation in tax rates and in bases for the numerous taxes, tax liability in the country is being determined largely by the level of income received rather than by the source of that income. As a result, the Panamanian system of taxing income places differential burdens on different income receivers. Placed in order of the lightest to the heaviest burden, the sequence is roughly: (1) civil servants, (2) private employees, (3) self-employed individual investors and private entrepreneurs, (4) investors in Panamanian corporations, and (5) owners of foreign corporations. For some tax purposes, these differential burdens may be weighted with respect to the

government's equity objectives and the desire to encourage development
by inducing higher levels of savings and investment. It is clear that
the exemptions stated in the tax laws are not designed for income distribution considerations but to stimulate industrial development and
to encourage the production for export.

Perhaps to offset the tendency of taxes of this sort to increase the concentration of income and wealth, the government has
(except in 1972) attempted to make the income tax more progressive.
However, this motivation on the part of the authorities toward equity
has not been backed by their skill in collecting the taxes. Therefore,
much of the reform in tax laws in the country has led only to increased corruption and widespread evasion. Tax evasion and corruption
have undoubtedly widened the income disparities rather than narrowed
them, since the resultant nonpaid incomes have distorted the investment pattern in favor of luxury consumption goods; this in turn has
created a self-generating growth spiral in that sector and a consequent
reduction of resources devoted to the nonluxury consumption goods
sector. This has caused domestic shortages in some luxury consumption goods, many of which the country is capable of producing but
which it must import.

The most glaring weakness in the Panamian revenue system
and one that has prevented income equalization is the failure to tax
income from capital on the same basis as that derived from labor.
Particularly deficient in this respect are measures to tax transfers
of wealth[20] effectively through the inheritance tax, which is a sieve
of loopholes, and the relatively lax taxation of capital gains under the
income tax. A failure to tax all capital gains under the income tax
destroys the neutrality of the income tax and directly benefits upper
income groups. The appropriate goal of the tax policy for Panama,
given the government's goals, is to obtain higher levels of investment, both public and private, but to do so in such a way that the
net effect is a more equitable redistribution of income and wealth.[21]

The main factors responsible for the failure of Panama's
tax system to attain its objective of a more equitable distribution
are:

(1) absence of a clear and comprehensive notion of what
constitutes income for tax purposes;

(2) failure to recognize that the ownership of disposable
assets confers a benefit on the owner over and above the income
that the property yields, and the failure to supplement taxes on income with taxes on net wealth;

(3) failure to secure the true aggregation of a man's (or a
family's) total property or income for tax purposes, owing (in part)

to defective provisions concerning the compulsory aggregation of family income, and to provisions concerning the transfer of income or property into trusts and settlements (quite apart from any illegal concealment of income);

(4) failure to secure the full reporting of income or property owing to the absence of an automatic reporting system for property income and property transactions; the failure to make the tax system comprehensive enough to ensure that it is self-checking in character. The current system makes possible the concealment of income and property through the registration of property in bogus names, or through anonymous holdings (like bearer bonds), or the system of blank transfers in the case of shares.

Our major conclusion is that some form of tax on wealth is the most effective way of using the tax system to improve the distribution of income, provided the technical problems of administering the tax are overcome. Taxes, however, cannot make the poor richer, which is, after all, the main concern of distributional policy. Even the complete removal of all taxes on the poorest members of a country would not make them much better off, simply because of the low absolute amounts involved. Futhermore, many of the poorest people, particularly those in rural areas, are at best marginally within the economic life of the country, and are thus little affected by taxes. While the regressive portions of the tax system ought to be reduced as much as possible, it is clear that if the country's main concern is with poverty as such, any fiscal corrective must be exercised primarily through the expenditure side of the budget.

GOVERNMENT BORROWING

Because Panama has no national currency (thus precluding inflationary financing), all government expenditures must be met by receipts from taxes or from borrowing. All fiscal operations of the government, therefore, have two distinct aspects and pose two distinct sets of problems. The first pertains to the effects on the economy produced by the raising of the funds, whether by taxation or by borrowing. The second concerns the effects on the economy of the expenditure of these funds, since every expenditure determines the allocation of manpower and materials between the private and the public sectors of the economy and exercises an influence upon the domestic price level and the level of total economic activity. The question of the desirability of a particular financial action of the government—for instance, whether revenues should be obtained by borrowing (internally or externally) or through taxation, or whether expenditures of a certain nature or impact should be increased or decreased—should be determined only after a complete analysis of the possible alternatives open to the government and the contribution of each to the government's basic objectives. The problem of public borrowing raises a particular set of problems.

Because Panama uses the U.S. dollar as currency, there is little difference between internal and external public debt—that is, all public debt is denominated in dollars. The major difference between internal and external debt has been the government's management of each.

For internal borrowing Panamanian governments have traditionally turned to the National Bank of Panama, the Social Security System, and suppliers and contractors to the government. [22] The National Bank operates like a private commercial bank, but it is government owned and the sole banking depository and lender to the public sector. It has been used by the central government (through the government's use of overdrafts at the bank) for the financing of the public sector's current budget deficits and to obtain short-term loans for financing some capital outlays. It has also typically converted its interest-free overdrafts from the bank into long-term loans at 6 percent interest, even when the National Bank has been forced to borrow funds at 8 percent to finance the loans. As a result of increased borrowing by the authorities, the amount of government bonds and loans held by the National Bank rose from B/4.9 million at the end of 1968 to over B/35 million by 1974.

The government's borrowing from the Social Security System has also been extensive. The short-term bills extended to the Social Security System in lieu of the government's employer obligations are periodically converted by the government into 20-year bonds at 6 percent interest. By the end of 1972, for example, B/12.9 million or 56 percent of the Social Security System's current assets and investments were in government or public agency bonds. The system's portfolio was far from optimal. The official bonds issued by the government and the public agencies were to mature in 20 years or more and the interest rates were lower than the rates on other comparable bonds.

The third market for government internal borrowing has been domestic suppliers or contractors. Capital projects not financed by the major international lending agencies have usually been financed with government bonds, which are issued by the authorities directly to contractors in payment for their work. As in the case of the Social Security System, these bonds usually have a 20-year maturity and pay 6 percent interest. The only reason contractors accept them is their fear that if they insist on direct payment in balboas or dollars, it will result in their losing government work (or not being paid at all). Presumably their concern over losing government work is so great that they are willing to accept these bonds, even though at the same time deposits in the commercial banking system are yielding up to 8 percent, and rates on commercial loans by banks vary from 9 to 10 percent. Because the yields on government bonds are low in comparison with other assets, the contractors have had to sell their bonds at varying discounts. These have never been lower than 15 percent and have usually been around 30 percent.

Recognizing that many bonds were sold well below par, the government, perhaps because of its embarrassment in not being able to float its bonds in the free market, has recently changed its amortization system. Rather than redeem all its bonds at par, however, the government holds auctions on bonds held by the private sector. It accepts offers from bondholders—offers that are ranked in decreasing order in terms of the lowest rate the holder is willing to accept for redemption. The process begins with the bondholder who will accept the lowest redemption price having his bonds redeemed at that price. Other bondholders then have their bonds redeemed at their offered price until the government's funds allocated for that year's bond redemptions are exhausted. Occasionally, even bondholders of expired bonds must wait for payment if funds for redemption—determined by the budget—are exhausted.

A major difference exists between internal and external government debt in Panama. With the exception of forced borrowing through government bonds by contractors, by the National Bank, and by the Social Security System, the government's recent net internal borrowing has been negative while its external debt has been rapidly expanding—more than $45 million between 1969 and 1973. Even the rapidly growing commercial banking system will accept only a small volume of government bonds and only because the leading banks consider it a public service.

Ironically, while the Panamanian branch of a multinational bank was recently declining the purchase of a 20-year Panamanian government bond at 6 percent interest, its home office was accepting 5-year Panamanian government securities with an effective rate of 10 percent. This is a direct result of the fact that Panama's currency is the U.S. dollar, and bank flows are unregulated. Panama must, under these circumstances, compete in the major international centers of the United States and Europe with creditworthy borrowers for its additional financial needs.*

To lower its borrowing costs, the Panamanian government must borrow more from the domestic private sector, and to do this it must first improve its internal creditworthiness. Several steps could be taken to accomplish this:

(1) Drop the direct link between projects or purchases and bonds or bills. This would lower the total costs of each project. As it stands now, contractors overcharge the government if they are paid in bonds. These same contractors usually offer bids about 30 percent lower for projects associated with the leading international lending agencies (which pay in cash) than for similar projects financed solely with domestic resources (that is, paid in bonds).

(2) Offer higher interest and shorter maturities.

(3) Redeem bonds at par when due.

(4) Reduce government borrowing directly from the National Bank or pay it the established market rate of interest.

(5) Make it clear that its borrowing from the Social Security System is simply a subsidy from the system and its membership.

(6) Establish a total budget system to determine borrowing needs, then issue bonds with terms attractive to the market.

CONCLUSIONS

The government of Panama has made a start in accomplishing its original ambitious objectives. It has, to a significant extent, increased the public social services provided to poorer Panamanians. Its revenue and expenditure policies have tended to reduce regional income disparities. It has begun a serious attempt at creating a diversified economy. It has created institutions such as rural village councils that will allow both Panamanian peasants and workers to increase their participation in economic affairs. And it has begun a series of important public infrastructure projects that will encourage the continuation of rapid economic growth in the urban areas if better fiscal policies are followed.

The government's spending policy, however, must be examined in the light of the country's special institutional conditions.

_____

*The author wishes to thank Robert Davenport of Stanford Research Institute for pointing out these facts.

Under the existing monetary system, fiscal deficits can only mean a transfer of funds from the private to the public sector of the economy. Thus, the great expansion of the internal public debt does not necessarily mean that the increase in fiscal expenditure will automatically bring about an increase in total expenditure and a corresponding revival of economic activity—which would have been the case if internal loans to the government came from funds that were not being used for expenditure, that is, from idle balances in the banking system. Moreover, the use of the balboa, which is equivalent to the U.S. dollar as the monetary unit, also means that there is nothing to prevent the conversion of internal into external purchasing power. Consequently, a great increase in public expenditure might have little effect on the domestic economy if, for example, it caused domestic inflation or balance-of-payments deficits. Either domestic inflation or a deficit in the balance of payments would produce a great drain on monetary reserves. An excessive expansion of fiscal expenditure might therefore only cause a contraction of private spending with no net impact on the level of national income, because of higher interest rates. The development of Panama as a financial center and the advent of world inflation and its impact on Panama have, in this respect, greatly complicated the task of the government.

NOTES

1. As expressed in its recent development plans. See Lineamientos del Plan Nacional de Desarrollo, 1974-1978 (Panama City: Direccion de Planificacion Economica y Social, 1973).

2. See Plan Trienal de Vivienda de Interes Social Plan de Trabajo para el ano de 1974 (Panama City: Ministry of Housing, 1973).

3. National Agricultural Policy Commission, "Politica de Desarrollo Agropecuario," mimeographed (Panama City: Ministry of Agricultural Development, Department of Sectoral Planning, 1973).

4. The effectiveness of this policy is evaluated in Gain Sahota, "Public Expenditure and Income Distribution in Panama," mimeographed (Panama City: Agency for International Development, 1972); National Agricultural Policy Commission, Politica de Desarrollo Agropecuario (Panama City: Ministry of Agricultural Development, Department of Sectoral Planning, 1973). An extremely interesting account of rural life and the government's programs in the provinces is given in James Wyche Green, "Panamanian District: A Case Study in the Sociology of Development," mimeographed (Panama City: Agency for International Development, 1969).

5. Sahota, op. cit., p.56.

6. Ibid.

7. Contraloria General, Hacienda publica y finanzas, various issues.

8. Joint tax program of the OAS/IDB, Fiscal Survey of Panama: Problems and Proposals for Reform (Baltimore: Johns Hopkins Press, 1964).

9. Calculated from Contraloria General, Hacienda publica y finanzas, various issues.

10. Fiscal Survey of Panama, op. cit., p.58.

11. Ibid.

12. Fiscal Survey of Panama, op. cit., chapter 4.

13. Ibid.

14. A reform resulting from the recommendations contained in the Fiscal Survey of Panama, op. cit.

15. Ibid.

16. Contraloria General, Hacienda publica y finanzas, 1973.

17. Ibid.

18. See Milton Taylor, "Toward the Redistribution of Income in Panama," mimeographed (Panama City: 1971).

19. The economic arguments are given in T. Scitovsky, "A Reconsideration of the Theory of Tariffs," in Papers on Welfare and Growth, ed. T. Scitovsky (Stanford: Stanford University Press, 1964).

20. Milton Taylor is the most knowledgeable individual in this area. See his "Toward the Redistribution of Income in Panama," op. cit., and his "A Proposal for a Net Wealth Tax in Panama," mimeographed (Panama City: no date).

21. Milton Taylor, "A Proposal for a Net Wealth Tax," op. cit.

22. See the Banco Nacional de Panama, Carta Economica, various issues. The effect of this borrowing on the financing of the Social Security System is given in Joseph Kessler, "Social Security in Panama," mimeographed (Panama City: Caja de Seguro Social, 1970), pp. 13-15.

9

**INFLATION
IN PANAMA**

The worldwide wage and price explosion of recent years has occurred largely because low interest rate and expansive fiscal policies were pursued by the United States between 1966 and 1969, while the rest of the world (including Panama, of course) with minor exceptions, maintained a rigid exchange-rate link with the U.S. dollar. This produced excess demand in the United States which spread, via the U.S. balance of payments and attendant monetary movements, to the rest of the fixed-exchange-rate world. Panama, along with other countries, was swept along on this inflationary wave, but at the same time may have undertaken several policies which gave its own inflationary spiral a further upward twist.

In order to evaluate the performance of the Panamanian authorities in dealing with world inflation, it is first necessary to examine the transmission mechanism of U.S. inflation into the Panamanian economy. As a first approximation, the proposition is advanced that the level of prices in Panama at a particular moment is determined solely by the quantity of money in circulation in the country. In turn, the country's balance of trade (which is a large component of the economy's balance of payments) depends on the relationship between domestic prices and those ruling abroad. Thus if the United States increases its money stock above that required for long-run equilibrium (as was the case in the late 1960s), the United States will have too high a price level, and an adverse trade balance vis-a-vis Panama. The chain of causation here, with regard to the transmission of price-level changes between the United States and Panama, is clear. An increase, for whatever reason, in the domestic money stock of the United States bids up prices there, and not until domestic prices in the United States have risen do that country's balance of trade and money begin to flow out to bid up prices in Panama. It is the flow of money that is the central factor in the transmission of price changes between the two countries and this is triggered by relative price-level discrepancies originating (because of its much larger size) in the United States.

Whether or not the Panamanian officials have pursued poor policies in reacting to these money flows and the monetary inflationary pressures in the country is certainly open to debate. The rate of inflation has been higher than in the United States. However, there are problems of observation and interpretation of the major price trends in Panama. The process of propagation of inflation in the economy involves substantial lags and a strong element of randomness in the adjustment of money wages and prices to preserve or restore the relative price relationships existing before the U.S. inflation. Further, for an important segment of the economy, such price and wage adjustments are made institutionally through price determination by the larger firms or industries and through collective bargaining. In these circumstances, wage and price adjustments are not continuous and small as pure theory would suggest, but discrete, large, and highly visible; and it is tempting to the casual observer to focus attention on the decisionmakers involved as being responsible for the inflation, and to attribute the change in their decisions toward inflation-producing ones to "abuse of monopoly power," "cost-pushfulness," "sociological change," and other phrases descriptive and emotive rather than analytical in nature. The temptation of cite these factors rather than the inflationary pressures generated by the explicit policies of the government is often strong, since Panama is a small and open economy and subject to inflationary pressures emanating from a large economy and from which it is forced to maintain a fixed exchange rate with the United States.

METHODOLOGY

To examine the role played by the authorities, inflation in Panama is reduced to two basic aspects: (1) the identification and classification of the various elements and categories involved in the process of inflation, and (2) analysis of their interrelationships. The first step therefore is to distinguish between the different inflationary pressures, to be followed by an analysis of the mechanisms by which inflation has spread throughout the different sectors of the economy, and continues after the fall of world inflation (the propagation mechanisms). This is a fundamental distinction, because the two types

of factors constitute separate logical categories; the propagation
mechanisms do not constitute the causes of inflation, but may keep it
alive and even contribute to its cumulative character. Moreover, the
mechanisms, as will be seen, are usually the most obvious features
of the inflationary process. This situation is largely responsible for
the current confusion in Panama which consists of taking those mechanisms as the real causes of inflation.

Because of Panama's monetary system, we accept from the
start the hypothesis that in the long run the chief factor causing Panamanian inflation is, as the monetarists contend, the increase in the
domestic money supply. Incorporating structural factors, the important questions for policy purposes however are: (1) the actual mechanisms through which this increase in the domestic supply of money
increases prices, and (2) the actual mechanism through which the
quantity of money increases. Involved in the approach to the issues
involving domestic inflation is first the identification and quantification
of those elements that contribute to the inflationary mechanism in
Panama. They include imported inflationary forces, domestic inflationary forces, and the government's anti-inflationary policies.

Of particular interest is the period from 1970 through 1972.
Admittedly, the oil crisis and other international developments
since 1972 have contributed to Panama's rising price level, but the
mechanism of inflation in Panama was established before these
latter events. To a certain extent their introduction makes an already complex process not only difficult to interpret, but in the end
yields little insight into the workings of the economy.

IMPORTED INFLATION

The magnitude of the current world inflation can be seen from
two price indexes of goods traded internationally—primary commodities and manufactured goods. With 1970 as the base year (1970 =
100), both indexes indicate that inflation had become a worldwide
phenomenon (Table 9.1). The implication for Panama was that the
country could thus no longer reduce the cost of its imports by re-
directing its imports from high inflation to low inflation countries
or from relatively expensive goods to cheaper substitutes.

Panama's remarkable history of price stability has been
partly the result of the operation of its relatively open economy,
and partly of the country's adherence to a quasi-gold-standard monetary system. This system with the U.S. dollar as the medium of
exchange has kept prices in line with those in the United States.

The current inflation in Panama began when the country's wholesale price index increased 7.2 percent annually in the period from September 1970 to September 1972 in contrast to 1.9 percent over the period 1961-70; similarly, the cost of living index has increased by 3.8 percent in the period September 1970 to September 1972 compared with 1.5 percent in the period 1962-70.[1]

TABLE 9.1

Index of World Inflation

1970 = 100	Primary Commodities	Manufactured Goods
1971	106	105
1972	120	113
1973	174	133
1974	272	162
1975	269	187

Source: United Nations, Monthly Bulletin of Statistics.

There is therefore evidence of an accelerating rate of increase in the general level of prices with very rapid increases occurring particularly in the first three quarters of 1972, owing to inflation abroad and the devaluation of the dollar. For example, the United States, Venezuela, and Japan account for roughly three-quarters of the goods imported to Panama. To illustrate this, a weighted average of the export price indexes with weights proportional to the participation of each country in Panama's total imports, has been constructed. This index (1966 = 100) together with this rate of increase is as follows:

1967	1968	1969	1970	1971	1972
102	103	105	109	111	116
(2.0)	(1.0)	(1.9)	(3.8)	(1.8)	(4.5)

This suggests that while imported inflation has been important in determining the rapid rise in domestic prices, other factors have also been at work.

The wholesale price index in Panama rose by 10.5 percent in 1973 as against 8.3 percent in the preceding year. Included in the index were increases of 11.6 percent in imports, 10.2 percent in industrial commodities, and 9.1 percent in agricultural commodities. (These figures are expressed as annual averages for 1972 and 1973.) From December 1972 to December 1973 the overall index and its components rose by 18.7, 20.2, 19.6, and 12.7 percent, respectively.[2]

Between 1966 and 1969 wholesale prices in Panama and the United States followed a fairly regular pattern, in that the Panamanian inflation was only about half that of the United States. Starting in 1969, however, the domestic price level (wholesale price index) accelerated in Panama, so that by 1974 it had easily overtaken that of the United States. Over time, therefore Panama's inflation rate was precisely the pattern one would expect. The country's monetary system, openness, and large volume of trade with the United States would, according to the monetarists, result in inflation in Panama mirroring that of the United States, much as inflation in California mirrors that of the United States. But the behavior of the components of the price index in Panama give a rather different picture than that associated with normal monetary adjustments. For example, during 1966-69 import prices were rising, but only half as much as the prices in the United States. At the same time, however, agricultural prices in Panama were rising on the average at twice the rate of inflation while industrial prices lagged far behind. After 1969 industrial prices escalated so rapidly, however, that by the end of 1972 prices in all sectors of Panama's economy had risen by about 25 percent (since 1966). This increase was roughly equal to the rise in both industrial and export prices in the United States.

A STRUCTURALIST EXPLANATION

The structuralist model* can be extended to industry and account for the movements noted above. In the late 1960s and early 1970s, industrial growth began to slow down in Panama. To stimulate production in that sector the government gave a number of inducements to firms, primarily increased protection from foreign competition. Such an expansion, it was hoped, would reduce the unemployment that was beginning to develop from the rapid expansion of the supply of labor in the face of a stagnant demand for workers.

---

*This model is not a position espoused by one person or group in Panama but is a synthesis of a number of ideas of economists and noneconomists, both within the government and in the private sector.

Employment figures for 1960 and 1970 would seem optimistic. Between these dates unemployment declined from 9.1 percent of the labor force to 7.1 percent. This apparent lowering of the unemployment rate, however, was somewhat misleading. In the first place, the decline in unemployment was to a large extent a result of decreases in unemployment in the metropolitan area, where unemployment dropped from 14.4 percent in 1960 to 9.8 percent in 1970. In contrast, unemployment in the rest of the country (primarily rural areas) declined only slightly—from 4.8 percent of the labor force in 1960 to 4.2 percent of the labor force in 1970.[3]

Second, the lowest level of unemployment was not in 1970, but in 1966, when 5.1 percent of the labor force were without jobs. The level of unemployment after 1966 began to increase to the 7.1 percent level of 1970.

Third, toward the end of the 1960s there was also an increase in the number of people without jobs for long periods of time. In 1968 approximately one-third of the unemployed had remained unemployed for more than five months; by 1970 nearly one-half of the unemployed were out of work for the same period of time.

Fourth, there was only minimal increase in employment in the agricultural sector. During the 1960s the rural sector employed 14,000 additional workers (Table 9.2). On the other hand, the number of additional people in the rural sector looking for work was around 66,000.[4] Given the age composition of the population (relatively young) and the high increase in the rate of population growth, therefore, it was clear to the authorities that the problem of unemployment would become much worse in the 1970s and 1980s.

Part of the problem in increasing employment, however, lay with the manufacturing sector. Between 1960 and 1970 this sector absorbed only 20 percent of the total labor-force increase, despite a high rate of growth during the period—over 9 percent annual growth in value added.

The economy's failure to create employment in manufacturing has been one of the chief concerns of the structuralists. They are concerned about the low labor absorption rates not only because of the serious social problems associated with urban unemployment or underemployment that are becoming evident, but also because of the implication for increased worsening in income distribution. Panama already has an unequal distribution of income, and the incomes of workers in industry are on the average substantially higher than the average for the country as a whole. The structuralists argue that unless the pattern of growth established in the 1950s and 1960s is broken, the country's income distribution will become even more concentrated.

TABLE 9.2

Employment and Average Productivity, by Economic Sector[a]

	1960	1963[b]	1964	1965	1966	1967	1968	1969	1970	1971
In Thousands of Workers										
Agriculture, forestry, and fishing	150	164	161	165	168	155	158	157	158	151
Mining	—	—	—	—	—	—	1	—	1	1
Industry	24	28	30	30	38	38	51	47	48	42
Construction	10	12	13	15	16	20	19	20	24	26
Electricity, gas, and sanitation	1	2	2	3	3	3	3	3	4	5
Commerce	26	34	34	34	34	40	41	47	49	59
Banking and finance	3	3	4	5	4	6	5	6	7	10
Transport, storage, and communications	9	9	9	11	12	13	15	16	16	18
Services	60	68	68	72	75	88	89	101	104	101
Canal Zone	18	20	20	20	22	23	23	23	22	24
Total employment	300	339	338	350	371	384	404	420	433	436
In Thousands of 1960 Balboas Per Worker										
Agriculture	0.64	0.69	0.74	0.80	0.83	0.94	0.98	1.03	1.02	1.11
Industry and mining	2.32	3.12	3.08	3.33	2.92	3.21	2.57	3.12	3.18	3.93
Construction	2.29	2.64	2.30	2.33	2.40	2.18	2.44	2.18	2.25	2.45
Electricity	8.40	5.55	6.10	4.83	5.00	5.43	6.30	7.83	6.50	5.94
Commerce and banking	2.35	2.72	2.88	3.04	2.92	2.63	2.81	2.75	2.88	2.54
Transportation	2.14	2.96	3.23	2.99	3.06	3.16	2.93	3.22	3.73	3.78
Services and public administration	1.35	1.41	1.44	1.46	1.50	1.37	1.42	1.31	1.41	1.58
Canal Zone	1.69	2.14	2.37	2.57	2.55	3.04	2.85	3.10	3.20	3.00
Total real productivity	1.39	1.60	1.67	1.76	1.79	1.88	1.91	1.99	2.07	2.23

[a] GDP at market prices divided by employment. Use of GDP at factor cost might have been preferable on theoretical grounds. As home ownership by definition utilizes no labor it perhaps would have been preferable to exclude its contribution to GDP in computing.

[b] Data for 1961 and 1962 are not available.

Source: Contraloria General, Direccion de Estadistica y Censo.

Because of the concentration of income, the growth of demand
for industrial products has been, according to the structuralists, insufficient to maintain the initial import substitution momentum. What
makes the situation in manufacturing even worse is the small size of
the domestic market, and many industries are forced to build substantially ahead of demand. Thus the existence of excess capacity
which is not being rapidly filled by growing demand, in turn, according to the structuralists, has raised prices (because of higher costs)
and dampened the incentive for private investment in the sector.

The process of declining growth in agriculture and manufacturing's inability to create jobs meant that labor productivity—
that is, value added per worker, rather than per hour worked—was
the critical link between employment and incomes in Panama. The
country was caught in a trap;[5] a lower rate of productivity increase
meant a greater labor absorption at a given rate of growth, but on
the other hand, a lower rate of productivity increase meant that
the economy would experience increasing income differences in the
country's various production sectors and regions.

The annual average rate of productivity growth between 1960
and 1971 was about 4.4 percent, reflecting in part the country's difference between the rates of growth of GDP and the labor force. For
example, the increase in productivity was higher than the national
average in manufacturing. Services (particularly urban), on the other
hand, experienced much lower increases in productivity—possibly
even declining somewhat. And agriculture in 1961 had an average
labor productivity of only about 45 percent of the overall average;
by 1971 it was about 50 percent of the average.

The major factors underlying the low productivity of the
Panamanian economy are, according to the structuralist line of
argument: (1) Panama's relative lack of basic social capital outside
the metropolitan area (the limitations and deficiencies of the national
road system are perhaps the greatest obstacles to any increase in
farm productivity); and (2) the scarcity (and resulting high cost) of
energy. Both factors have inflated the costs of industrial production
by limiting the size of the market and necessitating investment by
firms for services that should have been provided by the government. In addition, Panamanian industry is based largely on the
utilization of primary agricultural products that are extremely costly. Again, the structuralist argument emphasizes the primitive level
of the techniques used in agriculture as a cause of the low productivity
in this basic sector. The failure to apply such elementary methods
as breaking up the land, the inefficient distribution of land resources
among the various crops, the large proportion of agricultural activity that has remained outside the monetary sector, the persistence

of semi-nomadic farming, and deficiencies in the land tenure system
are the major causes of the rural sector's low productivity and thus
its high cost. The problems in agriculture have been aggravated by
the country's defective and costly marketing system of farm products.

Admittedly the post-1968 government began a major attempt
to lessen regional disparities in income through public expenditures.
However, the ability of the expenditures to reduce urban-rural disparities in income seems to have been limited as a result of the relatively high concentration of government investment in urban areas,
particularly in the metropolitan area.

Structuralists admit that the increasing concentration of
income could, of course, be avoided by various types of redistributive
policies of the government—redistribution by income groups, by
sector of the economy, and by regions. Progressive tax measures or
appropriate wage policies could be used to redistribute incomes a-
mong social groups; and government credit and fiscal policies could
redirect resources to neglected sectors (such as agriculture, housing,
road building) and to the more backward regions.

Potential domestic demand for industrial products exists
in Panama according to the structuralists because the import replacement process has occurred in an unbalanced fashion; that is, as
import replacement took place in industry, other sectors such as
agriculture, low-income housing, transportation, and infrastructure
were neglected, resulting by the late 1960s in severe bottlenecks.
At the same time a strong regional concentration of income and
industry took place. Although such regional concentration was eco-
nomical in the 1950s and up to the mid-1960s (taking into account
external economies to firms settling close to suppliers, to direct
infrastructure facilities, and to skilled labor supplies), it had a
self-reinforcing nature. Increasing regional concentration of wealth
now presents the country with the political need to redistribute income on a regional basis. All these forces according to the structuralists make it possible to generate new demand through government policies toward the industrial sector.

This is the main thrust of the structuralist argument as we
have constructed it: stagnant conditions in agriculture (a structural
problem) resulted in a migration to the metropolitan area; and the
rapid urbanization of Panama City, in particular, substantially increased the need for expanded government services. More precisely, the country needed an expanded infrastructure to make up
for the lag in government interest in the 1950s and 1960s; continued
growth required better roads, port facilities, power projects,
schools, and health services to complement the growing urban-in-
dustrial sector; and a substantial lag in the construction of these

services was beginning, according to the structuralists, to hinder
growth of the industrial sector. In brief, rapid urbanization in the
1960s required more government attention to the construction of low-
income housing, urban transportation, and sanitation. By the late
1960s the investment responsibilities of the government were beginning to increase at a rapid pace. In short, lagging government investment in these infrastructure activities, according to the structuralists, began to manifest itself in increased social tensions in the
cities and hampered the smooth growth of an integrated diversified
economy.

We can summarize our reconstruction of a structuralist
model by saying that inflationary pressures in Panama are basically
the result of lack of adaptation of domestic supply to a changing pattern and level of demand. This problem in a structuralist framework
is aggravated by the inflexibility and instability of exports, which do
not allow changing import levels to achieve sectoral equilibrium.
Neither do industrial prices move to equate demand and supply,
particularly if they have to move downward.

This all seems plausible. The structuralist-monetarist debate, therefore, is ultimately one of degree. The relative strength
of monetary pressure and structural conditions in determining the
pattern and rate of Panama's inflation can only be ascertained by
detailed examination of the type and prices of imports, agricultural
products, and industrial products.

The differential movements in the prices of imports, agricultural production, and industrial output should shed some light
on the inflationary mechanisms in Panama. In 1970, for example,
26 percent of the gross value of production in the industrial sector
was accounted for by inputs of imported goods. Domestically produced agricultural products, intermediate goods, and raw materials
accounted for 34 percent of the gross value. The timing of these
three prices then should provide a definitive test of the degree to
which the inflation can be described as resulting from monetary or
structural factors; that is, since the price of industrial output is
simply a weighted average of the prices of the various inputs, including the income generated in that sector (its value added or contribution to GDP), an index of the prices of these inputs should provide valuable information concerning the mechanism of inflation in
the country.*

---

*This was constructed for Panama by Professor Sjaastad.

DOMESTIC INFLATION

The indexes for the key sectors are obtained by dividing the
sector indexes of price by the overall price index. During the early
phases of the inflationary process (1970), the relative price of value
added in industry fell. At the same time the index for the price of
value added in agriculture rose (Table 9.3). Subsequently the industrial wholesale price index rose in 1971 and 1972, so that by the end
of 1972 its level had regained its 1966 value.

TABLE 9.3

Relative Prices, Wholesale Level, by Sector, 1966-72

Date	Imports	Industry	Agri-culture	Value Added: Index
March, 1966	100.0	100.0	100.0	100.0
December, 1966	99.8	100.0	101.0	99.3
December, 1967	100.4	98.8	102.7	94.5
December, 1968	100.0	98.7	103.7	93.6
December, 1969	100.5	98.0	104.7	90.8
December, 1970	101.9	96.5	105.1	86.0
December, 1971	102.0	97.8	101.7	91.8
December, 1972	100.3	99.6	100.8	98.2

Source: Larry Sjaastad, "Prices and Wages in Panama"
(Panama City: U.S. Agency for International Development, 1973), p.14.

Because Panama is a small buyer in international markets,
it is unable to influence the prices of its imports.[*] Also, agricultural prices have been subject to strict control during much of the
period under consideration. Therefore the key to understanding the
sudden spurt of inflation during 1971-72 lies in the behavior of industrial prices. Particular insight can be gained by studying the
details of the price changes from the end of 1970 to the end of 1972.

The areas of major price rise within the industrial sector
during 1971 and 1972 were processed food products (mainly meat

---

[*]This is a generalization. Even though Panama is such a
small country in its purchase of internationally traded goods, its
purchases may have some effect.

and fish), alcoholic beverages, fuels and lubricants, manufactured articles (jewelry, furniture, footwear), and miscellaneous manufactured articles.

The price rise of each can be explained by a somewhat different set of conditions. For example, the increases in food prices reflect rising world prices for fish and shrimp together with sharp increases in domestic cattle prices; the rise in prices of domestically produced alcoholic beverages to a large extent is the result of the increases in taxes on those items during 1972. The rise in prices of fuels and lubricants is due to increases in the world price of oil, and also to higher taxes imposed in 1972. The rise in the price of jewelry reflects the rising world price of sliver and gold, as individuals increased their holdings of these metals as a hedge against inflation, particularly in the European countries such as Germany.

The price index for value added in industry is constituted so that it is unaffected by changes in the prices of imports and domestically produced agricultural goods.[6] Therefore only the tax increases can be reflected in the index. It follows that much of the explanation of the dramatic rise in that index from December 1970 through December 1972 was due to modest but widespread increases in prices of most industrial outputs, with the major increases in prices of furniture, footwear, and miscellaneous manufactures. The rise in prices of items such as furniture and footwear, once inflation begins, is hard to control. They are not standardized as are products such as rice. Style changes and modifications in their design enable producers to increase prices easily, even though the government may be attempting to control prices.

There are at least two alternative hypotheses explaining the increase in prices in the industrial sector during 1971-72: (1) changes in government policy concerning labor and wage rates,* or (2) increases in general aggregate demand for Panamanian products.

The first includes changes in the legal and institutional framework concerning labor and wage rates—increases in minimum wages and the new labor code. Presumably this legislation increased labor costs that were in turn passed on to consumers in the form of higher prices.

The government's wage and price policies introduce an important point concerning the different mechanisms of inflation. In the monetarist view there is clearly no room for cost (wage) inflation

---

*A policy on wages or income was adopted under the post-1968 government.

because prices and wages always move to whatever level is necessary
to prevent shortages or surpluses in markets. Aggregate demand in
money terms is therefore determined by the supply of money, given
the level of output. On the other hand, to include cost inflation in a
structural explanation would not be a true reflection of their position.
Cost inflation* is not related at all to the usual causes of inflation
stressed by this school, such as the inability of the agricultural sector to expand food supply in line with increased profitability, instability
of the purchasing power of exports, deficiencies in the tax structure,
and so on. For policy purposes, inflation in Panama resulting from
pure cost increases decreed by the government should be considered
apart from a structuralist or from a modified monetarist explanation. †
It is particularly important to make this distinction when considering
policy alterations designed to cope with the country's inflation. In
this connection it is important to note that the basic relationships and
treaties between the Republic of Panama and the Canal Zone were not
changed during this period, and the policies of the government began
to become more oriented toward increases in wages through decree.

GOVERNMENT'S ANTI-INFLATION
POLICIES

Panama City and Colon have traditionally been the high-wage
areas in Panama. This is a direct consequence of the high salaries
paid to workers in the nearby Canal Zone. Prior to 1969, most wages
of Panamanian workers were determined without government intervention. Since that time, the government has intervened actively in
labor markets in an effort to increase real wages. In December 1971,
for example, employers were required by decree to pay an additional
month's wage to their workers (the "thirteenth-month" decree), in an
attempt to bring wages back to their real purchasing power. After
1971 the new month's salary was split into three payments: two direct

---

*Inflation resulting from rising costs, not necessarily
related to increased demand; that is, inflation that presumably could
occur through increases in wages or prices irrespective of the volume of money or credit.

†Cost inflation is sometimes included in the structuralist
explanation of inflation, particularly increases in costs resulting from
a devaluation. However, most structuralists would prefer to confine
their discussion principally to rigidities in supply and institutional
problems as the major causes of inflation.

payments to workers in April and December and a third through the Social Security System to be used by the new public mortgage bank. The government pursued these policies with little consultation with employers and without any study to examine the impact of its actions. As might be expected, the government's rapid shift in policy created substantial uncertainty and distrust among employers, especially since the December 1971 payment was for a full year's cash payment, and was announced only two months before being implemented. Most importantly, the timing of its implementation (December) affected the fiscal year profit expectations of most firms at a critical time, when they were planning whether or not to expand their investment in plant and equipment.

A second wage policy was to increase the direct taxation of wages, which was implemented by a 2 percent "educational insurance" decree passed in July 1971. This taxed employers 1.25 percent of their wage bill and the wages of employees by 0.75 percent.

A third government wage policy was the revision of the country's labor code. This code through rewriting became a detailed compendium patterned after the Mexican labor code.[7] It set regulations for conduct of employers and workers and significantly changed the traditional working relationships between employer and employee. The country had had a labor code for some time prior to 1971, but it had never been implemented. All but the minimum wage provisions had usually been ignored by both the government and employers. The post-1968 government, however, immediately began a serious attempt to implement its new labor code, especially those parts that favored the worker. The scope for action in this area was considerable.

The new code greatly enlarged the authority of the Ministry of Labor, which set up a national employment service to implement the code. In practice, the ministry may fine employers for infractions of the labor code; it regulates strikes, conciliates disputes, and appoints arbitrators. It is now even responsible for setting up or regulating day-care centers for children of female workers.

As could be expected, the response of employers to the government's labor policies was not favorable. Not only did unionization proceed rapidly, but many new unions began to demand that all the provisions of the new code be included in collective aggrements. In addition, for the first time many employers were forced to bargain collectively with their employees. Their response to workers' increased wage demands varied from industry to industry. Companies producing products such as refined oil products and cement, where labor costs make up only a small percentage of total cost, absorbed most pay raises and expanded output with only moderate increases in prices. Many bankers, some merchants, and owners of firms forced to produce with controlled prices either resisted the implementation of the code or deferred any new investment in their firms until the thrust and implication of the government's program became clearer.

Partially as a result of the government's income policies (wage and price controls), real wages increased about 8.7 percent between 1968 and 1972, or a little over 2 percent per year. In money terms the rise between 1968 and 1972 was about 22 percent, or 5 percent yearly. In effect, about 45 percent of the increased real output went to wages—a fairly high share compared with previous years when wages made up only about 25 percent of value added.* What strongly concerned many employers, however, was not the increase in real wages but the manner in which the wage increases were made, and the change from a relatively open-market wage system to a regulated one.

Along with the wage increases, which mostly affected urban workers, the government has followed a policy of attempting to control prices. Because Panama had relatively stable prices before 1970, both the government and businessmen were not accustomed to active price regulation. The scope for price regulation in Panama has always been rather limited, since many of the goods sold in Panama are imported or are produced largely from imported products. The prices of imports can not be altered significantly (at least in a downward direction) because they are set by world market forces. The government initially attempted to regulate the prices of locally produced agricultural products, but in December 1972, it passed a decree virtually freezing all prices. This decree was later modified to allow for exemptions when individual firms were able to prove cost increases were harmful to their profit structure.†

The government lacked the administrative machinery to assess these exemptions, but it succeeded in making some major

---

*Value added is the gross output minus intermediate inputs entering into the production process. Value added includes the incomes generated as a result of the productive process; that is, wages, rents, interest, and profits.

†Obviously the government was not in a position to enforce the decree. Thus while "official" prices remain constant, the "actual" prices which would be necessary for a thorough analysis are not available.

changes. In October 1973 it lowered most housing rents to the December 1972 level, and early in 1973 it lowered cattle and beef prices to half the world price. This freeze in combination with an export embargo meant that the income of cattle producers (including 10,000 medium and small producers), unlike that of urban workers, has been kept down by government policy.

The main beneficiaries of government wage and price policy until 1973 were, therefore, the already employed higher-income urban workers, although the government's lack of consultation with businessmen before announcing wage and price actions affected the investment climate adversely and retarded the growth of urban employment. *

The government was aware that the increase in the cost of living had an adverse effect on lower-income groups whose income had risen less rapidly than that of the urban workers. For this reason, at the beginning of 1974, the authorities began to consider a general wage increase as a means of countering the adverse redistribution effects of inflation.

At the end of March 1974 the government enacted three additional laws (Laws 32-34 of March 29, 1974)† on wages and prices, with the prime motive of forestalling what it considered to be adverse effects on low-income groups resulting from the continuing inflation. Law No. 33 raised salaries in the private sector by the following percentages with respect to their levels of Dec. 31, 1973:

Wage	Percent Raise
Up to B/0.60 per hour	15
B/0.61 to B/1.60 per hour	13
B/1.61 to B/4.50 per hour	13 to 4.7
Over B/4.50 per hour	0

Domestic workers received an increase of 10 percent of their nominal wage, and workers in the construction industry received an increase of B/0.05 per hour. (This is a 7 percent increase for a wage of B/0.70 per hour, the minimum wage established for construc-

---

*This occurred mainly as a result not only of this measure but of the continual changing of the "rules of the game" under which businessmen operated. The government at this time was experimenting with a number of various policies and changed them frequently.

†Most of the provisions in these laws were for urban workers. Rural workers were not greatly affected.

tion.) Law 33 also increased the minimum wage previously established by 10 percent (the increase in no case to be less than B/0.05 per hour), and fixed minimum wages for domestic, agricultural, and construction workers. For construction workers the law established a minimum wage scale based on geographical area, skill level, and type of construction work.

Law No. 32 raised the salaries of public employees as of June 10, 1974, by the following percentages:

Wages	Percent Raise
Up to B/125 per month	20
From B/125 to B/200 per month	15
Over B/200 per month	15 to 0

Finally, Law No. 34 provided that prices previously regulated by the government may be increased to meet the salary increases prescribed by Law No. 33. It also established a mechanism for regulating increases in other prices (those not previously regulated).

> ... firms... shall provide advance notification to the Office of Price Regulation, within one week, of increases ... and the time at which they become effective, and shall maintain documents and reports verifying that there has been an increase in costs that justifies them because of a decrease in real profit margins, for examination by the Office of Price Regulation.[8]

The government has evidently made an effort to minimize some of the possible adverse effects mentioned above. The laws provide for progressive wage increases to benefit those harmed most by the rise in the cost of living, and to reduce the average increase of wages in the economy, limiting it to approximately the increase in the general price level caused by exogenous factors. The increases and other provisions also are differentiated according to industries, professions, and geographical regions, in order to reduce the overall impact on the economy. Finally, the measure regulating price increases tends to control the inflationary spiral that might have resulted from increases in wages and other costs, for example, raw materials and fuels.*

---

*An implicit cost-push type of mechanism was assumed by the government.

At the same time, Law No. 32 will have an unfavorable effect on the prospects of public finances, resulting in an average annual increase of about 8 percent in salaries paid by the national government; it also will affect the finances of other public agencies. In addition, the salary measures will prevent the traditional balance of payments adjustment mechanisms from operating with full force, which means that larger deficits will continue to be financed by receipts on capital account primarily from the banking system, since the government has little ability to control the lending policies of the commercial banks.

IMPACT OF THE GOVERNMENT'S INCOME
POLICIES ON INFLATION

While it is possible that the rise in the indexes in the first quarter of 1972 could have been a result of the imposition of the government's thirteenth-month wage payments and other labor legislation in late 1972, it is unlikely that these factors could explain the rise in the price of industrial value added of more than 10 percent from the fourth quarter of 1971 to the third quarter of 1972.

Specifically, the index of the price of value added in industry indicates that industrial prices began to increase during the first quarter of 1971, well in advance of the introduction of the government's thirteenth-month wage and salary compensation plans, and nearly a year prior to the introduction of the new labor code.[9] Moreover, the increase in production costs resulting from the thirteenth-month salary increase could have had only a minor impact during 1972, as (1) it was introduced only at the very end of the year, (2) only one-half of the thirteenth month was required to be paid in 1971, and (3) firms already paying a bonus of two or more weeks of pay in December were not required to make any further payments under the rules of the thirteenth month. Up to 50 percent of commercial firms and 75 percent of industrial enterprises were in fact paying December bonuses prior to the introduction of the thirteenth-month rule. It is clear therefore that the increase in labor costs associated with the thirteenth-month wage payment had only a small impact on prices during 1971—perhaps no more than 2 percent. The government's actions in the wage areas, therefore, hardly constitute a major cause for inflation in industry.

This conclusion is supported by additional evidence. First, between 1965-69, there was an upward drift in nominal hourly earnings of over 4 percent per year. During that period there was a slightly larger upward drift in the value added per man-hour. These statistics suggest that productivity of labor in industry was increasing at more than 5 percent per year. As a result of the productivity increase (through lower labor costs per unit of output), wages could have risen by more than 5 percent per year in the 1965-70 period without causing industrial prices to rise more rapidly than did other prices in the economy (because productivity increases were lower in those areas).

Second, in 1971 there was a reverse of the rising trend in value added per man-hour. In that year value added per man-hour fell almost 7 percent, while wages rose by 5.7 percent (the historical average had been 4 percent). The increases in wages were heavily concentrated in food, tobacco, footwear, and construction materials. This rise in wages is not sufficient to explain, however, the rise in the average price of value added in industry by over 7 percent from 1970 to 1971 (Table 9.3). A rise of 5.7 percent in wages, even given the drop in productivity, would be consistent with price stability (insofar as value added is concerned).

To explain the 1971 industrial price-wage pattern (the behavior of the price of value added in view of only a modest increase in the rate of change of hourly earnings), the behavior of value added and labor's share over time must be examined. The year 1971 was average insofar as value added was concerned; the increase of 13.7 percent was very close to the historical rate of 13.3 percent; but there was a major difference in that the historical rate of change occurred simultaneously with a fall of about 1 percent per year in the price of value added. In 1971, however, this increase occured with a 7 percent rise in that price. It follows that value added must have been rising by more than 14 percent on the average during the 1965-70 period; however, in 1971 it increased by only 7 percent. At the same time that this slowdown occurred, labor's share of value added rose by 13 percent, after falling in previous years. Labor costs measured in terms of labor's share, rather than labor costs measured in terms of wages per man-hour of worker inputs, is therefore the key to explaining the price patterns in industry.

In Panama, labor's share of value added is defined as the ratio of the wage bill for production workers to value added, and as such is a measure of the labor costs of production. Clearly during 1971, labor costs, measured in terms of labor's share of value added, rose much more sharply than did labor costs measured in terms of wages per man-hour of production worker input. It is the rise in labor's share of value added, not labor costs measured in terms of wages per man-hour, that was partly responsible for the increase in the price of value added during 1971. Indeed, labor costs measured in this way explain about one-half of that increase. Since labor

accounts for less than one-quarter of value added for the average
Panamanian industrial firm, this conclusion at first seems implausible.
A detailed examination of the data, however, clearly explains the
observed price patterns. During 1971 labor costs, instead of falling
about 1 percent as had been the case historically, rose by 13 percent.
Hence labor costs in this sense were 14 percent higher during 1971
than they would have been had historical trends continued. This 14
percent increase represents an increase in the price of value added
of only about 3.5 percent.

The fact that labor costs, measured as labor's share, rose
so much more sharply than did wages per man-hour, while explaining
the pattern of industrial price changes, still seems puzzling. This
relative change in the two labor-cost measures indicates that somehow labor productivity declined during 1971. This means that the increase in earnings per man-hour, rather than being matched by an
increase in productivity (which is the reason for wage increases in
the first place), was accompanied by a fall in productivity. This
decline in productivity is reflected in an unusually large increase of
more than 20 percent in man-hours worked between 1970 and 1971.
Increases of this size were never even approached in the previous
five years. It follows that much of the increase in the quantity of
industrial output that was experienced in 1971 was due to increased
labor utilization.

The normal methods of increasing labor input, however, can
not explain this jump in man-hours worked in 1971. First, the increase
in labor inputs could not have resulted from increased capital formation (thus creating additional jobs) since most machinery had to
be imported and in 1971 imports of equipment actually fell. Second,
real industrial output expanded by only 7 percent in 1971 so that greater utilization of excess capacity is ruled out. The only other explanation for the increase in labor hours is that the industrial production of 7 percent in 1971 was achieved through the utilization of
more labor with a given capital stock, rather than through a general
expansion of industrial firms.

Apparently the 20-percent expansion in production labor input in Panamanian industry was brought about by firms drawing on
rural migrants, since their low level of skill would cause average
productivity to fall and labor costs to increase by an amount larger
than the rise in wage rates. There are two explanations for this
phenomenon. First, firms were apparently willing to hire rural
migrants in the hope that they would not become unionized or that the
firms would not have to extend the new provisions of the labor code
to them. Second, the government at the end of 1970 enacted a new
industrial incentives law.

The industrial incentives law* (decree 413) was meant to stimulate the declining manufacturing sector. Since 1962 the central government had given increasing importance to import quotas as protective measures for new industries, although quantitative restrictions on imports were initiated solely as an instrument of domestic protection. Quotas on a number of products (for example, brushes, hats, paper cups, sardines, butter, suitcases, shoes) were imposed between 1966 and 1970. Although it was the government's intention to liberalize import quotas, particularly for imports of construction materials in order to mitigate inflationary pressures, they continued to be prepared and approved by the National Assembly.

In the meantime the new industrial incentives law passed at the end of 1970 was a significant advancement in economic legislation. Among its strong points were: (1) uniformity in the level of tariffs; (2) a decreasing level of protection through time; and (3) the establishment of incentives for the utilization of labor, especially plants established for import replacement that were located in certain areas outside the metropolitan area—in David, Renacimiento, Santiago, Chitre, Los Santos, Las Tablas, Aquadolce, and Natay Penonume.

The incentives given to firms engaging in export activities were (1) the total elimination of duties on imported machinery, equipment and parts, raw materials, semi-manufactured products, and combustibles and lubricants; and (2) the total elimination of income taxes, export tariffs, and domestic sales taxes.

Manufacturing activities that involved replacing imports were given total exemption from the import tariff of machinery, equipment and parts, and partial exemption (decreasing through time) on the importation of raw materials and semi-finished products that were produced internally in sufficient quantity, acceptable quality or competitive prices. Most important, the import replacing sectors were granted reductions in their income tax of 10 percent of the total wages and salaries (with the exclusion of the administrative personnel). After the tenth year from the granting of these incentives, exemptions of wages and salaries from the income tax could not exceed 50 percent of the company's tax. The law, therefore, granted a subsidy to those firms that produced for the domestic market in certain areas in the country and used relatively large amounts of labor. †

---

*Explained in much more detail in Chapter 11.

†Because of the unreliability of the input-output table for Panama, this conclusion is quite crude, although probably accurate enough for our analysis. The lack of a reliable interindustry

The concept of effective protection was developed by economists to determine the total effect of tariff structures and other trade restraints on domestic firms. There is an important distinction in this area to be made between nominal and effective protection to the value added of a firm. The nominal rate of protection of a particular commodity is defined as the percentage excess of the domestic price over the world market price resulting from the application of protective measures. If tariffs are the only protective measures used and they are not prohibitive in the sense that they would exclude all imports, the domestic price of competing domestic commodities of identical quality will equal the sum of the c.i.f. import price and the tariff, and the nominal rate of protection will equal the ad valorem rate of tariff (tariffs expressed as a percentage of import value). The measurements in the area of effective protection are not only conceptually difficult, but nearly impossible to make without an accurate input-output table.[10]

The effective rate of protection is calculated as follows:

Using largely agricultural inputs of a dollar or its domestic equivalent, production inactivity j in sector A can be broken down into three parts,

$$1 = VA_j + MA_j + NA_j \tag{9.1}$$

where VA_j = value added, MA_j = cost of materials produced domestically, and NA_j = cost of raw materials not produced domestically. The tariff protection granted under the law allowed a firm such as A to increase its price to \$1.50 and distribute it as follows:

$$1.5 = V'A_j + 1.5\ MA_j + 1.2\ NA_j \tag{9.2}$$

where $V'A_j$ = new value added, $1.5\ MA_j$ and $1.5\ NA_j$ = cost of raw materials.

If the effective rate of protection (TA_j) is defined as the proportional change between the old value added and the new value added, then

$$TA_j = \frac{V'A_j - VA_j}{VA_j} \tag{9.3}$$

table for Panama has made the government's programs very difficult to design, particularly if one sector or group of workers is intended to be affected favorably by the government through its measures.

$$TA_j = \frac{1.5 - 1.5\ MA_j - 1.2\ NA_j - 1 + MA_j + NA_j}{VA_j} \tag{9.4}$$

$$TA_j = \frac{0.5 - 0.5\ MA_j - 0.2\ NA_j}{V'A_j}$$

$$= \frac{0.5(1 - MA_j - NA_j) + 0.5\ MA_j - 0.2\ NA_j}{V'A_j} \tag{9.5}$$

or

$$TA_j = 0.5 + 0.3\frac{(NA_j)}{(VA_j)} \tag{9.6}$$

To see the relative advantage that a firm using agricultural inputs would have over one using primarily manufacturing inputs, a similar calculation for the effective protection in activity i of sector B yields:

$$TB_i = 0.37 + 0.17\frac{(NB_i)}{(VB_i)} \tag{9.7}$$

The law therefore favored firm A (because of its use of raw materials) by 13 percent over firm B. The degree of relative discrimination, of course, depends on the proportion of raw materials in the aggregate value of firm A and firm B. The greater the proportion, the greater discrimination in favor of A.

Of particular interest in attempting to account for the manufacturing sector's rapid increase in labor utilization in 1971 is the discrimination given by the law between firms that received a tax reduction for the wages and salaries paid, and those that were not granted a deduction under this provision. The figure used in the following calculation is the 10-percent reduction in a firm's taxes on the wages and salaries paid in producing its products. As before;

V_j = aggregate value in activity j in a situation without tariffs, V'_j = the aggregate value added with a tariff, S_j = the labor subsidy for labor employment, and V''_j is the aggregate value with tariff and subsidy. It follows that:

$$V'_j = (1 + T_j) \tag{9.8}$$

$$V''_j = V'_j + S_j \tag{9.9}$$

$$S_j = 0.10a_1 V''_j \tag{9.10}$$

T_j is the effective tariff, a is the proportion of wages and salaries in V''_j. The new rate of effective protection is defined as

$$T''_j = \frac{V''_j - V_j}{V_s} \tag{9.11}$$

Using the previous values,

$$T''_j = \frac{V'_s}{V_j(1 - 0.10a)} - 1 \tag{9.12}$$

$$T''_j = \frac{1 + T_j}{1 - 0.10a_1} - 1 \tag{9.13}$$

$$T''_j = (T_j + 0.10a_1) \frac{1}{1 - 0.10a_1} \tag{9.14}$$

Equation 9.14 indicates the extent to which an enterprise could increase its effective tariff (T_s) if it used labor. For example, an intensive use of labor ($A_1 = .74$) protected by an effective tariff of 50 percent could increase its effective rate to 62 percent. To take advantage of this provision the firm had to be located in one of the designated provincial towns, for example, David, Los Santos.

It is clear, therefore, that a number of firms had a great incentive to increase their employment. In part this must account for the abnormal increase in the wage share in manufacturing in 1971. Recall that the law, Decree 413, was enacted in December 1970, and lasted only eight months of 1971 before being replaced by another decree.

The implementation of Decree 413 was slow, given the institutional arrangements existing in Panama. The National Assembly had to approve any new customs tariff or tariff rate change, while the Office of Price Regulation, on the other hand, could introduce import quotas without going through the legislative process. Thus in August 1971, to speed up the incentives to industry, a revised industrial incentives law (Decree 172) was enacted, perhaps to protect some industries in the Colon Free Zone, as well. This decree introduced a mixed system of import quotas to encourage industrial diversification, as well as to promote exports and import replacement. The main instruments of the law were a series of fiscal exemptions for export-oriented industries, but no tax incentives for employment were granted.

Decree 172 eliminated certain provisions of Decree 413 and accentuated its weakest aspects. For example, the new law increased the government's discretionary authority by leaving protection rates to the discretion of several of the government's autonomous agencies, and what is worse, by allowing judgment to be exercised ex post facto. It is too early to determine the actual amount of uncertainty caused by this provision.

The post-1968 government set up a number of new autonomous agencies to facilitate the greatly expanded role of the state. It was felt that these agencies could assume some of the burden of the central government, which at the time lacked the personnel to coordinate all of the government's activities. It is clear, however, that this policy of creating autonomous agencies could have only intensified the situation that produced it. If the central government was weak in evaluating the overall impact of its policies, a series of alternative mini-governments would only have weakened it still further. As one Panamanian official noted:

> Every three months we review the expenditures
> for each ministry for the next quarter. New per-
> sonnel are not hired, nor is equipment bought.
> If a serious deficit is foreseen, the President
> pulls out his list of priorities and new decisions
> are made. [11]

The nickname of the autonomous agencies in Panama is "Republicatitas" (little republics), which shows that they are seen as self-contained alternatives to the government within their areas. It is therefore hardly surprising that those who man them are strong believers in independence from the government. They have the power to set prices, quotas, and tariffs, hire people without following civil service regulations, cut through governmental red tape, and act more quickly than the central bureaucracy. Most would like to be as autonomous as possible. This freedom, of course, has its drawbacks; autonomous agencies are an easy prey for clientele groups where central control by the government is not present to offset local pressures.

The 1969 decree* that established the Office of Price Regulation, an autonomous agency, also created the Board of

---

*In 1969 a whole series of decrees were enacted, greatly expanding the number of autonomous agencies and the powers granted the existing ones.

Adjustments, another autonomous agency, composed of representatives of various ministries to determine commercial policy in the
light of national development priorities and to supervise the workings
of the Office of Price Regulation. However, the Board of Adjustments
remained a largely nonfunctional body. The result was that commercial policy was defined and implemented by several agencies on
a somewhat ad hoc basis and with little coordination at the national
level, in order to integrate commercial policy with development
goals. Thus, certain commodities produced by protected industries
were given both quotas and high import tariffs. After 1971 firms en-
joying this increased monopoly position had a much greater potential
to increase their domestic prices. Thus the patterns of wages, man-
hours worked, productivity changes, and so on, while somewhat unusual, can be easily explained and do not detract from our major
conclusion, that is, that increased labor costs by themselves had
little influence on industrial pricing in this period of inflation.

INFLATION AS CAUSED BY INCREASED
DOMESTIC EXPENDITURE

As there seems to be little evidence that increases in labor
costs in the form of unusually large wage-rate increases brought
about the rising industrial prices in 1971, one must look to other
factors for a more complete explanation of the rising prices. One
promising possibility (our second hypothesis) has already been mentioned, namely, excess demand for domestically produced goods
and services.

While it is true that Panama is an open economy and can
hardly insulate itself from international inflationary forces, the fact
remains that the rise in a number of consumer prices has been
higher than the rise in import prices. Hence, domestic forces have
reinforced the world rise in prices.

The high growth performance of recent years imposed a
severe strain on domestic supplies. Private sector consumption
grew at an average annual rate of 7.75 percent in real terms between 1968 and 1973, and 8.4 percent alone from 1970 to 1971. Private
investment expenditures grew by about 10.5 percent per annum during
the same period. And government expenditures on consumption and
investment grew at an average annual rate of 7.2 and 21.3 percent,
respectively. A small open economy like Panama's, without foreign
exchange constraints (assuming it can borrow internationally), need
not face serious development bottlenecks even at these high rates

of growth if it is able to import food, raw materials, and capital
goods. It can even import labor and capital. When import prices
are stable, such imports will help diffuse domestic inflationary
pressures brought about by excess demand for domestic factors,
goods, and services. When import prices are rising, however, inflation becomes inevitable. The first major physical bottleneck in
Panama, therefore, occurred in nontraded goods, particularly in
the construction sector. The boom of the late 1960s and early 1970s
led to acute shortages of land, construction materials, and workers.
Escalating land and property prices were aggravated by speculation.
Strong inflationary pressures were set up in the construction sector
after 1969 and the cost of new housing and new office buildings sky-
rocketed. Higher costs of land and property development were
aggravated by the trend toward more luxurious features in residential buildings and commercial offices. *

The construction boom began in 1971 and was partially financed by foreign funds brought in by the international banking system.
By 1972 construction permits in Panama City were up 55 percent over
their 1969-70 level. [12] Futhermore, foreign commercial bank lending
for construction purposes nearly doubled between 1970 and 1972.
Finally, the great growth in liquidity is reflected in the rapid increase in Panamanian bank deposits, both foreign and domestic.

Not only was the expansion of credit inflationary, but the
composition of bank loans also had an inflationary bias. Since most
loans were for housing, construction, and trade (products that cannot be directly consumed by workers), with little for agricultural
and industrial activities, production increased in areas that did not
provide goods that wage earners could consume.

More generally, during the period from September 30, 1972,
to September 30, 1973, credit from the banking system extended to
domestic activities expanded by almost 42 percent. Credit had already increased by 36 percent between the end of 1971 and the end of
1972 (see Chapter 7). Credit expansion by commercial banks therefore permitted a rapid rise in consumption and in real investment,
despite sharp increases in the general price level. Bank credit thus

---

*Regressions using monetary variables found a close re-
lationship between domestic expenditure and commercial bank credit.
Because of the problems involved in measuring the money supply,
these results are not presented. They are available from the author
upon request, however.

plays a dual role in the Panamanian context. On the active side, it is capable of stimulating consumption and investment spending in spite of higher prices, and passively it permits expenditures that are under consideration, independently of the rate of inflation.

Growth in investment demand, such as the construction boom, was met by an inflow of foreign capital that has appeared as an increase in the Panamanian money stock, and even though the trade gap is widening, it is continuing.

According to the monetarist theory, it was the favorable surplus on the current account (due to the lag between world inflation and that in Panama) that originally expanded (through a positive trade gap) the country's monetary supply.[13] This money supply, by increasing the domestic price level, should have caused (according to the monetarists) that money to flow out again. The country's development as a financial center has changed this mechanism. The trade gap has been growing rapidly, but that gap is now only a partial determinant of the availability of money in Panama; the private sector can now increase the money stock virtually at will through the banking system, and the demand for foreign funds for investment purposes bears no relation to the demand for funds to be held in Panama. The critical assumption in the monetarist assumption (the stable demand for money and its effect on the money supply) has been broken by the actions of the foreign banks.

From September 30, 1972, to September 30, 1973, bank credit to the external sector rose by 48 percent, even more rapidly than did internal credit, but less than the 62 percent increase between the end of 1971 and the end of 1972. Because total bank credit expanded at very similar rates in these two periods, by 1973 the system was giving preference to internal activities.

Thus conditions now exist in Panama in which an investment boom will be inflationary, not only because the boom increases the demand for local resources, but also and more importantly, because that boom will add to the stock of money in Panama. The continued increase in money will generate excess demand by putting pressure on prices of all domestic goods. This in turn will accelerate prices over the world rate of inflation. The extent of the inflation will depend on how long and at what level the commercial banks will extend credit to the domestic sector. Available evidence indicates that although most of the banks were originally set up in Panama to conduct foreign business, they have been quite willing to engage in domestic transactions.[*]

---

*As indicated by the number of branch banks in rural areas.

There are limits on the amount of credit that banks have extended to the domestic sector. Apparently, however, the limits have come from the amounts that Panamanians want to borrow rather than from the amount that banks are willing to extend internally.

Total bank deposits increased by 87 percent between the third quarter of 1972 and 1972, as against 67 percent between the end of 1971 and the end of 1972. This performance was due mainly to the 108 percent increase in deposits of foreign banks in Panama. Deposit liabilities went up much more rapidly than did bank credit, with the result that banking institutions increased their liquid assets—primarily in time deposits with foreign banks—by 112.8 percent in the first nine months of 1973. This indicated that in response to the extraordinary rise in total deposits, the demand for funds by internal borrowers has been insufficient to absorb all such deposits. For example, with respect to internal demand, the ratio of internal credit to the sum of local deposits and net external loans dropped from almost 100 percent at the end of 1971 to 77 percent at the end of 1972, and to 54 percent in the third quarter of 1973.

It seems evident that if there had been a greater internal demand for funds for investment in traditional sectors such as construction, funds could have been available to meet that demand.

CONCLUSIONS

From the preceding discussion it should be clear that most of the inflation that took place in Panama in the early 1970s is, as our tentative hypothesis indicated, best explained by the monetarist position that increases in money and credit were the chief cause of the country's rapid rise in prices. Government policies did not significantly increase inflation beyond the prediction of monetary theory. A number of structural factors were present, however, so that it is impossible at the present stage of our empirical knowledge to resolve the issues completely in favor of the monetarists; that is, we cannot say, for example, that 95 percent of the inflation could be accounted for by purely monetary factors. Our tentative conclusion derived from an examination of the inflationary mechanism in Panama is that despite the change in government priorities, with the increase in world inflation and the country's declining exports, little can be accomplished by changing the treaties with the United States, other than political satisfaction. The country's major economic problems are not caused by structural factors, the canal, or the treaties. The structuralist position does gove some insight into the problems facing the country. It seems, however, that further debate over

inflation will not advance the interests of the country; it will only
prolong the time until the government addresses itself directly to
defining and implementing a consistent set of policies toward the
goals it has set for the economy.

NOTES

1. Contraloria General Estadistica Panamena, Ingreso
Nacional, various issues.

2. The wholesale price index is used in this analysis because
it, in contrast to the consumer price index in Panama, is designed
in such a way as to facilitate identification of sources of inflation.
See Larry Sjaastad, "Prices and Wages in Panama," mimeographed
(Panama City: U.S. Agency for International Development, 1975)
pp. 1-3, for a critique on the limitations of price indexes in Panama.

3. Situacion y perspectivas del empleo en Panama, (Ginebra:
Oficina Internacional del Trabajo, 1974), part I, chapter B.

4. Ibid.

5. The word "trap" has a bad connotation. Some structuralists have used the idea of a trap for more advanced industrial
countries like Brazil to indicate a problem of income distribution
incapable of creating effective demand for the products produced in
industry. See N. Georgescu-Rogen, "Structural Inflation-Lock and
Balanced Growth," Economies et Societes 4, no. 3 (March 1970):
pp. 557-605. Because Panama is a relatively open country and does
not have a highly developed industrial structure, the situation discussed by Rogen is unlikely. Here, then, "trap" is used to indicate
simply a problem of short-run adjustment of supply and demand for
goods in general in the country.

6. For a detailed description of this index see Sjaastad,
"Prices and Wages in Panama," op. cit., pp. 5-9.

7. See Joseph Ramos, Labor and Development in Latin
America (New York: Columbia University Press, 1970) for an excel-
lent description of labor policies in other countries in Latin America.
For Mexico, a detailed description of the labor code and its evolution
over time is given in Roger D. Hansen, The Politics of Mexican
Development (Baltimore: Johns Hopkins Press, 1971).

8. Law no. 34, March 29, 1974, Article II.

9. Based on Sjaastad's analysis. See his "Prices and Wages
in Panama," op. cit., pp. 9-21.

10. For examples of these measurements, see Bela Balassa, The Structure of Protection in Developing Countries (Baltimore: Johns Hopkins Press, 1971). The example here should be considered in this light. It is simply an approximation of the likely changes that the law would bring about.

11. Quoted from Naomi Caiden and Aaron Wildavsky, Planning and Budgeting in Poor Countries (New York: John Wiley, 1974): 72-73.

12. Sjaastad, "Prices and Wages in Panama," op. cit., has a detailed description of the construction boom of the early 1970s. It might be noted that the decline in construction was one of the many factors bringing on the recession of 1974 and 1975 many private individuals over-expanded their building of luxury apartments during the early 1970s.

13. Ibid. This is Sjaastad's version of the monetarist mechanism, which the author also subscribes to.

10

MECHANISMS
IMPLICIT IN
PANAMANIAN GROWTH

The Panamanian economy experienced a remarkable evolution in the post-1955 period. Compared to most developing countries, Panama's rate of growth was exceptional, and in Latin America surpassed only by Mexico. The rate of inflation was low and steady. These are only two of the many economic accomplishments that have been referred to as "The Panamanian Miracle."

While the days of the so-called Panamanian miracle appear to be ending, it is possible that the country's current economic problems are only temporary. Beginning in 1971 the rate of growth began to decelerate, while the rate of inflation accelerated. The question now asked is whether this situation is just a temporary setback or a sign of things to come.

Previous chapters have given some indication of the mechanisms at work in the Panamanian economy. These insights are now used for four purposes: (1) to interpret the country's recent development performance; (2) to indicate in qualitative terms some of the requirements of accelerated growth; (3) to provide a framework for the discussion of the policy options available to the authorities, and the ability of these policies to enable the government to achieve its basic economic and social objectives; and (4) to serve as the basis of a quantitative (econometric) model (Appendix C) which will in turn be the basis for the forecasts of the economy (made in Chapter 11) during the next decade (1974-84).

ECONOMIC POLICY OBJECTIVES

It is possible that Panama's natural growth rate at present is 6 to 6.5 percent per year—well ahead of the country's 3 percent rate of population growth—and that given present conditions, this rate of income expansion may be expected to continue. But such a growth rate may not necessarily imply a sufficient rate of structural change to ensure that development—as a broader concept—will continue to take place at a pace and in a manner satisfactory to the authorities and the majority of the population.

As General Torrijos has stated,[1] the objectives of the government include eight major programs:

1. to strengthen national self-determination through the intensification of the utilization of the country's natural resources and its geographic position, including the Canal Zone;

2. to reach the national development and transformation at the lowest social cost;

3. to stimulate economic growth and maintain an adequate balance between production and national consumption;

4. to obtain social, economic, and political integration with an emphasis toward decentralization, economic as well as political;

5. to speed up economic progress and social betterment of the poorest groups in the urban and rural areas and increase their participation in the benefits of development.

6. to better substantially the incomes of the most marginal groups;

7. to reduce quickly the unemployment or underemployment in urban as well as rural areas;

8. to obtain the participation of the whole nation in the process of national development.

Whether Panama will be able to return to a path of high sustained growth, while at the same time fulfilling these eight basic guidelines, depends on: (1) an accurate identification by the authorities of the areas in which government policy will have to be taken; (2) how large a contribution can be expected from the major potential sources of growth (labor, capital, and production); and (3) what factors will govern and limit the rate of growth. Panama's future is surrounded by many political uncertainties, and any attempt to make a forecast of the economy over the next decade must be based on a number of assumptions that may in fact never come true. The ideal policy, as outlined below, must be comprehended as the best policy that the Panamanian government could possibly pursue under the given basic institutional setup and the known natural and human resources. It is natural to assume that a country with independence as the cornerstone of its revolution, and with neutralism and nonaligment as the basis of its foreign policy, will prefer to base its economic development mainly on its own resources and efforts.

Three development problems in Panama stand out in importance in determining the country's future development: (l) ascertaining to what extent the sources of growth are to be found in the steady accumulation of capital or in the progressive transformation of old ways into new; (2) increasing exports; and (3) limiting population growth so as to facilitate the adjustment of the country's income distribution to an equitable pattern.

THE GROWTH RATE

Several approaches to the analysis of the Panamanian economy are possible. From a methodological standpoint, they can be grouped under two main headings: neoclassical, and structuralist (or Keynesian). The neoclassical or supply (sources-of-growth) approach to the analysis of Panama's economic growth attempts to adapt concepts of functioning of an economy that were initially formulated for the study of mature industrial societies (such as the United States and Western Europe). The structuralist approach, on the other hand, attempts to identify the specific constraints on growth in each country under consideration—Panama is this case—that affect economic adjustments and the choice of development policy. As was noted in the discussion of the recent inflation in Panama, the structuralist approach tends to concentrate on explaining phenomena such as balance-of-payments disequilibrium, unemployment, and worsening income distribtuion on the basis of particular properties of demand and supply functions, and other specifications of economic behavior (an unresponsive agricultural sector, for example).

Panamanian Growth—A Neoclassical Explanation

In determining the limits to growth, using the neoclassical or sources of growth approach, a production function in which substitution between capital and labor is possible was selected. This type of production relationship allows the national output to be broken down into its separate components, that is, capital, labor, and a residual (or technical progress). This relationship between output and its components is given by:

$$Y = AK^a L^{(1-a)} \tag{10.1}$$

where K = capital stock, L = labor, Y = income, and A denotes factors other than capital and labor that contribute to income.

In order to gauge more precisely the prospects for future growth in Panama by using this approach, the highest average growth rate actually sustained for a prolonged period was taken as a first approximation for the country's growth possibilities. The period chosen for finding the country's growth limit in this way is somewhat arbitrary. It seems natural to select the 1960s, however, since this was a period of rather stable conditions. The revolution of 1968, although politically important, had few immediate consequences for economic development; the land reform after 1968 had an impact mainly on the distribution of wealth and income, and was more a social than an economic reform. There were no significant treaty changes during this period.

The sources-of-growth analysis requires information on the growth rate of net domestic product at factor cost (NDP), the growth rate of employment, the growth rate of the capital stock, and the relative shares of capital and labor in NDP. For the 1960s NDP grew at approximately 8 percent annually (in real terms). Data on the capital stock is not available for Panama. An estimate of the size of the country's capital stock can, however, be estimated indirectly through examination of the rate of return on investment.

In making an estimate of the capital stock, the following procedure was used: let b = the share of non-labor income in NDP, r = the net rate of return on capital, Y = NDP, and K = the value of the stock of capital. It follows that:

$$b = rK/Y \tag{10.2}$$

Given estimates of b, r, and Y, we can solve for K, the value of the capital stock for each year. Accordingly, the capital stock was estimated by assuming to net (of depreciation) rates of return on net investment, that is, 15 and 20 percent. These values are plausible in the light of the experience of other countries and independent studies on investment in Panama.

The shares of labor and nonlabor earnings in NDP (60 and 40 percent, respectively) were derived as follows. The Contraloria General de la Republica, Direccion de Estadistica y Censo gives a breakdown of GDP at factor cost into (a) compensation of employees, (b) income from property, and (c) income from farms, professions, and self-employed workers. In the computations category (c) was divided between labor and property incomes by using two assumptions: (1) the share of family workers and self-employed workers are assumed to be equal to property incomes, and that of employees to labor income, and (2) that the imputed wage of family workers and self-employed workers was the same as the average wage earnings of employees. With these assumptions the average wage bill was multiplied by the ratio of family and self-employed workers to employees to obtain the wage component of income from farms, professions, and self-employed workers. The property income component was obtained as a residual (Table 10.1).

The sources-of-growth analysis indicates that the residual contribution to growth, or the growth of total productivity, appears to have been responsible for 17-26 percent of the observed 8 percent annual increase of the NDP. This analysis makes no allowance for significant price and wage increases however. Adjustment for such changes would reduce the importance of the growth of total productivity. For example, during this period the wages of many Panamanian workers in the Canal Zone were brought up to the U.S. minimum wage scale. This accounted for approximately 0.7 percent of the 8 percent rate of annual growth. In addition, education and migration during the 1960s accounted for approximately 1.5 percent of the 8 percent rate of growth.

In short, it is possible to explain a very large share of Panama's observed growth, with only 1.2 percentage points out of 8.0 being accounted for by factors we did not directly quantify.[2] This value for the residual elements in growth can be interpreted as increases in productivity and efficiency. The conclusions derived from this analysis are that Panama's growth of the 1960s was at an exceedingly high rate, and that it was largely a result of increases in investment and employment.

With respect to the increase in wages and salaries of workers in the Canal Zone, it is highly unlikely that the 1970s will witness an increase as dramatic as that of the 1960s when Canal Zone wages were brought up to the standard dictated by the U.S. minimum wage legislation. This illustrates the importance of the arrangements concerning canal revenues that will be reached by a new agreement

TABLE 10.1

Growth Rate of Net Domestic Product (NDP)
at Factor Cost and Sources of Growth, 1960-1970

	Net Rate of Return on Capital = 15 percent	Net Rate of Return on Capital = 20 percent
Annual exponential growth rate of NDP	8.00	8.00
Labor		
Annual exponential growth rate	4.35	4.35
Contribution to NDP growth rate (row 2 x 0.6)	2.61	2.61
Relative contribution to NDP growth rate (row 3 + row 1)	32.6	32.6
Capital		
Annual exponential growth rate	8.33	10.00
Contribution to NDP growth rate (row 5 x 0.4)	3.33	4.00
Relative contribution to NDP growth rate (row 6 + row 1)	41.6	50.0
Residual		
Contribution to NDP growth rate (row 1 - row 3 - row 6)	2.06	1.39
Relative contribution to NDP growth rate (row 8 + row 1)	25.8	17.4

Source: Computed by author.

between the governments of Panama and the United States. These terms must be more favorable for Panama than those currently prevailing in order to sustain the country's growth. If they are significantly above the current $2 million annual payment, this will tend to offset or even outweigh the reduction in the contribution of Canal Zone wage increases to Panama's rate of economic growth.[3]

The sources-of-growth analysis, while helpful in gaining insights into the country's past growth, is not very helpful in determining the level of economic expansion likely to take place during the next decade. Sources-of-growth analysis is primarily related to the country's possibility of increasing employment, improving the quality of labor, expanding the stock of real capital, and employing better and more suitable techniques and technologies. Almost by definition, Panama cannot grow faster than its physical capacity permits. But it certainly may grow more slowly, depending partly on its ability to take advantage of its physical potential and partly on its ability to finance growth expenditures in such areas as real investment, education, and health. It is not easy to determine the upper limit of the country's growth rate, and perhaps, strictly speaking, no rigid upper limit can be identified. Yet it is obvious that for meaningful projections, such a limit would have to be estimated. (See Appendix D for an illustration of the problems involved in making these estimates for the agricultural sector in Panama.)

Another major defect in attempting to make a forecast using the supply or sources-of-growth approach is that these models, by themselves, are not sufficient to identify the policies required to solve the problem of imbalance in the economy, particularly that caused by high population growth. Also no causal mechanisms are assumed in the models—we know how much investment took place, its distribution between the private and government sectors, and what its contribution to growth was; but we do not know why it took place. The supply model is incapable of furnishing any insight into this very relevant question, and the types of policy needed to make investment change as the authorities feel necessary.

Also, the supply models assume implicitly that there is complete convertibility between domestic and foreign resources. As shown in Chapter 3, this might be the case for Panama, although no definitive answer can be given. There is reason to believe that owing to the numerous structural problems referred to in previous chapters, foreign and domestic resources in Panama are not completely convertible. In that country there is a serious constraint on growth operating independently from domestic constraints, namely the trade gap. Under a foreign trade constraint, it is not possible for the economy fully to convert a domestic surplus into domestic fixed-capital formation, since growth is limited by a lack of imports of capital machinery. A foreign exchange (or import) constraint could take place even though there was scope for mobilizing larger domestic resources for investment. Unless substantial increases in the domestic capacity to produce capital goods and industrial materials occur, Panama, so as to sustain growth in GDP and investments, will have to increase its exports in order to import the capital goods and raw materials needed for development.

To summarize, the success of the Panamanian economy in accelerating its rate of growth without inflation in the 1960s cast some doubt on the significance and extent of the structural problems that had been identified in the analysis of inflation. However, in the past few years, the importance of structural rigidities has been reemphasized by several new phenomena: the limited ability of the economy to absorb the growing labor force, the apparent worsening of the income distribution, and—most recently—the disruption of world trade caused by increased oil and food prices, which will require a substantial adjustment in the country's productive structure. In short, development policy in Panama in the early 1970s seems to be constrained by a number of structural factors. These structural elements require a more explicit analysis of the possibilities for short-term adjustment, and for longer-term adjustment and for longer-term changes in the economic structure itself, than can be provided by the neoclassical or sources-of-growth analysis.

Panamanian Growth—A Structural Explanation

The methodology used below in making a structural analysis of the Panamanian economy is based on a set of rather intuitive hypotheses. The approach can be summarized as consisting of three stages: formulation of hypotheses, empirical testing, and the elaboration of more complete models. For Panama this sequence can be illustrated for two of the basic elements stressed in structuralist systems: the importance of exports in determining the overall rate of growth, and the concept of a dual economy.

Exports in Panamanian Growth

It is clear that the high rates of growth of the export sector have provided a strong stimulus to the economy. However, the precise nature and magnitude of that stimulus is not easy to quantify, since a number of other factors contributing to growth were simultaneously at work. To obtain a more complete explanation of the forces determining Panama's growth, the relationship between exports and investment must also be examined. Between 1950 and 1973 the growth rate of exports (in constant 1960 prices) was 5.2 percent compared with GNP growth of 6.5 percent a year. In current prices the rates were 7.8 and 12.7 percent, respectively. The growth of the second demand element, gross investment (public and private, and change in stocks), was 9.4 and was greater than that of exports in 15 of the 23 years. Investment, however, remained a smaller proportion of the GNP throughout the period. Government consumption increased (in constant prices) at a lower rate than did GNP, and thus can be ruled out as a prime stimulus. Imports grew at a fairly rapid rate (6.7 percent a year), so that import replacement does not seem to have been a major factor in income growth.

The best way to determine the importance of demand elements such as exports and investment in Panamanian growth, and at the same time to decide if exports did act as an independent force, is to identify, in an econometric model, the essential features of the Panamanian economy. The model can then be used to simulate the past performance of the economy, and the contribution of each source of demand (exports, investment, and consumption) can be identified. Ideally the model includes the following sets of equations:

(1) a production function and a factor supply schedule that determine output capacity, in addition to capital and skilled labor. Essential imports would be considered a productive factor;

(2) aggregate demand equations that give the level of consumption, public and private investment, government expenditure, exports, and imports;

(3) equations for monetary demand and supply and the determination of money wages, which yield the price level.*

If the Panamanian economy were perfectly competitive (with flexible wages and prices) and if the country's demand for investment or for its exports were very responsive with respect to interest rates or prices, national income would be determined by the first set of equations, that is, by the supply model role that exports could play in Panamanian growth under such a system would be to stimulate or allow increases in factor supplies. For example, a rapid growth of exports might encourage investment if foreign investors were particularly sensitive to developments in the export sector in making their investment decisions; or exports might increase the country's savings if they raised the income of groups

---

*Monetary equations were not used because of the difficulties involved in measuring the money supply.

that save a higher portion of their additional income. Finally, exports in Panama could, under these assumptions, play an important role by increasing the country's capacity to import essential, noncompeting items, in which case the sector would have a major role in contributing to full employment output. If, however, as is assumed in the structural model developed here, the Panamanian economy were characterized by rigidities, that is, inflexible wages or prices (particularly downward), then the sources-of-growth or factor-supply equations could not determine the country's equilibrium level of national income. National income, and hence the degree of capacity utilization, would in that situation depend on the aggregate demand and monetary equations. In the case where rigidities exist in the economy, exports, in addition to their function as a major determinant of the country's factor supplies (that is, investment), would also determine the level of aggregate demand and thus national income.

From the analysis in previous chapters it is clear that a number of rigidities do exist in the Panamanian economy. The supply model therefore must be rejected as a tool for projecting the economy, or giving an accurate explanation of the historically observed rate of growth in Panama.[*] By their nature, supply models assume perfect competition in the economy—a rather unrealistic assumption in the light of the fact that the post-1968 government has played a large role in setting wages, in the high levels of unemployment, and in the protection given to industry.

A structural or Keynesian aggregate-demand model emphasizing the second set of equations for historical analysis and projection purposes[†] above was therefore developed (see Appendix C). To determine if Panama has been characterized by export-led growth, simulations using this model and actual exports were carried out for the period 1950-73 (Tables 10.2 and 10.3). These simulations yielded growth rates close to those actually observed for GNP (10.0 versus 10.2), consumption (7.8 versus 8.8) and imports (10.0 versus 11.2), but were high in duplicating the rates for investment (19.0 versus 15.4). Thus, if the export-investment causality is accepted,

---

[*]This is probably too strong a statement. The author feels, however, that the model is simply not amenable to the types of policy recommendations he wishes to make.

[†]Supply factors are introduced later through the production function—the capital output ratio.

TABLE 10.2

Contribution of Keynesian Demand Sources to Panamanian Growth, 1951-62
(in millions of 1960 balboas)

	1951	1952	1953	1954	1955	1956	1957	1958	1959	1960	1961	1962
Total consumption	1.5	11.5	-3.2	10.4	3.7	4.5	13.2	0.2	2.1	8.1	6.7	5.5
Private consumption	(0.2)	(7.8)	(-0.7)	(9.8)	(5.0)	(3.9)	(14.0)	(-0.5)	(1.9)	(6.2)	(5.9)	(3.9)
Public consumption	(1.3)	(3.7)	(-2.5)	(0.6)	(-1.3)	(0.6)	(-0.8)	(0.7)	(0.2)	(1.9)	(0.8)	(1.6)
Total investment	-3.5	0.5	6.0	-3.2	1.9	3.3	0.1	2.2	2.7	-1.7	4.6	2.7
Private investment	(-1.6)	(-0.5)	(2.3)	(0.9)	(0.8)	(1.7)	(2.1)	(0.4)	(1.8)	(-0.7)	(1.9)	(0.6)
Public investment	(-0.8)	(0.9)	(-0.7)	(-0.5)	(1.0)	(1.6)	(-2.6)	(0.5)	(2.2)	(-0.9)	(2.2)	(0.7)
Change in stocks	(-1.1)	(0.1)	(4.4)	(-3.6)	(0.1)	(—)	(0.6)	(1.3)	(-1.3)	(-0.1)	(0.5)	(1.4)
Exports	-2.8	(—)	2.5	-1.5	3.0	-0.1	0.8	-1.7	1.7	3.0	4.8	6.5
Imports	3.8	-6.4	1.0	-2.0	-2.9	-2.3	-3.3	0.3	0.4	-3.0	-4.6	-6.0
Net factor payments	-0.4	0.3	-0.2	-1.9	-0.2	—	-0.4	1.9	-0.2	—	0.5	0.3
GNP	-1.3	5.9	6.2	1.8	5.9	5.5	10.7	2.8	6.4	6.2	11.7	8.7

Note: Figures in parentheses indicate sub-components of the above figure.
Source: Compiled by author.

174

TABLE 10.3

Contribution of Keynesian Demand Sources to Panamanian Growth, 1963–73

(in millions of 1960 balboas)

	1963	1964	1965	1966	1967	1968	1969	1970	1971	1972	1973
Total consumption	9.2	5.6	7.4	2.1	7.2	2.7	9.1	5.1	7.9	2.2	7.8
Private consumption	(8.3)	(5.1)	(6.8)	(0.9)	(5.9)	(1.8)	(9.2)	(3.3)	(6.6)	(1.0)	(7.7)
Public consumption	(0.9)	(0.5)	(0.6)	(1.2)	(1.3)	(0.9)	(-0.1)	(1.8)	(1.3)	(1.2)	(0.1)
Total investment	2.5	-1.9	2.6	6.5	1.3	3.0	3.4	4.6	3.9	5.9	-0.8
Private investment	(1.8)	(-1.6)	(2.7)	(7.0)	(0.1)	(2.1)	(1.8)	(2.4)	(4.0)	(-1.2)	(3.5)
Public investment	(0.7)	(-0.5)	(-0.4)	(-0.4)	(1.1)	(0.6)	(1.2)	(2.4)	(-0.2)	(6.8)	(-4.1)
—Change in stocks	(—)	(0.2)	(0.3)	(-0.1)	(0.1)	(0.3)	(0.4)	(-0.2)	(0.1)	(0.3)	(-0.2)
Exports	4.0	0.1	4.9	3.6	3.8	2.9	2.7	1.8	1.8	—	1.1
Imports	-7.0	0.6	-5.4	-4.3	-3.4	-1.4	-6.4	-4.4	-4.6	-1.8	-1.2
Net factor payments	0.1	0.8	-1.9	-0.1	-1.2	-0.3	—	-0.1	-0.5	-0.1	-0.8
GNP	8.8	5.1	7.4	7.7	7.8	6.8	8.7	7.0	8.4	6.5	5.9

Note: Figures in parentheses indicate sub-components of the above figure.
Source: Compiled by author.

exports can be said to explain most of Panamanian growth during
the last decade.

Still, within the structural or Keynesian framework one can
get a clear picture of the respective influences of exports and investment by looking at the growth rates of the country's national income
aggregates for short periods. From 1950 to 1955 exports measured
in balboas at current prices grew at the rate of 2.9 percent, with
investment at 9.4 percent, and GNP at 4.2 percent. During this
period, export growth was attributable almost entirely to goods and
not to services to the Canal Zone. In 1956 and 1958 there were marked drops in export growth so that the 1954-59 rates were 2.4 percent
for exports, 6.1 percent for GNP, and 14.7 percent for gross investment. Thus, up to 1959 it would appear that exports, investments,
and income, while varying in rates of growth, tended to expand together. However, in 1959 the export boom began and was sustained,
with the exception of a slight drop in its rate of growth in 1964.
During this five-year period (1959-64) exports increased at a rate of
13.4 percent a year, due largely to the jump in service exports in
1960 and the explosive growth in banana exports. During the same
period, investment grew at a lower rate of 8.6 percent a year, leading to the conclusion that exports were largely responsible for the
GNP growth of 8.1 percent for this period. Increased exports alone
accounted for over 43 percent of increased GNP, while investment
accounted for slightly under 20 percent. However, from 1966-73
public and private investment became the most important stimulant,
growing at 17.5 percent a year. Exports grew by only 8.9 percent a
year. The contributions to growth of investment and exports during
this period were 40.0 and 31.8, respectively.

A structural model, therefore, gives a somewhat different
picture of the Panamanian growth experience than that presented by
the neoclassical or supply model (sources-of-growth approach).
We have already noted in Chapter 2 that the country was able to survive a period of declining exports (a major source of demand) because the other major sources of aggregate demand, consumption
and investment, did not decline significantly—a common pattern in
Panama. The statistical estimates of the basic determinants of
aggregate demand in Panama show this basic stability (Appendix C).

Exports and Dualism in Panama

Having established that export growth was at the least a very
important stimulus to Panamanian growth over the years from 1950
to 1973, if not the only one, the next step is to ask how this growth

has affected the dualism (the coexistence of modern and backward sectors of the economy) that prevades the economy. In a country with the limited resources of Panama, growth may not be enough. Greater equalization of income and the integration of the national economy to reduce regional disparities of income have become important goals. Hence, the quality of development is now seen by the government to be as important as its rate. The export sector in Panama could contribute to the alleviation of dualism in the following ways: (1) by creating jobs, both directly through its own growth and indirectly through its stimulation of other industries, which have the capability of absorbing agricultural labor; (2) as a consequence of (1) by reducing the number of workers per acre in agricultural areas and thus increasing the output and incomes per worker in agriculture; (3) by offering higher incomes than were paid in the sectors from which labor was drawn, thus contributing to a more equal distribution of income; and (4) by opening up productive opportunities in lower income regions, thus helping to diffuse economic activity throughout the country.

The first means of alleviating the dualism in Panama is obvious enough and can be expected to operate with any new or expanding industry, but it may not operate to a significant degree. The combination of items (2) and (3) implies the necessary condition that the expanding sector be one of higher marginal productivity of labor than the one losing labor. The fourth expresses the hope that, in the case of natural-resource-based industries, the development of additional export activities does not lead to an intensification of whatever geographical concentration already exists.

There is little evidence that in the development of the Panamanian economy the export sector has contributed very much to the improvement in the country's pattern of income distribution. The two most dynamic export activities—services to the Canal Zone and the export of bananas—are carried out in enclaves, which intensifies the existing geographic dualism.

The only possible contribution of the export industry to an equalization of income, therefore, would be through their providing enough jobs at sufficiently high salaries to absorb surplus labor from rural areas in the metropolitan area. This would raise a substantial group of workers from subsistence to a middle-income category on the income scale, thus improving the income distribution.

One piece of evidence of the effectiveness of the export sector in accomplishing this goal is the change in the country's distribution of national income (presented in Table 10.4). While wages and salaries and professional earnings in total income fell markedly during the 1950s and 1960s as a fraction of national income, other family and noncorporate income remained about constant. The largest movement was in corporate savings which increased its share of national income from 3.9 percent in 1950 to 14.4 percent in 1972, since industrial protection from foreign competion was accelerating during this period and employment in the Canal Zone was constant. These data indicate that exports did not contribute to the equalization of income but that the foreign sector as a whole probably caused a marked deterioration in the income of lower-income groups relative to that of higher-income groups.

It would appear then that exports contributed very significantly to the growth of Panama, but not in alleviating the country's dualism. The export-led growth in Panama has been growth of only part of an economy, but it is still a significant phenomenon, because the country's growth from 1955 to 1971 was very rapid and sustained, and left the country with considerably more resources at its disposal than lower rates of growth would have provided. But the examination of the Canal Zone's contribution to the country's growth should be viewed against this background: its contribution to the urbanized economy may have been great but its effects on the mass of rural society have been marginal.

CONCLUSIONS

The conflict between the neoclassical and structural approaches to the identification of the mechanisms in Panama's growth is perhaps most acute in the area of external policy. The neoclassical approach tends to exaggerate the benefits of trade to the Panamanian economy, since it does not explicitly consider the effects of uncertain export prices and the difficulties of shifting resources to meet changing market conditions, or export's adverse impact on income distribution.

The structuralist concept of development developed above (as characterized by rigidities that limit economic adjustments) requires an analytical framework, in which external policy is more closely linked to domestic resource allocation, than does the neoclassical view which minimizes these restrictions. An attempt to formulate and quantify these relationships was started in Chapters 2 and 3, and Appendix A. Appendix C continues this line of thought with the empirical estimation of the basic macroeconomic relationships in the economy. On the basis of this work the following

TABLE 10.4

Distribution of National Income, 1950–72
(in millions of balboas)

	1950	1955	1960	1965	1970	1972
Net national income	210.2	266.4	336.5	539.1	840.8	1,034.9
Wages, salaries, and professional earnings	178.5 (85.0)	226.5 (85.0)	266.5 (79.2)	428.4 (79.5)	677.4 (80.6)	799.3 (77.2)
Other family and noncorporate income	14.5 (6.9)	18.4 (6.9)	23.1 (6.9)	26.4 (5.0)	36.4 (4.3)	62.0 (6.0)
Corporate savings	8.3 (3.9)	10.0 (3.8)	30.4 (9.0)	56.9 (10.6)	73.2 (8.7)	115.0 (11.1)
Direct taxes on private corporations	2.0 (1.0)	6.5 (2.4)	7.7 (2.3)	14.6 (2.7)	36.4 (4.3)	39.4 (3.8)
General government income	7.5 (3.6)	6.0 (2.3)	10.0 (3.0)	17.0 (3.2)	25.0 (3.0)	37.7 (3.6)
Interest on public debt	0.6 (0.3)	1.0 (0.4)	1.5 (0.5)	4.2 (0.8)	7.6 (0.9)	18.5 (1.8)

Note: Figures in parentheses indicate percentage of national income.
Source: Controller General.

179

conclusions concerning the mechanisms involved in the Panamanian economy can be drawn:

(1) There is general compatibility among all the economic policy measures in the sense that the available policy instruments appear capable of eliminating any potential contradictions between different objectives. Furthermore, Panamanian economic policy under the current government is potentially consistent in the sense that the policy tools, if used correctly, will exert a favorable impact on the government's goals in the direction desired.

(2) A high rate of economic growth has resulted from heavier investment by the federal government, reorientation of productive resources toward more profitable sectors, and promotion of exports.

(3) There will be an increase in employment over and above past trends, if the economy expands rapidly, and if growth is re-oriented toward those activities that are most strongly labor inten-sive, such as agriculture and tourism services.

(4) Income distribution will be more equitable if federal spending continues to concentrate on the lowest-income groups and if this expenditure is financed to a greater extent by taxes from the highest-income groups. On the other hand, reorientation of the economy toward the agricultural sector, by generating more jobs for the poorest groups (unemployed and underemployed) will directly benefit the lower-income segments of the population. These two endeavors represent definite changes under the new Panamanian economic policy.

(5) The balance-of-payments current account and the ser-vice rate on external debt should improve, even if the economy ex-pands as fast as in the past, since imports will be down (because of the change in demand profile caused by the redistribution of income). The main balance-of-payments problem in Panama, in any case, has not resulted from a rapid increase in imports due to accelerated growth, but from the decline recorded in the ratio between exports and GDP. Export promotion measures, as well as the heavier federal investment in agriculture and reorientation of the private sector toward this area, can be expected to produce a more rapid growth of Panamanian exports than in the recent past. However, the government should take steps to increase domestic savings and thereby reduce the external savings required to date to finance total investment levels.

The probable qualitative impact of the various policy in-struments on the country's main goals is illustrated in Table 10.5.

TABLE 10.5

Qualitative Impact of Economic Policy Instruments on Goals

Instruments	Goals					
	Increase in Growth Rate	Reduction in Balance-of-Payments Deficit on Current Account	Improved Income Distribution	Expanded Employment	Reduction in Rate of Service of External Debt	Reduction of Inflation
Export promotion	+	+	?	+	+	+
Increase in federal government investment outlays	+	?ᵃ	+	+	?ᵃ	-
Increase in direct personal taxes	-	+	+	-	+	+
Increase in taxes on public enterprises	-	+	?	-	+	+
Reorientation of productive resources	+	+	+	+	+	+
Improved administration of the public debt	0	+	0	0	+	+
General impact of instruments on goals	+	+	?ᵇ	+	+	+

ᵃCould favorably affect the balance of payments of public services, such as tourism and the farm sector.
ᵇDoubtful, although more favorable than if the instruments were not used.
+ indicates favorable impact.   ? indicates doubtful impact.
- indicates unfavorable impact.   0 indicates slight impact, if any.
Source: Compiled by author.

181

        While the direction of the government's policies is fairly
clear, additional quantification of their impact on the government's
expressed goals will be needed for their successful implementation.
Such quantitative estimate of the major forces at work in the Panamanian economy will also permit an identification of the influences
that the Canal Zone and associated treaties have on the economy—
information necessary before productive negotiations on a new treaty
can proceed further.

                                NOTES

        1. Taken from various speeches. See, however, Lineamie-
ntos del Plan Nacional de Desarrollo, 1974-1978(Panama City:
Direccion de Planificacion Economica y Social, 1973) for a statement
of the country's major objectives. An excellent summary is given
in Nicolas A. Barletta, Memoria Que Presenta a la Asamblea
Nacional de Representantes de Corregimientos (Panama City: Ministerio de Planificacion y Politica Economica, 1973)
        2. See Larry Sjaastad, "Prospects for Economic Growth in the
1970s: Panama," mimeographed (Panama City: United States Agency for
International Development, 1972), and Arnold C. Harberger The Past
Growth and Future Prospects of the Panamanian Economy (Panama
City: Direccion General de Planificacion y Administration, 1972) for
similar results.
        3. Ibid.

11

There is no law of development guaranteeing that once a satisfactory rate of economic growth is achieved it will continue indefinitely, but past progress is probably the best available guide to the future. Thus the high and sustained rate of economic growth attained in the 1955-71 period leads to the presumption that such a rate is repeatable in the future for Panama. The analysis contained in previous chapters thus warrants the presumption that Panama will be able to survive the current slump and regain the momentum built up during the 1960s, and that growth in the 1970s and 1980s, while perhaps not as high as in the 1960s, is not an impossible target. Perhaps the most important lesson in the previous chapters is that economic development in Panama is feasible and is unlikely to be constrained by the canal treaties per se, given sound policies and a stable environment. The government's goals can probably be achieved without heroic sacrifice, unparalleled wisdom, or un-foreseeable good fortune.

Past growth implies that substantial development efforts are needed in Panama, and that such efforts are likely to be reward-ed. Effort alone is not enough, however. What is required is en-lightened effort. Heroic sacrifices can be misdirected.

In the forecasts below an attempt is made to estimate the feasible growth of GNP in real terms and the trade-gap projections for Panama for the period 1974-84 using econometric techniques coupled with a pragmatic approach, on the basis of the study of the economy in earlier chapters. Both approaches depend on the struc-tural characteristics of the economy observed in the past and on judgment and common sense as to future development and policies, and thus should not be taken in isolation from each other. In fact, econometric techniques help to avoid inconsistencies in economic policies and policy objectives and indicate where these policies can be most effective.

DESCRIPTION OF THE MACROECONOMIC MODEL OF PANAMA

The two-gap approach adopted in this study involves, generally speaking, the estimation for an assumed rate of growth of (1) the difference between investment requirements and potential savings (the savings gap), and of (2) the difference between import requirements and potential exports of goods and services (the trade gap). This approach involves estimating the minimum level of domestic savings and investment as well as the minimum level of imports required to achieve a given rate of growth of GNP. Once the postulated relationship between domestic resources, import requirements, and the growth rate of GNP is quantified, the magnitude of the gap associated with various assumed growth rates is determined and appropriate methods for bridging the gap are studied in order to enable the assumed growth rates of GNP to be achieved.

In examining the savings-investment gap, the focus is on the resource requirements for growth, with no differentiation being made between domestic and foreign resources. These are treated as though they are perfectly interchangeable. This assumption implies that there is no obstacle to increasing fixed capital formation if the required (for the assumed rate of growth) domestic savings are mobilized. The trade gap, on the other hand, assumes that domestic output is not freely substitutable for imports—which is, as earlier chapters have indicated, the case in Panama. The trade gap approach recognizes that Panama is not self-sufficient in either capital goods or raw materials, and thus recognizes that imports of necessities not produced at home play a crucial role and represent a constraint on the growth of GDP. In other words, where the country faces difficulties in exports or capital inflow, the efforts to increase domestic savings (such as increases in domestic tax) may not suffice to ensure the expansion of investment required to achieve a certain growth rate of output because the required imports cannot be acquired from abroad.

Ex post, the two gaps must be equal; ex ante, however, they may not be identical. The larger of the two gaps is the dominant one

and thus the binding constraint on growth. Obviously, the discrepancy
between the two estimates results from the neglect of variable adjustors and can thus help in identifying the type of adjustors required.
If the trade gap is dominant, the adjustors are export promotion,
import replacement, increased consumption, lower growth rates of
GNP, or a combination of them. If the savings gap is dominant, the
adjustors are increased domestic savings, reduced investments or
increased imports.

Assumptions Used in the Model

The projections below entail a large number of assumptions.
The approach in this respect has incorporated the following
characteristics:

(1) As far as possible a number of assumptions have been
used that are close to those of the macro-unit of the Ministerio De
Planificacion y Politica Economica, which have been in their longer-
range forecasts. *

(2) In general, optimistic assumptions have been made with
regard to the future. This affects not only implicit assumptions
about such factors as a new canal treaty, but quantitative elements
such as net foreign capital inflows.

(3) Although there are indications that the Panamanian
economy may be going through a turning point, and behavioral relationships are shifting in a way that may make growth increasingly
difficult, optimistic assumptions have been made that the past behavior patterns will hold for the future.

Given these assumptions the model is designed to examine
the feasibility of the economy actually achieving the main objectives
of the post-1968 government:† (1) the highest rate of growth permitted by existing resources and the pressing immediate needs of
the population; (2) the safeguarding of relative price stability within

---

*The author wishes to thank William Byerts of the University
of Chicago for providing some preliminary forecasts of the major
macro elements in the economy to be used by the ministry.

†Ideally one would wish to use a linear programming approach to identify the constraints on Panamanian growth. The absence of a reliable input-output table for the country makes this
approach impossible.

the limits set by the country's institutional constraints and price
movements abroad; and (3) the maintenance of a reasonably small
deficit in the balance of payments.

Results of the Macro Model

To see a number of different aspects of the economy, the
model is formulated under different assumptions as to the rate of
growth of exports—2, 4, 6, and 8 percent annually. Rates of growth
of GNP of 4, 6, and 8 percent are projected together with the rate
of growth of exports, and two gaps[1] are determined for each combination of exports and income growth (Table 11.1). The level of
total investment is not determined by the summation of the behavioral
relations (equations in Appendix C), but instead is assumed to be a
function of the rate of growth itself (equation 2, Appendix C).*
The macro model (Table 11.1 shows that for an 8 percent
growth of GNP the trade gap at the different rates of export growth
is usually larger than the savings gap. This larger trade gap points
out a problem of insufficient domestic demand to attract foreign
financing of the trade deficit. In other economies (with a central
bank) the monetary authorities, by expanding the money supply, could
generate sufficient domestic demand. Of course, additional foreign
exchange would have to be found to fill the trade gap.
In Panama, however, the closing of the trade gap must lie
in the discovery by the banking community of a sufficient number of
domestic investment projects so as to be economically viable at the
borrowing rates currently prevailing in the international capital
markets.
If the commercial banks find these projects, and are in turn
not constrained by government controls from extending credit to these
areas, they will divert some of their funds from foreign branches to
Panama. In the process they will finance the required level of

---

*For each rate of GNP growth—8, 6, and 4 percent annual-
ly—exports were projected at 8, 6, 4 and 2 percent annually. Due
to space limitations, only the 8 percent GNP growth simulations are
presented. The other simulations are available from the author upon request. In general these simulations give results similar to
those corresponding to those in Table 11.1.

TABLE 11.1

Domestic and External Gaps, 1974-84, Macro Model III
(in millions of 1960 balboas)

	1974	1975	1976	1977	1978	1979	1980	1981	1982	1983	1984
Variation I (8 percent increase in exports)											
GNP	1045.1	1128.7	1219.0	1316.5	1421.9	1535.6	1658.5	1791.2	1934.5	2089.2	2256.4
Total investment	222.2	240.0	259.2	280.0	302.4	326.5	352.7	380.9	411.4	444.3	479.8
Savings (ex-ante)	212.0	229.8	249.0	269.7	292.1	316.2	342.3	370.5	400.9	433.8	469.3
Savings (ex-post)	201.3	217.2	235.0	254.6	276.4	300.2	326.3	354.7	385.5	418.9	455.3
Savings (ex-ante) - Total investment	-10.2	-10.2	-10.2	-10.3	-10.3	-10.3	-10.4	-10.4	-10.5	-10.5	-10.5
Savings (ex-post) - Total investment	-20.9	-22.8	-24.2	-25.4	-26.0	-26.3	-26.4	-26.2	-25.6	-25.4	-24.5
Exports	362.6	391.6	422.9	456.7	493.3	532.7	575.3	621.4	671.1	724.8	782.7
Imports	241.9	362.9	392.5	424.5	459.0	496.4	536.7	580.1	627.2	677.9	732.7
Net factor payments	32.4	35.0	37.8	40.8	44.1	47.6	51.4	55.8	60.0	64.8	69.9
Exports - Imports	88.3	-6.3	-7.9	-8.6	-9.6	-11.7	-12.8	-14.2	-16.1	-17.9	-19.9
Variation II (6 percent increase in exports)											
Savings (ex-post)	201.4	217.2	235.1	254.8	276.4	300.1	326.4	354.6	385.5	419.1	455.3
Savings (ex-post) - Total investment	-20.8	-22.8	-24.1	-25.2	-26.0	-26.4	-26.3	-26.3	-25.9	-25.2	-24.5
Exports - Imports	81.5	-20.7	-31.0	-41.5	-53.7	-68.2	-83.3	-100.5	-120.1	-141.5	-165.3
Variation III (4 percent increase in exports)											
Savings (ex-post)	201.3	217.1	235.0	261.7	276.5	300.2	326.4	354.7	385.5	419.0	455.3
Savings (ex-post) - Total investment	-20.9	-22.9	-24.2	-18.3	-25.9	-26.3	-26.3	-26.2	-25.9	-25.3	-24.5
Exports - Imports	74.8	-35.8	-54.2	-73.6	-95.6	-120.8	-147.5	-177.4	-219.8	-256.6	-297.1
Variation IV (2 percent increase in exports)											
Savings (ex-post)	201.3	217.2	235.0	254.6	276.5	300.1	326.3	354.6	385.5	419.0	455.0
Savings (ex-post) - Total investment	-20.9	-22.8	-24.2	-25.4	-25.9	-26.4	-26.4	-26.3	-25.9	-25.3	-24.8
Exports - Imports	68.1	-48.6	-74.6	-101.9	-132.2	-166.3	-202.5	-242.3	-286.0	-333.5	-376.9

Note: An 8 percent growth rate of GNP is assumed.
Source: Compiled by author.

domestic credit expansion and the trade deficit simultaneously.
Whether the two gaps are brought into equality depends therefore on
the likelihood of such an increase in domestic aggregate demand.

On a macroeconomic level there are five ways in which this
increasing demand could conceivably be effected:

(1) Government expenditure, especially on investment projects, might increase.

(2) The private sector might finance more expensive current
consumption by running down their savings, especially their real
money balances (particularly if consumer prices rise faster than
the overall price level).

(3) The economy's rate of growth in constant prices could
fall.

(4) Increases in expenditure on certain imports such as
petroleum products could produce a substitution effect away from
other imports, and a reduction in expenditures on imports complementary to (in this case) petroleum products, such as cars, tires,
and others.

(5) Since changes in inventories are considered part of investment, the economy, in the short run, could experience a change
in inventory levels held by private retailers and wholesalers.

The short-run adjustments and options open to the country
are rather limited. Given the government's fiscal problems, the
balancing of the gaps will probably not be arrived at by (1), and only
a small amount of leeway is possible in (4) and (5). A fall in growth
below 6 percent might not be politically feasible nor desirable from
the point of view of employment creation and income distribution.
This eliminates (3) as a practical solution. This leaves only (2),
that is, the erosion of constant nominal money balances by a strong
inflation not fully anticipated or perceived by the private sector. In
the short run this would place the economy in danger of a liquidity
squeeze if banks run afoul of shifting expectations and confidence.
Fortunately, Panama's banking system has enough contingency credit
to fall back upon.

In Panama, all banks participating in the domestic banking
system must comply with the contingency credit portion of the banking laws. These regulations require banks to keep available sufficient emergency financing abroad. Those funds in turn may be
utilized at the discretion of the banking commission to lend to any
member of the system that experiences a 10 percent drop in its
liabilities over any six-month period.

Since (2) and (5) above are means available for only short periods of time, most of the responsibility for adjustment in the longer run will have to come from government expenditure, substitution in imports, or a fall in the growth rate. A likely chain of events is that during the period 1976-78, price adjustments within the economy may reduce consumption. After 1978 new government export-oriented investment activities currently being undertaken will result in the trade gap being reduced to the level of the savings gap. This investment will widen the savings gap, hence increasing domestic demand, while increasing exports and reducing the trade gap. Finally a constant, nominal, crude oil price eroded by domestic inflation will enable a further reduction in the trade gap to occur by lowering the real cost of petroleum to Panamanian consumers.

SECTORAL PROJECTIONS

Recent empirical work has indicated that the level of per capita income and the size of the domestic market are closely related to the level and structure of production.[2] These relationships have been shown to hold over a wide range of countries with different natural-resource endowments. The implication is that a country has a particular (or comparative) advantage in producing various goods at each stage of its development and this advantage changes systematically as the level of development (or per capita income) and the size of the market in the country change. Further, if a country's actual sectoral structure is different from the normal pattern, there must be something specific, such as an economic policy or other special constraint, that keeps the country from following a normal pattern of development. Obviously, when a small country possesses a unique resource such as oil, the nation's economic structure may differ from the predicted sectoral composition. This difference can also occur if the country has developed within a unique legal or political environment. In this case the economic environment may either prevent or encourage the production or the import of products that would have been reached under relatively competitive conditions.

Obviously, Panama would have a somewhat different sectoral composition of output if the Canal Zone and related institutions had never existed. If we assume that Panama would, under those circumstances, follow a normal pattern of growth, its productive structure would resemble the "predicted" composition.

It is apparent (Table 11.2) that the country's agricultural development has followed a relatively normal pattern; that is,

TABLE 11.2

Comparison with Normal Growth Patterns, 1950-70
(percent GDP current prices)

	Primary	Industry	Transport and Communications	Services
1950				
Actual	28.9	14.4	3.9	52.8
Predicted	27.5	27.7	7.0	37.8
1953				
Actual	28.4	16.4	4.0	51.3
Predicted	26.9	28.2	7.0	37.9
1955				
Actual	29.2	15.2	4.6	51.0
Predicted	26.0	28.8	7.2	38.0
1957				
Actual	25.8	17.9	4.5	51.8
Predicted	24.8	29.7	7.4	38.2
1960				
Actual	23.2	20.6	4.6	51.4
Predicted	24.9	29.6	7.3	38.2
1963				
Actual	21.3	23.5	5.1	50.1
Predicted	22.6	31.4	7.7	38.4
1965				
Actual	21.7	23.9	5.3	49.1
Predicted	21.7	32.1	7.8	38.4
1968				
Actual	20.2	25.5	5.7	48.5
Predicted	20.2	33.3	8.0	38.4
1970				
Actual	18.3	26.1	6.7	49.0
Predicted	19.4	33.2	8.1	38.2

Sources: "Actual" calculated by the author from Contraloria General de la Republica, Direccion de Estadistica y Censo, Ingreso Nacional, various issues; "Predicted" calculated by the author from formulas given in Hollis Chenery, "Patterns of Industrial Growth," American Economic Review (September 1960).

increases in per capita income and population have stimulated production in this sector to a degree similar to that in most other countries. The notable exceptions are services and industry, where Panama deviates significantly from a normal growth pattern.

To the extent that the level of income and the size of the
Panamanian market result in cost differentials between sectors and
also their relative competitiveness in international markets, the
difference between actual and predicted economic structure should,
in the long run, be eliminated. Two reasons could explain the per-
sistent divergence: (1) economic policy of the Panamanian government has intentionally created the differences that exist, or (2) there
are economic reasons other than population and per capita income
that are responsible for this difference—that is, institutions associated with the canal, Canal Zone, and associated treaties.

The obvious explanation for the higher than expected percentage of services in GDP is the proximity of the Canal Zone. The
geographical advantage of the country makes the real cost of Panamanian imports into the Zone relatively inexpensive. The competitive advantage Panama has in supplying the Zone, together with the
future of Zone activity, also explain Panama's relatively high level
of service exports.

Theoretically, since Panama's economic structure differs
from the typical or predicted structure (even though caused primarily
by legal and political factors), a disequilibrium exists and should
set up forces that would tend to move the economy toward the normal
structure. In the case of Panama this might be reflected in a divergence of actual profit rates from normal rates of return in various
sectors. If so, there should be a changing pattern of costs and profit rates of firms in the various sectors, to reflect more accurately
the country's level of per capita income. The country's population implies a level of skills, relative factor prices, and size of domestic
market. Given the values of these variables, the profitability of producing various goods domestically would be determined by the price of
imports. Panama maintained low levels of industrial protection
through most of the 1950s and 1960s. Domestic firms also faced
competition from firms in the Canal Zone (before 1955). This, together with the country's relatively high wage scale, accounts for
the country's very low ratio of domestic production to imports of
various manufactures. When the Canal Zone industries shut down
in the late 1950s and trade barriers (mainly quotas) increased in the
1960s, some investors undoubtedly found costs for some firms lower
than the cost of importing similar products. When the Panamanian
entrepreneurs expanded capacity the ratio of domestic production

TABLE 11.3

Projected Normal Growth Patterns, Selected Years, 1950-72
(in millions of 1960 balboas)

	1950	1955 Predicted	1955 Actual	1959 Predicted	1959 Actual
Agriculture	74.5	88.6	86.0	105.2	98.7
Mining	0.6	0.7	0.9	0.9	1.1
Consumer manufactured goods	19.7 ⎫	24.7 ⎫	n.a. ⎫	31.8 ⎫	38.6 ⎫
Intermediate manufactured goods	0.6 ⎬ 23.5	0.8 ⎬ 32.9	⎬ 33.2	1.0 ⎬ 38.6	2.1 ⎬ 49.4
Capital manufactured goods	3.2 ⎭	7.4 ⎭	⎭	5.8 ⎭	8.2 ⎭
Construction	10.6	13.1	13.5	16.7	17.9
Utilities	3.2	4.0	4.5	5.3	6.5
Transportation and communication	10.0	12.5	13.4	16.1	18.0
Other services	134.8	166.2	163.2	209.5	200.6
Total	257.2	318.0	314.7	392.3	392.2

	1965 Predicted	1965 Actual	1968 Predicted	1968 Actual	1972 Predicted	1972 Actual
Agriculture	125.8	132.2	148.0	154.0	184.8	172.0
Mining	1.6	1.8	2.0	2.1	2.7	2.7
Consumer manufactured goods	66.1 ⎫	65.4 ⎫	84.9 ⎫	86.4 ⎫	117.2 ⎫	108.7 ⎫
Intermediate manufactured goods	4.8 ⎬ 89.1	11.8 ⎬ 98.1	6.2 ⎬ 115.8	16.1 ⎬ 131.6	8.7 ⎬ 112.1	24.1 ⎬ 177.0
Capital manufactured goods	18.2 ⎭	20.9 ⎭	24.7 ⎭	29.1 ⎭	36.2 ⎭	44.6 ⎭
Construction	35.1	34.9	44.4	47.3	60.4	71.8
Utilities	13.7	14.5	17.8	18.9	25.0	34.2
Transportation and communication	30.4	32.9	38.9	43.9	55.4	72.2
Other services	321.7	302.7	404.1	374.3	545.2	503.8
Total	617.4	617.3	771.0	771.2	1035.6	1045.2

Sources: "Actual" calculated by the author from Contraloria de la Republica, Direccion de Estadistica y Censo, Ingreso Nacional, various issues; "Predicted" calculated by the author from formulas given in Hollis Chenery, "Patterns of Industrial Growth," American Economic Review 50, no. 3 (September 1960): 624-54.

to imports increased. This is reflected in the projected normal
growth patterns (Table 11. 3).

As indicated, while the share of manufacturing in GDP remained low during the 1950s and 1960s, it grew faster than predicted
by the normal country development criterion. The slowdown of manufacturing output in the early 1970s may mean, however, that a new
impetus to growth in the sector may be needed. Conceivably, this
could come from a new treaty agreement, as was the case in the
1955 treaty.

The important question now facing Panama is: would an
alternative treaty arrangement be effective in significantly changing
(within, say a decade) the country's sectoral development pattern to
a more normal pattern of growth. Increased production for local
consumption is the obvious way of modifying the country's historical
relationship between the rate of growth of domestic expenditure and
the rate of sectoral growth. Two mechanisms are available for
effecting this. One is a deliberate changing of consumption patterns
away from imported goods either by voluntary individual decisions
or by government policy (for example, government expenditure).
There would be no strain on the balance of payments if this shift
were caused by a change in expenditure patterns from imports to
local products, as long as increases in supply were planned ahead.
No change in the treaty would be required for this change in policy,
although the scope for action here is probably limited. The alternative is some limited application of a disequilibrium system involving the financing of construction expenditures or investment in
productive activity through expansion in the money supply. This
would involve the use of controls to suppress the resulting inflation
and the deterioration in the country's balance of payments. This
alternative offers, as was seen in the inflation and stagnation of the
early 1970s, little promise for the country.

The country's sectoral development has, however—despite
the fact that it does not correspond to a normal pattern—followed a
close enough pattern with domestic income increases (GDP) to form
the basis for projections of sectoral output, given a rate of growth
of GNP.

The income elasticities for the expansion of sectoral output, given a 1 percent change in GDP for 1950-59 and 1960-73, are
as follows:

	1950-1959	1960-1973
Agriculture	0.7447	0.6623
Mining	0 9399	0.8789

	1950-1959	1960-1973
Manufacturing	1.5390	1.2417
Construction	1.4199	1.2073
Utilities	1.4545	1.6408
Transportation and communication	1.4344	1.4704
Commerce	0.8393	0.9945
Finance	1.5000	1.6565
Housing	0.4565	0.8423
Public administration	1.0501	1.0015
Other services	1.0592	0.7861
Canal Zone services	0.5991	0.9310

The 1960-73 GNP-sector growth coefficients were used in the projections for the 8 percent GNP growth (Table 11.4). Using trends in employment and productivity during the 1960-71 period by sector, projections of these variables were also made on one 8 percent GNP growth (Table 11.5).

In terms of employment, the main implications of the projected patterns of growth are:

1. At a 4 percent average annual rate of growth of GDP, employment opportunities would expand by only 2.41 percent.

2. At a 6 percent rate of GNP growth, employment opportunities of only 4 percent annually would be created—approximately the rate of increase in employment expansion needed simply to employ new entrants in the labor force.

3. At an 8 percent rate of real GDP growth, employment opportunities would expand at a rate of 5.9 percent—fast enough to employ new entrants in the labor force, but in addition to upgrade the productivity, and thus the per capita income, of a number of existing workers.

RECOMMENDED DEVELOPMENT STRATEGY

On the basis of the above results, it seems that several implications for Panama's future growth stand out. These include certain much debated issues in Panama, such as the role of foreign capital, the trade-off between employment and growth, the implications for growth of the government's attempt at attacking poverty,

TABLE 11.4

Sectoral Output, 1974–84
(in millions of 1960 balboas)

	1974	1975	1976	1977	1978	1979	1980	1981	1982	1983	1984
Agriculture	180.2	190.6	201.6	213.3	225.6	238.6	252.4	267	282.5	298.8	316.1
Mining	2.8	3	3.2	3.4	3.7	4	4.2	4.5	4.9	5.2	5.6
Manufacturing	182.6	199.2	217.4	237.1	258.7	282.2	307.9	335.9	366.4	399.8	436.1
Construction	69.6	75.8	82.6	89.9	98	106.7	116.2	126.6	137.9	150.2	163.6
Utilities	35.3	39.1	43.4	48.1	53.4	59.2	65.6	72.8	80.7	89.5	99.3
Transportation and communication	73.7	81.1	89.5	98.5	108.6	119.6	131.8	145.2	160	176.2	194.1
Commerce	147.9	159.5	171.9	185.3	199.8	215.4	232.2	250.3	269.8	290.9	313.6
Finance	44.7	49.6	55.1	61.1	67.8	75.2	83.5	92.7	102.8	114.1	126.6
Housing	72.7	77.8	83.1	88.9	95.1	101.7	108.7	116.2	124.3	132.9	142.1
Public administration	27.6	29.8	32.1	34.6	37.4	40.3	43.5	46.9	50.6	54.5	58.8
Other services	141.8	151.1	161	171.6	182.9	195	207.8	221.5	236.1	251.6	268.2
Canal Zone services	77.8	83.6	89.8	96.5	103.7	111.4	119.7	128.7	138.2	148.5	159.6
GDP	1056.7	1140.2	1230.7	1328.3	1434.7	1549.3	1673.5	1808.3	1954.2	2112.2	2283.7

Note: An 8 percent growth rate of GDP is assumed.

Source: Compiled by author.

and the possible trade-off between inflation and growth. Needless to say, each of these issues has many complicated aspects—economic as well as sociopolitical—and our model is not geared to provide an intensive analysis of each issue. As emphasized before, however, the models are presented only to clarify a few misconceptions.

Foreign Capital and Growth in Panama

In recent years the role of foreign capital in Panama's development has come under increasing scrutiny. In particular, it has been argued that foreign capital has stifled domestic savings, and thus reduced the growth prospects of the country.[3] This argument is generally based on some presumption as to the adverse effects that foreign capital would have on local entrepreneurs; that is, foreign capital would preempt the areas in which local businessmen would be likely to invest, thus causing them to save less (due to fewer attractive investment possibilities). The analysis in Chapter 3 indicated, however, that this has not been the case—that foreign capital and domestic savings have been complementary in Panama.

In the macro-model system of equations it is also clear that both savings and GNP growth rates are increased by external savings, and also that increases in foreign capital inflows cause domestic savings, investment, and income to increase. There is therefore no evidence of any possible adverse effect on the country's development stemming from foreign capital.

Employment and Growth

The results of the model suggest that any adverse relationship between employment and growth is unlikely. A conflict between increased employment and income growth may be valid in some abstract theoretical models of growth,[4] but Panama seems to have large amounts of labor available for more productive work. There is no reason to believe that both employment and productivity cannot be expanded through proper government policy implementation. For example, if the country's growth is constrained by foreign exchange, as it appears to be at all politically acceptable levels of growth, employment-creating techniques can be introduced in a manner that will not increase the foreign exchange gap. As a result, higher growth will, under these conditions, be associated with more rapid employment creation.

TABLE 11.5

Employment and Average Productivity, by Economic Sector, 1974-84

	1974	1975	1976	1977	1978	1979	1980	1981	1982	1983	1984
Thousands of Workers											
Agriculture	159.4	162.6	166.0	169.7	173.7	177.8	182.4	187.2	192.4	197.8	203.5
Mining and manufacturing	58.7	62.6	66.9	71.3	76.2	81.5	87.2	93.5	100.1	107.2	114.9
Construction	35.3	38.6	42.2	46.1	50.4	52.2	60.3	65.9	71.9	78.7	86.0
Utilities	7.3	7.8	8.3	8.8	9.6	10.1	10.9	11.7	12.7	13.5	14.8
Commerce and finance	101.9	109.7	118.0	126.8	136.4	146.8	157.9	170.0	183.1	197.2	212.4
Transportation and communication	26.0	27.8	30.1	31.9	34.3	36.8	39.6	42.6	45.8	49.3	53.1
Services and public administration	133.7	142.3	151.2	160.8	171.1	181.9	193.4	205.7	218.8	232.6	247.4
Canal Zone services	20.8	21.5	22.4	23.2	24.2	25.2	26.3	27.4	28.6	30.0	31.4
Total employment	543.1	572.9	605.1	638.6	675.9	712.3	758.0	804.0	853.4	906.3	963.5
Thousands of 1960 Balboas Per Worker											
Agriculture	1.13	1.17	1.21	1.26	1.30	1.34	1.38	1.43	1.47	1.51	1.55
Mining and manufacturing	3.16	3.23	3.30	3.37	3.44	3.51	3.58	3.64	3.71	3.78	3.84
Construction	1.97	1.96	1.96	1.95	1.94	1.94	1.93	1.92	1.91	1.91	1.90
Utilities	4.84	5.01	5.23	5.47	5.56	5.86	6.02	6.22	6.35	6.63	6.71
Commerce and finance	1.89	1.91	1.92	1.94	1.96	1.98	2.00	2.02	2.03	2.05	2.07
Transportation and communication	2.83	2.92	2.97	3.09	3.17	3.25	3.33	3.41	3.49	3.57	3.66
Services and public administration	1.81	1.82	1.83	1.84	1.84	1.85	1.86	1.87	1.88	1.89	1.90
Canal Zone services	3.74	3.89	4.01	4.16	4.29	4.42	4.55	4.70	4.83	4.95	5.08

Note: An 8 percent growth rate of GDP is assumed.
Source: Compiled by author.

In addition, employment-oriented policies have the potential in Panama to work through factor price changes in the price of labor vis-a-vis capital, increase the demand for labor, and reduce the country's capital import requirements. By lowering the relative price for labor, therefore, it may be possible to further increase both employment and GNP growth simultaneiously.[5] Similarly, if the employment problem is attacked through changing the pattern of growth (toward the rural sector, for example), such that it reduces the demand for capital and imports, the government can obtain more rapid rates of both employment and growth.

Poverty and Growth

Our conclusions on poverty and growth are rather similar to those on employment and growth. If the government's income growth policy is oriented toward simply transferring resources from the urban rich to the urban poor, there may be a conflict between growth and equity. However, the majority of the poor in Panama live in the rural areas, and make their living from agriculture. In general, rural farmers have a high propensity to save. High rates of rural savings are evidenced by the great number of branch offices of the foreign banks in rural areas. Given this high level of rural savings, any government policy that raises the productivity and income of the rural poor, particularly those in agriculture, would not reduce the country's saving potential. An equally important fact is that, in general, income generation in agriculture requires less capital and fewer imports than the expansion of manufacturing. Rural policies would thus reduce the foreign exchange gap (for the same rate of national income growth). It is therefore possible for the government to improve the conditions of the poor and at the same time achieve a higher growth rate. In fact it is very likely that rates of growth much lower than those in the 1960s would undoubtedly hurt the poor. A higher growth rate, while necessary for an attack on poverty, is not however a sufficient condition for helping the lower-income groups. The answer lies in restructuring growth toward the provinces. The implication of the analysis presented above is that the country should not attempt to aid the poor at the expense of development of the country as a whole, but to attack poverty through restructuring the country's growth.

Inflation and Growth

The results suggest that, if used as positive instruments of economic policy, consumer goods price increases vis-a-vis the general price level could help the country overcome any possible saving constraint on economic growth. For example, instead of assuming that the country must fill the largest resource gap by a foreign capital inflow, the country can close the gap by means of a policy of price controls over a number of investment goods; that is, it could allow the prices of consumption goods to increase domestic savings. The rise in the relative price of consumption goods could be gradual to see how far the resource gap could be narrowed before further borrowing took place.

CONCLUSIONS

In view of the country's high population growth, and of uncertainties as to (1) the ability of the economy to expand exports at a rate comparable to that achieved in the 1960s, (2) the status of the canal, and (3) the new and complex issues arising from growth itself—the changing social and political aspirations of the population—continued rates of high income growth are essential for Panama. To maintain the 8 percent growth rate of the 1960s—perhaps the minimum necessary to absorb the expanding population into productive employment—the rate of investment will have to be higher. Fiscal reform will have to take place, together with other essential measures, if the country is to avoid balance-of-payments strains. Agricultural and industrial policy will have to be more carefully administered and coordinated than in the past. Education and other social reforms will need to be more intensive and purposeful. Gross inequalities in income and wealth will have to be redressed, and new policies will have to be worked out for urban development—particularly the problem of insufficient housing and communications in the metropolitan area that has developed as a result of the massive rural-urban migration of the 1960s and early 1970s. Regional imbalances must be seriously approached under programs correlated to overall development programs and long-range objectives. The government must face these issues and work out the necessary planning machinery to ensure optimum utilization of Panama's many positive trends and experiences in development.

Economic developments in Panama during 1974 and 1975 were the most serious in the past quarter-century, owing largely to world inflation and recession. Internal factors, such as the collapse of the construction boom and the end of the period of relatively easy import replacement opportunities in the early 1970s, have also contributed to the country's slowdown. In 1974 economic growth was halved to 3.5 percent and decreased further to 2 percent in the first half of 1975. Inflation was nearly 17 percent during 1974 but was reduced sharply to 1.8 percent in the first half of 1975, partly as a result of the government's stabilization measures—mainly a reduction in its expenditures.

Since late 1974 a number of longer-run measures have been taken to stimulate the country's recovery. Of particular significance is the government's capital investment program which will provide for a more self-sustaining economy and one with a greater export potential. It is estimated that the projects involved in transforming the country will provide greater employment, increased earnings of over $350 million, and import savings of $60 million. The projects cover energy, transport, fishing, sugar, cement, and copper mining.

The new investment program is far beyond Panama's own resources, and foreign finance is being obtained from both international development agencies and banks. As a result of this borrowing, the country's foreign debt is expected to rise from $68 million in 1975 to nearly $100 million in 1976. The government, however, believes that the program of direct and indirect investment will return Panama to the path of export-led growth.

If the analysis in this study is correct, Panama is quite likely to regain the growth momentum of the 1960s, although the next phase of the country's economic expansion will probably be characterized as one of development of the entire economy, not simply of a narrow segment.

Marxists often argue that the world is in a continual state of change. Following their line of argument, revolutions occur in nations when the institutions of the country are incompatible with the "new economic realities," that is, when these institutions cannot accommodate the new demands placed on the economy by such changes as technology, new economic priorities, new social movements, and so on. Panama's institutions have changed only minimally since the treaty of 1903 and the monetary agreement of 1904. The country has had a revolution, but hardly one resulting from a process described by Marx. While the country's leaders often like to refer to themselves as Marxists, the early twentieth century institutions within which they are currently pursuing their policies still seem best for the country's future advancement.

NOTES

1. The theory of the two-gap model is given in Jaroslav Vanek, Estimating Foreign Resource Needs for Economic Development (New York: McGraw-Hill, 1967).

2. See Hollis B. Chenery, "Patterns of Industrial Growth," American Economic Review 50, no. 3 (September 1960): 624-54. and Hollis Chenery and Moises Syraquin, Patterns of Development: 1950-1970 (London: Oxford University Press, 1975).

3. See the general discussion contained in Keith Griffin, Underdevelopment in Spanish America (Cambridge, Mass: MIT Press, 1969), ch. 3.

4. Frances Stewart and Paul Streeten, "Conflicts Between Output and Employment Objectives in Developing Countries," Oxford Economic Papers 23, no. 2 (July 1971): 145-68. Walter Elkan "On the Apparent Benefits of Higher Productivity: an Arithmetical Illustration," Journal of Development Studies 7, no. 4 (July 1971): 435-39.

5. As an illustration two levels of net capital formation can be assumed—B/. 30 million and B/. 45 million. In the first instance the number of workers expands over the 1970 level by some 13 percent in manufacturing when wages are held constant, while the expansion rate is 12 percent when wages increase at 5 percent, 11 percent when wages increase at 10 percent and so on. Thus for each percentage increase in wages in Panama about 26 new jobs in manufacturing will be sacrificed. See Del Fitchett, "Capital-Labor Substitution in the Manufacturing Sector of Panama," mimeographed (Panama City: U.S. Agency for International Development, 1973).

CONSTRAINTS ON GROWTH, 1945–46

The following variables are of relevance in identifying the mechanisms and constraints on Panamanian growth and in testing the hypothesis set forth in Chapter 2:

Y = gross national product

C^P = private consumption expenditure

C^g = government consumption expenditure

C^T = aggregate consumption expenditure ($C^P + C^g$)

I^p = private investment expenditure

I^g = government investment expenditure

I^T = aggregate gross domestic capital formation ($I^p + I^g$)

X = exports of goods and services

M = Imports of goods and services (including net factor payments)

F = net foreign capital inflows

S = gross national savings

Three identities from the Panamanian national income accounts summarize the structure of the model (t = current year values, t − 1 = previous year values).

$$Y_t = C^P_t + C^g_t + I^p_t + I^g_t + X_t - M_t \qquad (A.1)$$

$$Y_t = C^T_t + S_t \qquad (A.2)$$

$$F_t = I^T_t - S_t \qquad (A.3)$$

From these three identities it follows that

$$F_t = M_t - X_t \qquad (A.4)$$

The actual saving function (that recorded in the national income accounts) is:

$$S_t = a_1 + b_1 Y_t + b_2 F_t \qquad (A.5)$$

The actual import functions are:

$$M_t = a_2 + b_3 Y_t + b_4 F_t \tag{A.6}$$

and

$$X_t = \bar{X}_t \text{ (exports determined exogenously).} \tag{A.7}$$

It is reasonable to assume that the actual magnitudes of savings and imports recorded in the national income accounts for the period were not the values individuals necessarily desired; a lack of either foreign exchange or domestic savings may have prevented individuals from obtaining the desired level of savings or imports. Under these circumstances, a trade gap would be the chief constraint on growth if the deficiency (in the desired sense) of foreign exchange exceeds the excess of required investment over potential savings for a given level of income. Inflows of foreign capital in Panama are positive under this condition and are equal to the trade gap. In this case the actual imports achieved at any point of time are the levels that individuals in the country desire. This relationship is given by:

$$M_t = a_2 + b_3 Y_t \tag{A.8}$$
$$b_4 = 0 \text{ in (A.6)}$$

Three cases are possible in this situation:

(a) when $I_t^T - S_t$ (the savings gap) is zero. This occurs when the amount individuals are willing to save is equal to the of investment necessary to maintain the level of GNP in that year, and $M_t - X_t$ (the trade gap) is positive.

(b) when $I_t^T - S_t$ is positive (though smaller than $M_t - X_t$).

(c) when $I_t^T - S_t$ is negative.

In the first case the desired level of domestic saving in Panama would be given by:

$$S_t = a_1 + b_1 Y_t \tag{A.9}$$

and is equal to the required investment.

In the first case (a), if Panama were able to attract foreign capital into the country to fill the trade gap, and since the two gaps must be equal (again because of national income account definitions), there would be a fall in savings below the desired level, an increase in investment, or both. If realized investment in Panama during this period were equal to the desired level, that is, the minimum level required for the attained level of income, all the adjustment would take place through changes in savings. Realized savings would have to fall short of the potential or desired levels by an amount equal to F. F would then be a complete substitute for savings; that is, inflows of foreign capital would not lower domestic savings levels. If such a situation did in fact prevail during the period examined, econometric measurements (using the national account figures) of the determinants of savings as incorporated in equation A.5 would be biased and we would obtain an estimate of b_2 close to unity with a negative sign. The estimate of b_1 in equation A.8 would be an approximation to the marginal propensity to save (the increase in domestic savings that resulted from an increase in income). Similarly, an attempt to estimate imports in equation A.6 would yield an estimate of b_4 close to zero. A positive value for b_4 would be an indication that actual imports exceeded the required level, or that the realized level of income was below the potential level, given the amount of imports that year.

In the second case (b) the desired savings gap is positive but less than the trade gap: $I_t^T - (a_1 + b_1 Y_t) < M_t - X_t$.

If investment requirements were incapable of being altered during this period, the actual savings would be potential savings by an amount equal to the excess of the desired trade gap over the desired savings gap. If the savings gap is large, then F will be mostly a complement to domestic savings, and the reduction in realized savings would be small. The extent to which F acted as a substitute for savings might have gone from zero—when the savings gap was as large as the trade gap—to the full value of F when there is no difference between desired savings and investment (the potential savings gap is zero). In equation A.5, b_2 would lie between minus unity and zero:

$$b_2 = -(M_t - E_t) - (S_t - I_t^T)/(M_t - E_t) \qquad (A.10)$$

If this case $(I + S < E^{-M})$ had persisted for several years in Panama, then an econometric estimation of equation A.6 yields an estimate of some weighted average of b_2. Under the assumptions that have been made, F would be equal to E - M so that it would be possible to obtain an estimate of the magnitude of an average potential (desired) savings gap. An estimate of the potential marginal propensity to save would again be given by b_1. The interpretation of b_4 remains the same as in the first case.

In the third case (c), the negative savings gap differs from (b) only in the sense that b_2 would be less than minus unity.

When the savings gap is binding in Panama, foreign capital is no longer a substitute for domestic saving but a complement. The actual amount of savings under these circumstances is equal to that desired and $b_2 = 0$. F is now equal to the savings gap $S_t - I_t^T$). Since $M_t - E_t$ is smaller, imports must increase exports and decrease from their desired level so that the identities A. 3 and A. 4 are preserved. Actual exports may fall short of the potential if a significant proportion of the goods or services exported can be consumed domestically, or if some inputs required for producing those exports can be employed in the production of goods for the domestic market.

Imports will exceed the minimum required levels in the presence of foreign capital inflows: b_4 will be positive (but smaller), the greater the downward adjustment in exports. In the case when the inputs into the export sector are highly specialized and if, as in this case, Panama's domestic use of exportable products is relatively low and not responsive to price changes, the value of b_4 should be close to $[(I_t^T - S_t) - (F_t + M_t)]/(I_t - S_t)$ indicating that part of the foreign capital has gone to increase imports.

The exports of Panama have always fluctuated fairly widely. These movements are due largely to influences outside the country's control. During periods of high export growth we should expect the savings gap to be binding; when exports, however, are low in relation to their trend—as was the case after World War II—the trade gap would be the more likely effective constraint. In the presence of altering savings and trade gaps, an examination of the constraints on Panamanian growth becomes very difficult. One of the two gaps has been predominantly binding: and we may obtain some evidence of this by regressing equations:

$$S_t = a_1 + b_1 Y_t + b_2 F_t \qquad (A. 5)$$

and

$$M_t = a_2 + b_3 Y_t + F_4 F_t \qquad (A. 6)$$

A value of b_1 close to -1 together with a value of b_4 not significantly different from 0 (a "t" value less than about 2) would be an indication of the trade gap having prevailed in that period. If this were the case in Panama, potential saving would be given by $a_1 + b_1 Y_t$. On the other hand, if b_1 turns out to be close to zero and b_4 is significantly positive, then this indicates that the savings gaps were binding. In this case the observed savings are probably close to the potential levels. When b_1 is significantly negative (but its absolute value is less than unity) and b_2 is significantly positive, the two gaps have alternated as constraints during the time period under consideration; that is, the savings and trade gaps were alternating on binding constraints. Under these circumstances, neither savings nor foreign exchange has been the predominant or exclusive constraint on growth. In this situation it is still possible to obtain some idea of the country's potential savings ratios. For example, if in those years when exports were highest (with respect to their trend) and savings ratios were also high, then it could be concluded that in those years the savings gap would be the constraint. In this case, the observed savings ratios would be the same as the potential ones.

Estimates of the critical equations from the data in Table 2.1 yielded:

$$S_t = 9.4864 + 0.1030\ Y_t - 1.0026\ F_t \qquad\qquad \text{(A.11)}$$
$$ (1.4856) \qquad (8.8435)$$

$$r^2 = 0.94$$
$$DW = 1.1$$

$$M_t = 40.5151 + 0.1750\ Y_t - 0.0522\ F_t \qquad\qquad \text{(A.12)}$$
$$ (2.0301) \qquad (0.3599)$$

$$r^2 = 0.85$$
$$DW = 1.1$$

Here, as in the other equations estimated for Panama, the "t" ratio is given below the estimated parameters. This ratio is a means whereby one can assess the likelihood that the coefficient is significantly different from zero. Given the number of observations used, the values of the "t" ratio should be greater than about 2.0 to indicate the significance of the coefficient.[1] The Durbin-Watson[2] statistic is a measure of the degree of serial[3] correlation in the unexplained portion of the dependent variable. A value of 2.0 indicates no serial correlation, while values less than 1.0 or greater than 3.0 tend to indicate a substantial amount present. The r^2 is a measure of the "goodness of fit." A value of 1.00 indicating the dependent variable is completely explained by the selected independent variable. The symbols are the same as on page 202.

The results of equation A.10 together with the F in equation A.11 being not statistically different from zero confirm the original hypothesis concerning Panama's inability to withstand the fall in Canal Zone exports after World War II. In other words, the trade gap was totally binding during this period.

MACROECONOMIC RELATIONSHIPS, 1945-56
(in millions of 1950 balboas)

$$C_t^P = 4.3994 + 0.4022\ T_t + 0.5191\ C_{t-1}^P \qquad\qquad\text{(A.13)}$$
$$\ (2.9415)\quad\ (3.3557)$$

$$r^2 = .98 \qquad\qquad DW = 2.1$$

$$C_t^T = -11.9939 + 0.4815\ Y_t + 0.5247\ C_{t-1}^T \qquad\text{(A.14)}$$
$$\ (2.99303)\quad\ (3.2812)$$

$$r^2 = .98 \qquad\qquad DW = 2.1$$

$$C_t^g = C_t - C_t^P \qquad\qquad\qquad\qquad\qquad\qquad\text{(A.15)}$$

$$I_t^P = -34.3341 + 0.1092\ Y_t + 0.3594\ M_t \qquad\text{(A.16)}$$
$$\ (4.2220)\quad\ (4.2492)$$

$$r^2 = .87 \qquad\qquad DW = 1.7$$

$$I_t^P = -8.0577_{t-1}^P + 0.4361\ Y_t + Y_t\ 0.0871 \qquad\text{(A.16')}$$
$$\ (1.7031)\qquad\ (1.9441)$$

$$r^2 = .85 \qquad\qquad DW = 1.2$$

$$I_t^T = -21.3923 + 0.1134\ Y_t + 0.7216\ I_{t-1}^T \qquad\text{(A.17)}$$
$$\ (3.0149)\quad\ (3.6614)$$

$$r^2 = .88 \qquad\qquad DW = 1.2$$

$$M_t = 34.6923 + 0.2866 + 1.0445\ I_t^P \qquad\qquad\text{(A.18)}$$
$$\ (3.0602)\ (3.0379)$$

$$r^2 = .83 \qquad\qquad DW = 1.4$$

$$I_t^g = I_t^T - I_t^P \qquad\qquad\qquad\qquad\qquad\qquad\text{(A.19)}$$

$$Y_t = I_t^P + I_t^g + C_t^P + C_t^g - M_t + E_t \qquad\qquad\text{(A.20)}$$

In each of equations A.13, A.14, and A.16, consumption or investment expenditures are determined as a function of GNP and expenditure in the previous year. These relationships indicate not only the major short-run changes in expenditure, but several deterrents of longer-run stability. This can be easily demonstrated by the following derivation. In the case of private consumption, let $\bar{C}_t^p = a + bY_t^Y$ be the long-run private consumption function. Implicit in this definition is the assumption that consumers, given an increase in their incomes, will consume a relatively small proportion in the current year,[4] and will spread over a number of years the additional consumption made possible by their higher income.

The parameter b then becomes the long-run increment of consumption that results from a change in income. The adjustment to a higher level of income takes place in the following manner:

$$(C_t^p - C_{t-1}^p) = (\bar{C}_t^p - C_{t-1}^p) \tag{A.21}$$

Substituting $\bar{C}_t^p$ by $\bar{C}_t^p = a + bY_t$ gives

$$(C_t^p - C_{t-1}^p) = Z(a + bY_t - C_{t-1}^p \qquad \text{or} \tag{A.22}$$

$$C_t^p = Za + ZbY_t + (1 - Z)C_{t-1}^p \tag{A.23}$$

Estimates of the parameters in this equation give the short-run changes in consumption resulting from a change in income (Zb) and similarly the long-run changes (b).

For private consumption the estimated coefficients were:

$$Zb = 0.1934, \quad Z = 0.4809, \quad \text{and} \quad b = 1.001$$

The short-run change in consumption resulting from a change in income is 0.1934; that is, if GNP were to increase by B/1 million, personal consumption expenditures would increase by B/140,300 in the same year. Eventually, consumers would adjust their consumption to the higher level of income so that their long-run consumption would increase by B/1.001 million. In the case of total investment, the short- and long-run responses to a change in income are 0.1134 and 0.4073 respectively, values a bit more stabilizing than those of private consumption. Nevertheless, the high long-run response of investment contributed significantly to the country's economic stability after the war.

NOTES

1. See Daniel Suits, "Forecasting and Analysis With an Econometric Model," <u>American Economic Review</u> 52, no. 1 (March 1962) pp. 104-32, for a discussion of the statistical values associated with econometric models.

2. J. Durbin and G.S. Watson, "Testing for Serial Correlation in Least Squares Regression," <u>Biometrica</u> 7, no. 3 (1951): 251-64.

3. See ibid. for a definition.

4. Long- and short-run consumption as defined by Thomas Mayer in his <u>Permanent Income, Wealth and Consumption</u> (Berkeley: University of California Press, 1972) chapters 1 and 2.

There are a number of strategies available for increasing the level of investment in Panama. During the period 1950-67 four different approaches to capital formation were taken by developing countries,[1] each yielding a rate of sustained growth:

(1) high capital inflow: more than 35 percent of investment financed by aid or other foreign sources for at least the first decade;
(2) high primary exports: levels of primary exports at least 50 percent above normal values (and typically twice as high);
(3) moderate capital inflow: external financing to the extent of 10 percent of investment during most of the period; and
(4) low external dependence: none of the above.

These four successful strategies are distinguished primarily by the varying patterns in resource allocation through which the growing economy is transformed over time to meet the needs of development patterns of high-growth countries have great similarities. In virtually every case, rapid growth has been accompanied by a rising savings rate, which permits the inflow of capital to be reduced (unless the growth rate accelerates further). This experience contrasts with that of slower-growing countries and suggests that there is a greater profitability of investment at higher rates of growth, and that this factor has a significant effect on the supply of savings. Increased self-reliance has therefore accompanied rapid growth; only in the slow-growing countries has dependence on aid tended to be perpetuated.

Panama falls in the high-aid category (Table B.1). It and the seven other countries in this group have been able to achieve high growth rates on the basis of large amounts of external capital. All are small (except Korea) and have received support for a variety of political reasons. Theoretically they started the period (1950) in difficult political circumstances and with unfavorable resource bases. Capital inflow averaged between 5 and 10 percent of GNP for substantial periods and was largely public. In most all cases there was a substantial rise in investment in the second decade, reduced dependence on capital inflow, and a shift toward private sources of financing.

TABLE B.1

A Classification of Development Strategies of High-Growth Countries

Country	GNP Growth (percent)		Population Growth (percent)	Per Capita GNP Increase, in percent (1950-67)	Investment Ratio		External Finance		Capital/Output Ratio	Export Growth (percent)	
	1951-59	1960-67			1950-55	1960-65	1951-59	1960-67		1951-59	1960-67
A-Strategy: High Aid											
Israel	11.5	7.5	4.8	2.23	.310	.237	.68	.52	3.2	21.0	15.0
Taiwan	8.2	9.4	3.3	2.21	.138	.220	.37	.21	2.0	7.0	20.0
Jordan	8.8	8.2	3.1	2.00	—	.165	1.00	1.00	1.6	15.0	10.0
Greece	6.2	7.3	0.9	2.41	.177	.249	.46	.36	3.1	12.0	12.0
Puerto Rico	5.5	8.1	1.5	2.52	.196	.252	.80	.79	3.3	7.0	10.0
Korea	5.4	6.9	2.8	1.48	.120	.164	.67	.63	2.7	7.0	27.0
Panama	4.4	8.5	3.1	1.56	.107	.191	.53	.29	2.4	4.0	9.0
B-Strategy: High Primary Exports											
Thailand	6.9	7.5	3.0	1.98	.181	.213	.13	.07	2.6	2.7	12.7
Trinidad	9.0	6.4	2.9	2.15	.229	.264	.24	.31	—	10.8	12.7
Jamaica	8.3	4.5	1.8	1.50	.135	.217	.51	.21	3.3	13.1	6.5
Malaysia	—	6.7	3.0	1.77	—	—	.82	.13	3.0	0.4	2.2
Iran	—	7.8	2.7	1.60	—	.172	—	0.00	2.2	1.2	9.9
Nicaragua	5.7	6.8	3.1	1.64	.171	.175	.23	.18	2.4	10.2	9.2
Venezuela	8.3	4.2	3.8	1.51	.251	.189	.07	-.21	3.2	8.3	0.7
Ivory Coast	—	19.1	2.6	—	—	.172	-.31	-.12	—	3.6	11.5
Iraq	5.8	7.2	2.8	1.49	.215	.173	-.11	-.13	—	15.6	4.3
Zambia	6.0	6.0	2.9	1.46	.240	.259	0.00	-.36	4.0	—	—
Rhodesia	6.7	5.3	3.2	1.38	.352	.175	.47	.02	3.6	—	—
C-Strategy: Moderate Capital Inflow											
Mexico	6.0	6.5	3.3	1.60	.130	.161	.09	.12	2.4	5.5	5.4
Turkey	6.8	5.3	2.7	1.75	.166	.164	.14	.17	2.7	5.2	7.0
UAR	6.2	5.5	2.8	1.83	—	.142	—	.27	—	0.0	3.0
Peru	4.7	6.5	2.7	1.74	.198	.203	.16	.08	4.2	6.6	12.8
Philippines	6.1	4.7	3.2	1.41	.119	.182	.19	.18	2.0	2.8	9.0
Pakistan	2.9	6.1	2.2	1.24	(-08)	.13	—	.25	(2.5)	0.1	6.7
Sudan	4.3	7.3	2.8	1.49	.053	.113	-.15	.19	2.4	7.3	2.6
Nigeria	3.5	6.0	2.1	1.44	—	—	-.02	.42	—	6.8	5.3
D-Strategy: Low External Dependence											
Japan	8.1	11.0	1.0	2.89	.252	.268	0.00	0.00	3.5	16.6	12.6
Yugoslavia	8.9	6.6	1.2	2.55	.314	.375	—	.01	—	13.6	16.2
Spain	5.1	8.7	0.8	2.24	.179	.213	.06	—	—	—	15.3
Bulgaria	8.8	7.3	0.8	2.22	—	.392	—	—	—	14.6	15.2
Brazil	5.9	4.5	3.1	1.43	.135	.150	—	.09	—	0.3	2.8

Note: Data for Pakistan are for 1951-55.

Source: H. Chenery, "Targets for Development," in The Widening Gap, ed. B. Ward (New York: Columbia University Press, 1971).

In fact, the purpose and ultimate aim of the high-aid strategy is to permit a developing country such as Panama to expand the sectors that can grow most readily without having to worry about balance-of-payments problems in the near future. In most of these countries aid has substituted initially for agricultural production, but both industry and primary production have grown very rapidly. The effect on trade is to bypass the normal stage of specialization in primary exports and to develop manufactured exports or services (tourism) instead.

Success in a high-aid strategy normally requires the recipient country to be in a position to make a substantial reduction in its dependence on capital inflows after a decade or so. As Table B.1 indicates, Panama brought about such a reduction by high rates of growth of both savings and exports, and the growth rates of both increased in the second decade.

A second feature of this strategy of importance to Panama is that it is the rapidly growing countries that become attractive to private investment. Private foreign capital has become available for local use whereas a decade earlier the country had held little interest for foreign investors. Because of the success of this strategy, private capital and hard loans have increasingly replaced concessional lending in the country.

NOTE

1. Analysis based on Hollis B. Chenery, "Targets for Development," in The Widening Gap, ed. B. Ward. (New York: Columbia University Press, 1971).

Examination of the Panamanian economy indicates that a
Keynesian or demand approach to the analysis of the country's future
growth potential is theoretically justified and can yield a number of
insights into likely constraints on the economy's development—insights
not provided by the sources-of-growth approach (the supply model).
Many of Panama's problems are simply a result of lack of adaptation
of domestic supply to a changing pattern and level of demand.

DESCRIPTION OF THE MACROECONOMIC
MODEL OF PANAMA

The model developed below is designed to obtain further
insight into the nature of the mechanisms at work in the Panamanian
economy. These mechanisms are determined by four sets of forces:
(1) the behavior of individuals and institutions (endogenous variables),
(2) the country's technological know-how, (3) the policies and development plans of the government, and (4) the numerous economic forces
outside the country's influence or control (exogenous variables).

The econometric relations in Table C.1 have been computed
on the basis of past time series data for investment, consumption
and international trade. Admittedly this procedure has the disadvantage that the parameters thus estimated have been influenced by
former (pre-1968) government policies and conditions that may not
be relevant or of the same importance for the projection period.
In designing the model, however, several safeguards have been
introduced that will, it is hoped, guarantee the reliability of the
forecasts. First, the model is estimated and constructed in terms
of five-year moving averages. The use of moving averages not
only reduces the influence of a number of random elements on the
estimated parameters (thus assuring a more reliable estimate),
but also assures the continuity of the forecasts with the past trends
in the economy. All the coefficients were statistically positive at
the 95 percent level and autocorrelation was removed using the
Cochrane-Orcutt technique.

TABLE C.1

Basic Macroeconomic Relationships
(in millions of 1960 balboas)

$$C_t^P = 7.5597 + 0.1403\, Y_t + 0.8476\, C_{t-1}^P$$

$$C_t^g = -2.0441 + 0.0314\, Y_t + 0.8148\, C_{t-1}^g$$

$$C_t^T = C_t^P + C_t^g$$

$$I_t^g = -2.9597 + 0.0139\, Y_t + 0.8971\, I_{t-1}^g$$

$$I_t^P = -30.4206 + 0.69851\, I_{t-1}^g + 0.0840\, C_{t-1}^P + 0.3316\, E_t$$

$$I_t^P = -6.5117 + 0.0314\, Y_t + 0.9741\, I_{t-1}^P$$

$$\Delta S_t = 2.9954 + 0.1154\, I_t^P$$

$$I^T = I^P + I^g + \Delta S$$

$$M_t = 6.8379 + 0.9928\, I_t^P - 0.2970\, F_t + 0.2857\, Y_t$$

$$E_t = \bar{E}_t$$

$$F_t = I_t^T - S_t$$

$$S_t = Y - C_t^T$$

$$Y_t = Y_t^{GDP} + NFP_t$$

$$NFP_t = \overline{NFP}_t$$

$$Y_t = C_t^P + C_t^g + I_t^P + I_t^g + \Delta S_t + \bar{E}_t + \overline{NFP}_t - M_t$$

where:

Y_t = GNP		E_t = exports	
NFP_t = net factor payments		M_t = imports	
C_t^g = government consumption		ΔS_t = change in stocks	
C_t^T = total investment		t = current year	
I_t = government investment		$t-1$ = previous year	
I_t^P = private investment		S = savings	
I^T = total investment		C_t^P = private consumption	

Source: Compiled by the author.

The estimated demand (see Table C. 1) relationships allow
for the identification of not only short-run (one year) changes in
expenditure, but their longer-run values. The short-run change in
consumption resulting from a change in income is 0.1403; that is,
if GNP were to increase by B/1 million, personal consumption
expenditures would increase by B/140,300 in the same year. Eventually, consumers would adjust their consumption to the higher
level of income so that their long-run consumption would increase by
B/920,600 million. In the case of government consumption (C_f^g), the
short- and long-run responses to a change in income are 0.0319 and
0.3181, respectively—values much less stabilizing than those of
private consumption. Investment also follows this pattern in Panama.
The short-run response of private investors to an increase in income
is 0.0314, while their long-run adjustment is 1.2124, indicating a
strong response by the private sector to high rates of income increase. For the government's investment the short-run responses
are 0.0139 and 0.1385. Again, the private sector is playing a much
more stabilizing role than is the government.

Admittedly, the model presented above has been formulated
at a high aggregate level, and it is hoped that as more data become
available (particularly an input-output table), an elaborate model
involving sectoral breakdown at a reasonably disaggregated level
can be developed.

Within the given limitations, the model is nevertheless useful in many ways. It furnishes estimates of important structural
parameters of the Panamanian economy. In quantifying economic
forces in the economy, the model throws into sharper focus the
structural characteristics of the economy, previously discussed,
but in a less crystallized way. The pattern is found to be the same
using different time periods. This lends additional credibility to
the conclusion that there are a number of elements of stability in the
Panamanian economy. Above all, in treating the functioning of the
economy as a system of simultaneous relations that bind the major
variables together, the model provides a framework within which
the interdependence and interactions among these variables can be
schematically traded.

The reduced form of analysis (derived from the solving of
the equations in Table C. 1 simultaneously) in Table C. 2 restates the
dilemma of development policy in Panama in quantitative terms.
Having no substantial natural resource endowment of any kind, the
country has to import in order to realize investment, to satisfy

TABLE C. 2

Impact–Multiplier Matrix Derived from the Macroeconomic Model

Endogenous Variables	Exogenous Variables			
	E_t	C^P_{t-1}	C^g_{t-1}	I^g_{t-1}
GDP	0. 86581	0. 85600	0. 79529	1. 11673
GNP	0. 83251	0. 82307	0. 76470	1. 07378
NFP*	0. 03330	0. 03292	0. 03059	0. 04295
C_p	0. 11680	0. 96308	0. 10729	0. 15065
C_g	0. 02614	0. 02584	0. 83881	0. 03372
I_p	0. 33160	0. 08400	0. 00000	0. 6985
I_g	0. 01157	0. 01144	0. 01063	0. 91463
ΔS	0. 03827	0. 00969	0. 00000	0. 08061
M	0. 65857	0. 23806	0. 16144	0. 76137

*NFP = . 04 Y GNP

Note: The impact of a one–unit change in an exogenous (or predetermined) variable on an endogenous variable can be found by locating the number corresponding to the row and column of selected endogenous variables; for example, a B/1. 000 increase in exports will increase imports by B/0. 6607.

Source: Compiled by the author.

consumption, and to produce goods for the domestic export market. *
There is a leakage at many points in the cycle of income generation,
and the multiplier effects of investment and exports are dampened. †
Given the relatively narrow domestic market, efforts to develop
capital goods industries would be frustrated unless access to a
considerably large foreign market could be secured. With maximum
income growth as the basic consideration, the promotion of high
skill and high wage industries would seem to be the optimal development policy to pursue.

   The Panamanian economy has undergone important changes
in the last decade or so. To the extent that the country is poor in
natural resources, has a relatively narrow domestic market, and
is heavily dependent on foreign trade, its development is highly
sensitive to change in external stimuli. However, the public-sector
investment programs, together with a fairly successful industrialization policy, have been effective in maintaining economic stability
and in promoting growth. The initiation of development programs with
their positive impact upon the economy have given the country a fair
amount of internal maneuverability. One would suspect that in the longer run the pace and pattern of growth of the economy would be set
partly by internal policy maneuvers, and partly by the configuration of
external developments. Note that between the periods 1945-56 and 1950-
73 the country became a bit less dependent on the foreign sector (compare Tables C.2 and C.3). For example, an increase in exports by
one dollar in the earlier period (Table C.3) increased GNP by 1.7015
dollars, while in the 1950-73 period the increase was only 86 cents.

   With respect to private investment (Table C.2), the hypothesis
put forward is that it is induced partly by public-sector infrastructural
investment and partly by access to export markets. In the context
of the recent development of the Panamanian economy, it seems
reasonable to assume that the bulk of private investment in the form
of imports of machinery and equipment and nonresidential construction
has taken place in the manufacturing sector. It is our belief that
investment in industries was made partly in response to the infrastructure and other incentives provided by the public sector; that is,
a forward linkage[1] mechanism was involved reducing the costs of

---

   *A basic assumption implicit and necessary for the
application of the two-gap model used here.

   †A leakage in the form of increased imports. This tends
to reduce the size of the income generated by an expansion of
expenditure.

firms and thus stimulating investment. On the other hand, the relationship between public-sector investment (equations 4, 5 and 5' of Table C.1) and private investment could also imply the working of a backward linkage[2]— that some infrastructural investment was called forth by private investment projects under consideration or construction, an obvious example being the extension of cement and electricity production to meet the increased demand of industries.

TABLE C.3

Impact-Multiplier Matrix 1945-56

Endogenous Variables	Exogenous Variables				
	E_t	E_{t-1}	C^P_{t-1}	C^T_{t-1}	I^T_{t-1}
Y_t	1.7015	-.7807	2.5615E-7	.8928	1.2278
C^P_t	.6844	-.3140	.5191	.3591	.4938
C^T_t	.8193	-.3759	1.2792E-7	.9546	.5912
C^g_t	.1350	-.0619	-.5191	.5955	9.7366E-2
I^P_t	.2975	.0284	2.6277E-8	.1561	.2147
I^T_t	.1930	-.0885	3.1919E-8	.1012	.8608
I^g_t	-.1045	-.1169	5.6426E-9	-5.4844E-2	.6462
M_t	.3107	.3163	2.7446E-8	.1630	.2242

Note: See description in Table C.2.
Source: Compiled by the author.

As to the government's component of fixed capital formation, it is our hypothesis that the public housing program introduced by the government after 1968 played the dual role of demand formation and supply creation similar to that of imports, but in a manner somewhat different from most developing countries. In these countries imports are eventually replaced by domestic products, whereas in Panama, private- and public-sector building programs are in a broad sense complementary, with the former catering to the higher-income groups and the latter taking care of mainly the lower-income groups.

THE ROLE OF DOMESTIC INVESTMENT
THE CAPITAL/OUTPUT RATIO

Also with regard to domestic investment, the country's higher growth rates have been based on greater investment. It follows that during these periods, that part of gross investment used to replace old equipment and to construct social overhead facilities usually represents a rather small share of the total. The result has been fairly high levels of overall capital productivity in Panama. Yet this capital/output ratio has recently increased, indicating a decrease in the productivity of investment.

To show that the country's capital/output ratio may be influenced by the growth in overall economic activity, the equation for the incremental capital/output ratio (ICOR) can be written as:

$$K = K' + zr \tag{C.1}$$

where K = gross ICOR, K' = net ICOR showing the effect of net investment, z = share of current income devoted to replacement, and r = rate of growth of GDP. An estimation of equation (1) yielded:

$$K = 4.4463 - 22.5609 z \tag{C.2}$$
$$(2.6)$$

The ICORs (shown in Table C.4) for Panama indicate that Panama has made relatively effective use of its investment; Panama's ICOR averaged 2.88 for the period. This compares favorably with the value of 3.0, the average for a country at Panama's level of development. [3]

Three observations can be made about the level and movement of ICORs in Panama: (1) the overall ICOR in Panama was low by international standards through the early and middle 1960s; (2) the overall ICOR has been rising rapidly in recent years; and (3) by 1973 the overall value for the ICOR was higher than the level for most rapidly growing countries, but was still lower than that in a number of countries at similar stages of development, and not significantly out of line with the average of developing countries.

There are several likely explanations for the observed productivity of capital in Panama. One major change in the pattern of demand during the latter 1960s was an acceleration in the rate of growth of public consumption. This increased from a 1.7 percent rate of growth during the 1950s to 7.9 per year between 1960 and 1968. This, together with the relatively low level of public fixed

TABLE C.4

Incremental Capital/Output Ratio, 1955-73
(in millions of 1960 balboas)

Year	Incremental Capital/Output Ratio
1955	4.05
1956	3.00
1957	2.61
1958	3.11
1959	2.71
1960	2.86
1961	2.31
1962	2.49
1963	2.25
1964	2.41
1965	2.32
1966	2.55
1967	2.73
1968	2.93
1969	2.79
1970	3.02
1971	3.19
1972	3.49
1973	3.93

Source: Compiled by the author.
Note: Five-year moving averages.

investment during the 1950s (with public savings even lower), indicates that the acceleration of public expenditure during 1955-68, therefore, encouraged high levels of private investment. Until 1968 the public sector restricted itself to satisfying a minimum of infra-structure requirements, some social investments (water, housing, and schools), and a greater share of social services; this explains the overall low value for the capital/output ratio. The upswing in investment outlays in the early 1970s occurred in both the public and private sectors. The expansion of public-sector expenditures was so great that it led to a 50 percent increase in the central gov-ernment's overall deficit.

Much of the increase in public expenditures in the early 1970s was directed toward providing the basic infrastructure nec-essary to stimulate such private investments. The government until 1971 channeled much of its investment into certain areas to achieve social aims, such as improved housing and health services. This pattern of investment was to the detriment of activities more directly connected with the strengthening of productive capacity. The result was an increasing capital/output ratio, beginning in 1969. This trend in government expenditure changed in 1972 when an increasing amount of resources was assigned to industry and commerce (al-though resource levels were maintained in the transport and health sectors and in the housing sector). In the industrial sector a high rate of project execution was recorded, more than three-quarters of the budgeted funds being used to complete the contribution of La Victoria sugar mill (B/15 million), and most of the remainder to expand and improve the export capacity of the Colon Free Zone. This should help stabilize the capital/output ratio.

The explanation for these trends requires more intensive study, by sectors, than we have been able to provide. Unfortunately, investment figures by sector in Panama are not available. However, we can suggest some plausible explanations of the observed trends in the aggregate capital/output ratio. One possible explanation is that Panama inherited some excess capacity from the period prior to 1960. In the early years after 1960 output could thus be increased without much input of capital; hence, the declining trend to 1965. By 1966, as the slack in the economy was taken up, more and more capital was required for increases in output. Another possible explanation is that during the period after 1965 factor prices became distorted, so that capital was made increasingly cheap compared to labor. This in turn encouraged a high capital-intensive structure.

A more important question, of course, is whether the capital/output ratio will increase or decrease during the next decade. With the continued development of the country's economy, particularly industry, there will be greater possibilities than in the past because

of the use of modern techniques of production and wider utilization of
the technology being developed in the advanced countries. Moreover,
the infrastructure currently being constructed by the government
and that already in existence, such as roads, irrigation, and electricity, will be more fully utilized. All these factors, of course,
will contribute to an increase in the productivity of existing capital
and that accumulated in the future. There is thus no inherent reason
for the capital/output ratio to continue to increase in Panama.

There are reasons to believe that the capital/output ratio
in Panama tends to be lower at higher rates of GNP growth: (1) During
periods of rapid growth, the country's productive capacity becomes
more fully utilized; during periods of slowdown much of the additions
to the capital stock are not utilized to their full potential; and (2) increases in factors other than capital—labor, available resources,
and technology—play a large part in determining the growth of output, and to some extent these elements vary independently of
investment.

NOTES

1. As defined by A.O. Hirschman, The Strategy of Economic
Development (New Haven: Yale University Press, 1958).

2. Ibid.

3. See Hollis B. Chenery and Peter Eckstein, "Development
Alternatives for Latin America," Journal of Political Economy 78,
no. 4 supplement (July/August 1970): 966-1016.

The problems involved in measuring the country's growth potential are best illustrated by a survey of the country's unused resources (unused resources being interpreted broadly to include underemployment of the existing labor force).

There is no question that Panama does have a significant amount of underutilization in its labor force. In fact, a characteristic feature of Panama's unemployment problem is that it takes the form of underemployment and low earnings rather than overt total unemployment. Underemployment, measured by the number of people in the labor force involuntarily working less than 35 hours per week or earning less than the official minimum wage (B/25 per week), is extremely high. While in 1970, only 7.1 percent of the labor force was classified as unemployed, the proportion of people underemployed was estimated to be between 25 and 30 percent of the labor force.

When the numbers of the employed and the underemployed are taken together and expressed in terms of the fully employed equivalent on the basis of 35 hours per week worked, or minimum wage or salary earned, the employment ratio is quite low, ranging from 69 percent of the labor force in agriculture to a high of 92 percent in utilities, with the average for all sectors at 73 percent. These ratios, expressed as an effective unemployment ratio, are equivalent to 31 percent in agriculture, 15 percent in manufacturing, about 20 percent in commerce and services, and 27 percent for all sectors.

For example, in 1970 rural areas in Panama had a population of 575,924 according to the 1970 Census of Agriculture. The average family size was 5.5 in the agricultural sector and was distributed by farm size approximately as follows:[1]

Farm Size (hectares)	Population
0.0- 0.5	72,000
0.5- 4.9	225,000
5.0- 49.9	224,000
50.0-499.9	45,000
500 and over	15,000

223

Clearly, family workers on some of the smaller farms are unlikely to be fully employed. While some of this excess labor is utilized as hired labor on large farms and in off-farm employment, substantial underutilization surely remains.

Since underemployment is defined in Panama as the percentage by which available labor time exceeds labor requirements (23.6 percent in 1970-71), this figure provides some indication of the amount of labor that could be withdrawn from the agricultural sector without reducing production and without substituting other inputs; it represents the equivalent of about 44,000 full-time workers. It should be emphasized that this calculation is based on the annual labor requirements. Rapid withdrawal of this number of workers probably would create serious labor shortages in periods of peak seasonal requirements in some areas.

In terms of the available evidence, therefore, it is clear that the country has the potential for utilizing its resources more intensively. The point remains that it is extremely difficult (simply from a survey of the country's unused resources) to place any precise figure on the country's potential for growth during the next decade. Panama has the same advantage that all other underdeveloped countries have in lagging behind the highly developed countries, thus having the opportunity to achieve rapid growth through simple limitation of more advanced productive techniques. It might be argued that the relative abundance of underemployed workers would, through assimilation of these new techniques in the rural sector, help Panama grow very rapidly during the next decade. Rapid growth, however, is conditioned also by the existence of relevant skills possessed by the labor force, and here Panama does not appear to have the numbers of technicians required for the easy assimilation of new methods of production. Similar arguments apply to the existence of unused capacity in industry. Unused capacity may be a symptom of underdevelopment itself and is not necessarily a source of easy progress. It is difficult, therefore, to point to or precisely measure any particular physical circumstances that should make it easy for Panama to obtain and keep as high a rate of growth as in the 1960s.

NOTE

1. National Agricultural Policy Commission, Politica de Desarrollo Agropecuario (Panama City: Ministry of Agricultural Development, Department of Sectoral Planning, 1973):43.

Anderson, Robert B., et al. Interoceanic Canal Studies, 1970.
Washington, D.C.: Atlantic-Pacific Interoceanic Canal Study
Commission, 1970.

Balassa, Bela. The Structure of Protection in Developing Countries.
Baltimore: Johns Hopkins Press, 1971.

Baldwin, Robert. Foreign Trade Regimes & Economic Development:
The Philippines. New York: Columbia University Press, 1975.

Banco Nacional de Panama. Carta economica, various issues.

Barletta, Nicolas Ardito. Que presenta a la Asamblea Nacional de
Representantes de Corregimentos. Panama City: Ministerio
de Planificacion y Politica Economica, 1973.

_____. "Bases para el desarrollo de la region de Colon," Mimeographed.
Panama City: Ministerio de planificacion y politica economica,
1974. (Informe preliminar)

Biesanz, John and Mavis. The People of Panama. New York: Columbia
University Press, 1955.

Caiden, Naomi and Aron Wildavsky. Planning and Budgeting in Poor
Countries. New York: John Wiley, 1974.

Campos, Roberto. "Inflation and Balanced Growth." In Economic
Development for Latin America, edited by Howard Ellis.
London: MacMillan, 1963, pp. 82-109.

Chenery, Hollis B. "Patterns of Industrial Growth," American
Economic Review 50, no. 3 (September 1960): 624-54.

_____. "Targets for Development," in The Widening Gap, edited by
B. Ward. New York: Columbia University Press, 1971.

_____, and Peter Eckstein. "Development Alternatives for Latin
America." Journal of Political Economy 78, no.4 supplement
(July/August 1970): 966-1016.

_____, and Moises Syraquin. Patterns of Development: 1950-1970.
London: Oxford University Press, 1975.

Christian, James. "A Macro-Sectoral Survey of the Economy of
Panama." Mimeographed. Panama City; Ministerio de Planificacion y Politica Economica, 1970.

Clapp and Mayne, Inc. Estudio sobre ZLC: Importancia Economica,
Problemas que Enfrenta y Posibilidades de Expansion. San
Juan, Puerto Rico: Clapp and Mayne, 1968.

Clare, Emilio. "Apuntes de Politica Economica." Mimeographed.
Panama City: Universidad de Panama, Facultad de Administracion Publica y Comercio, 1970.

Coale, Ansley and Edgar M. Hoover. Population Growth and Economic
Development in Low-Income Countries. Princeton, N.J.: Princeton University Press, 1958.

Cohen, Arie. "Establishment of an Industrial Free Zone at the
Tocumen International Airport." Mimeographed. Vienna:
United Nations Industrial Development Organization, 1973.
(restricted).

Comision de Caminos Aeropuertos y Muelles. "A Four-Year Program
for Administrative Reorganization, Personnel Training, Rehabilitation and Maintenance of Public Highways." Mimeographed. Panama City, 1975.

Contraloria General de la Republica, Direccion de Estadistica y
Censo. Hacienda publica y finanzas, various issues.

_____. Estadistica Panamena boletin 417. Panama City, 1971.

Contraloria General, Estadistica Panamena. Ingreso Nacional,
various issues.

Cooper, Richard. Currency Devaluation in Developing Countries.
Princeton, N.J.: Princeton University Department of Economics,
International Finance Section, 1971.

de Grazia, Nicholas J. "A Study of the Establishment of Organized
    Equities Markets in the Republic of Panama: Conclusions and
    Recommendations." Mimeographed. Panama City: U.S. Agency
    for International Development, 1973.

Demas, William. The Economics of Development in Small Countries.
    Montreal: McGill University Press, 1965.

____. Papers. In The Economic Consequences of the Size of Nations,
    edited by Austin Robinson. London: Macmillan, 1963.

Diaz-Alejandro, Carlos F. Less Developed Countries and the Post-
    1971 International Financial System. Princeton: N.J.: Prince-
    ton University Department of Economics, International Finance
    Section, 1975.

Direccion de Estadistica y Censo. Estadistica Panamena, serie "0".
    Panama City: Contraloria General de la Republica, 1971.

____. Estadistica Panamena, serie "D" (Balanza de Pagos) various
    issues.

____. Sexto Censo de Poblacion y Segundo de Vivienda. Panama,
    February 1965.

____. Septimo Censo de Poblacion y Tercero de Vivienda. Panama,
    November 1971.

Direccion General de Planificacion y Administracion Departmento
    de Planificacion. "Informe Economico." Mimeographed.
    Panama City, 1972.

Durbin, J., and G.S.Watson. "Testing for Serial Correlation in
    Least Squares Regression." Biometrica 7, no. 3 (1951): 251-64.

Elkan, Walter. "On the Apparent Benefits of Higher Productivity:
    An Arithmetical Illustration." Journal of Development Studies 7,
    no. 4 (July 1971): 435-39.

Enke, Stephen. "The Economic Aspects of Slowing Population
    Growth." Economic Journal 76, no. 1 (March 1966): 44-56.

Eshag, Eprime. "The Relative Efficacy of Monetary Policy in Se-
    lected Industrial and Less Developed Countries." Economic
    Journal 81, no. 2 (June 1971): 294-309.

Fitchett, Del. "Capital-Labor Substitution in the Manufacturing Sector
    of Panama." Mimeographed. Panama City: U.S. Agency for
    International Development, 1973.

Frank, Thomas M., and Edward Weisband. "Panama Paralysis,"
    Foreign Policy no. 21 (1975-76): 168-87.

Friedman, Milton. "The Role of Monetary Policy." American
    Economic Review (March 1968).

_____. The Optimum Quantity of Money and Other Essays. Chicago:
    Aldine, 1969.

_____. Money and Economic Development: The Horowitz Lectures of
    1972. New York: Praeger Publishers, 1973.

Georgescue-Rogen, N. "Structural Inflation-Lock and Balanced
    Growth." Economies et Societes (March 1970).

Green, James Wyche. "Panamanian District: A Case Study in the
    Sociology of Development." Mimeographed. Panama City:
    U.S. Agency for International Development, 1969.

Griffin, Keith. Underdevelopment in Spanish America Cambridge,
    Mass: MIT Press, 1969.

Griffin, Keith and J.L. Enos. "Foreign Assistance: Objectives and
    Consequences." Economic Development and Cultural Change 18,
    no.3 (April 1970): 313-27.

Haberler, Gottfried. "International Aspects of U.S. Inflation." In
    A New Look at Inflation: Economic Policies for the Early
    1970s. Washington, D.C.: American Enterprise Institute,
    1973.

Hahn, Joung. "The Effect of Foreign Resources on Domestic Savings,"
    South African Journal of Economics 42, no.1 (March 1974):
    85-94.

Hansen, Bent. Long- and Short-Term Planning in Underdeveloped
    Countries, Professor Dr. F. de Vries Lectures. Amsterdam:
    North-Holland Publishing Company, 1967.

Hansen, Roger D. The Politics of Mexican Development. Baltimore:
    Johns Hopkins Press, 1971.

Hanson, Simon G. Five Years of The Alliance for Progress: An
    Appraisal. Washington, D.C.: Inter-American Affairs Press,
    1967.

Harberger, Arnold C. "Memorandum sobre Incentivos Fiscales."
    In Estudios sobre Politica Arancelaria, Incentivos y Comercio
    Exterior. Panama City: Direccion General de Planificacion,
    1970.

_____. "Some notes on Inflation," and "Reflections on the Monetary
    System of Panama." Reprinted in Chicago Essays in Economic
    Development, edited by David Wall. Chicago: University of
    Chicago Press, 1972.

_____. "The Past Growth and Future Prospects of the Panamanian
    Economy." Mimeographed. Panama City: U.S. Agency for
    International Development, 1972.

_____. "On Measuring the Social Opportunity Cost of Labor." In
    Benefit Cost Analysis, edited by Arnold C. Harberger et al.
    Chicago: Aldine, 1972.

Harris, Louis. "Panama." In Political Forces in Latin America,
    edited by Ben G. Burnett and Kenneth F. Johnson. Belmont,
    California: Wadsworth, 1968.

Hirschman, A.O. The Strategy of Economic Development. New
    Haven: Yale University Press, 1958.

Instituto Panameno de Turismo. Estudios Sectoriales: Potencial de
    la Industria de Turismo. Panama City: Direccion General de
    Planificacion y Administracion de la Presidencia, Departmento
    de Planificacion, 1970.

Inter-American Committee on the Alliance for Progress. The
    Creation of a National Monetary System in Panama. Washing-
    ton, D.C., 1966.

International Monetary Fund. International Monetary Fund Yearbook.
    Washington, D.C.: International Monetary Fund.

____. "Colon Free Zone Serves the Region." IMF Survey 4, no. 3 (February 3, 1975): 45-47.

James, Preston E. Latin America. 4th ed. New York: Odyssey Press, 1969.

Johnson, Harry. "Panama as a Regional Financial Center: A Preliminary Analysis of Development Contribution," Economic Development and Cultural Change 24, no. 2 (January 1976): 261-86.

____. "Secular Inflation and the International Monetary System," Journal of Money, Credit and Banking 4, no.1 (February 1973): 509-23.

____. Inflation and the Monetarist Controversy. Amsterdam: North-Holland Publishing Company, 1972.

Joint Tax Program OAS/IDB. Fiscal Survey of Panama: Problems and Proposals for Reform. Baltimore: Johns Hopkins Press, 1964.

Joshi, Vijay. "Saving and Foreign Exchange Constraints." In Unfashionable Economics—Essays in Honour of Thomas Blough, London: Weidenfeld and Nicolson, 1970.

Kafka, Alexandre. "The Theoretical Interpretation of Latin American Economic Development." In Economic Development for Latin America, edited by Howard Ellis. London: Macmillan, 1963.

Kane, Edward J. Economic Statistics and Econometrics. New York: Harper and Row, 1968.

Kessler, Joseph. "Social Security in Panama." Mimeographed. Panama City: Caja de Seguro Social, 1970.

Kindleberger, Charles P. "Liberal Policies vs. Controls in the Foreign Trade of Developing Countries." Mimeographed. Washington, D.C.: U.S. Agency for International Development, 1967.

Landau, Luis. "Saving Functions for Latin America." In Studies in Development Planning, edited by Hollis Chenery. Cambridge, Mass.: Harvard University Press, 1971.

Larravide, Alvaro E. "Monetary Discipline and Growth—The Case
of Panama." Finance and Development 7, no. 2 (1970): 44-50.

Leith, J. Clark. Foreign Trade Regimes & Economic Development:
Ghana. New York: Columbia University Press, 1974.

Lineamientos del Plan Nacional de Desarrollo, 1974-1978. Panama
City: Direccion de Planificacion Economica y Social, 1973.

Lloyd, Peter J. International Trade Patterns of Small Nations.
Durham, North Carolina: Duke University Press, 1968.

Looney, Robert. "The Impact of Alternative Treaties on the Economy
of Panama." 1975 (rough draft).

Machlup, Fritz. "Three Concepts of the Balance of Payments and
the So-called Dollar Shortage." Economic Journal 60, no. 1
(March 1950): 46-68.

Magnifico, Giovanni. European Monetary Unification for Balanced
Growth: A New Approach. Princeton, N. J.: Princeton
University Department of Economics, International Finance
Section, 1971.

Makin, John. Capital Flows and Exchange-Rate Flexibility in the
Post-Bretton Woods Era. Princeton, N. J.: Princeton
University Department of Economics, International Finance
Section, 1974.

Mamalakis, Markos J. "The Export Sector, Stages of Economic
Development, and the Savings-Investment Process in Latin
America." Economia Internazionale 21, no. 1 (February
1968): 56-62.

Mayer, Thomas. Permanent Income, Wealth and Consumption.
Berkeley: University of California Press, 1972.

_____. "The Relative Efficacy of Monetary Policy in Selected Industrial
and Less-Developed Countries: A Comment." Economic
Journal 82, no. 328 (December 1972).

McKinnon, Ronald I.and Wallace E.Oates. The Implication of
    International Economic Integration for Monetary, Fiscal,
    and Exchange-Rate Policy. Princeton, N.J.: Princeton
    University, Department of Economics, International Finance
    Section, 1966.

Meade, J.E. The Theory of International Economic Policy. Vol. I.
    The Balance of Payments. London: Oxford University Press,
    1951.

Merrill, William C., et al. Panama's Economic Development: The
    Role of Agriculture. Ames, Iowa: Iowa State University Press,
    1975.

Michalopoulos, Constantine. "Imports, Foreign Exchange, and
    Economic Development: The Greek Experience." In The Open
    Economy, edited by Peter Kennen and Roger Lawrence.
    New York: Columbia University Press, 1968.

Ministerio de Planificacion y Politica Economica. Lineamientos del
    Plan Nacional de Desarrollo, 1974-1978. Panama City, 1973.

Ministerio de Salud. "Proyecciones Cuadrienales de Salud."
    Mimeographed. Panama: Panama City, 1972.

____. "La Participacion de la Comunidad in los Programas de Salud."
    Mimeographed. Panama City: 1972.

Ministry of Education. Statistics for the Analysis of the Education
    System. Panama City, 1973.

National Agricultural Policy Commission. Politica de Desarrollo
    Agropecuario. Panama City: Ministry of Agricultural Develop-
    ment, Department of Sectoral Planning, 1973.

Panama Canal Company. Annual Report. Balboa Heights, Canal
    Zone, various issues.

Plan Trienal de Vivienda de Interes Social and Plan de Trabajo
    para el ano de 1974. Panama City: Ministry of Housing, 1973.

Pringle, Robin. "Banking in the Land of Balboa," The Banker 125, no. 56 (October 1975): 1195-1201.

Rahman, M.A. "Foreign Capital and Domestic Savings: A Test of Haavelmo's Hypothesis with Cross Country Data." Review of Economics and Statistics no.1 (February 1968): 137-38.

Ram, Bali. "Net Internal Migration by Marital Status for Panama: Females, 1950-1960." Social and Economic Studies 20, no.3 (September 1971): 326-30.

Ramos, Joseph. Labor and Development in Latin America. New York: Columbia University Press, 1970.

Rosenfeld, Stephen. "The Panama Negotiations—A Close-Run Thing." Foreign Affairs 54 (1975): 1-13.

Schultz, T.Paul. Population Growth: Investigation of a Hypothesis. Santa Monica, California: The Rand Corporation, 1969.

Scitovsky, T. "A Reconsideration of the Theory of Tariffs." In Papers on Welfare and Growth, edited by T.Scitovsky. Stanford: Stanford University Press, 1964.

Sahota, Gian. "Public Expenditure and Income Distribution in Panama." Mimeographed. Panama City: U.S. Agency for International Development, 1972.

Shourle, Arun. "The Use of Macro-economic Regression Models of Developing Countries for Forecasts and Policy Prescription: Some Reflections on Current Practice." Oxford Economic Papers 24, no.1 (March 1972): 1-35.

Situacion y perspectivas del empleo en Panama Ginebra: Oficina Internacional del Trabajo, 1974.

Sjaastad, Larry. "Prices and Wages in Panama." Mimeographed. Panama City: U.S. Agency for International Development, 1973.

_____. "Possibilities for Panama's Participation in the Andean Common Market." Mimeographed. Panama City· U.S. Agency for International Development, 1970.

_____."Prospects for Economic Growth in the 1970s: Panama." Mimeographed. Panama City: U.S. Agency for International Development, 1972.

Sowelem, R.A. Towards Financial Independence in a Developing Economy: An Analysis of the Monetary Experience of the Federation of Rhodesia and Nyasaland, 1952-1963. London: George Allen & Unwin, 1967.

Stanford Research Institute. A Review of World Shipbuilding and Merchant Ship Fleet Trends. Menlo Park, California: Stanford Research Institute, 1967.

Stavrou, Jarilaos. "Macro de Referencia Macroeconomico." Mimeographed. Panama City: Direccion General de Planificacion y Administracion, 1972.

Stewart, Frances and Paul Streeten. "Conflicts Between Output and Employment Objectives in Developing Countries." Oxford Economic Papers 23, no. 2 (July 1971): 145-68.

Suits, Daniel. "Forecasting and Analysis With an Econometric Model." American Economic Review 52, no. 1 (March 1962): 104-32.

Svennilson, I. "The Concept of the Nation and its Relevance to Economic Analysis." In The Economic Consequences of the Size of Nations, edited by E.A.G. Robinson. London: Macmillan, 1963.

Taylor, Lance. "Short-Term Policy in Open Semi-Industrialized Economies: The Narrow Limits of the Possible." Journal of Development Economics 1, no. 2 (September 1974): 85-104.

Taylor, Milton. "Toward the Redistribution of Income in Panama." Mimeographed. Panama City: 1971.

_____. "A Proposal for a Net Wealth Tax in Panama." Mimeographed. Panama City: no date.

Treadway, Peter. The Feasibility of Creating an Underwriting Market-Making Fund in Panama. Washington, D.C.: Organization of American States, 1974.

United Nations Economic Commission for Latin America. Analysis
    and Projections of Economic Development, VII, The Economic
    Development of Panama, Panama City: United Nations
    Economic and Social Council, 1959.

____. The Economy of Panama and the Canal Zone. Vols. I and II.
    Mexico City: Economic Commission for Latin America, 1972.

U.S. Department of State. Friendship and Cooperation: General
    Treaty Between the United States of America and Panama,
    and Exchange of Notes. Signed at Washington, D.C., March
    2, 1936.

____. Mutual Understanding and Cooperation: Treaty, with Memoran-
    dum of Understanding Reached Between the United States and
    Panama. Signed January 25, 1955.

U.S. House of Representatives, Committee on Government Operations.
    A Review of Alliance for Progress Goals. Washington, D.C.:
    Government Printing Office, 1969.

U.S. Senate. Resolution 301. 93rd Congress, 2nd Session,
    March 29, 1974.

Valles, Jean-Paul. The World Market for Bananas, 1964-1972.
    New York: Praeger Publishers, 1968.

Vanek, Jaroslav. Estimating Foreign Resource Needs for Economic
    Development. New York: McGraw-Hill, 1967.

Wallich, Henry. Monetary Problems of an Export Economy—The
    Cuban Experience 1914-1947. Cambridge, Mass.: Harvard
    University Press, 1950.

Weil, Thomas E., et al. Area Handbook for Panama. Washington,
    D.C.: U.S. Superintendent of Documents, 1972.

Weisskopf, T.E. "The Impact of Foreign Capital Inflow on Domestic
    Savings in Underdeveloped Countries." Journal of Inter-
    national Economics 2, no.1 (February 1972).

____. "An Econometric Test of Alternative Constraints on the Growth
    of Underdeveloped Countries." Review of Economics and
    Statistics 54, no.1 (February 1972).

Whitman, Marine von Neuman. International and Interregional Pay-
    ments Adjustment: A Synthetic View. Princeton, N.J.:
    Princeton University, Department of Economics, International
    Finance Section, 1967.

ROBERT E. LOONEY is assistant professor of economics at the University of Santa Clara. He has been a faculty member of the University of California at Davis, development economist at the Stanford Research Institute, and senior economist for Louis Berger International. He has served as economic adviser to the governments of Iran and Panama.

Dr. Looney has published a number of articles in professional journals and is the author of The Economic Development of Iran, 1959-1981 (Praeger, 1973), and Income Distribution Policies and Economic Growth in Semi-Industrialized Countries: A Comparative Analysis of Iran, Mexico, Brazil, and South Korea (Praeger, 1975).

Dr. Looney earned his B.S. and Ph.D. degrees from the University of California, Davis.

RELATED TITLES
Published by
Praeger Special Studies

INCOME DISTRIBUTION POLICIES AND ECONOMIC
GROWTH IN SEMI-INDUSTRIALIZED COUNTRIES:
A Comparative Analysis of Iran, Mexico, Brazil,
and South Korea

> Robert E. Looney

AGRICULTURAL MODERNIZATION THROUGH
PRODUCTION CONTRACTING: The Role of the
Fruit and Vegetable Processor in Mexico and
Central America

> J. David Morrissy

DEPENDENT INDUSTRIALIZATION IN LATIN
AMERICA: The Automotive Industry in Argentina,
Chile, and Mexico

> Rhys Owen Jenkins

ECONOMIC GROWTH AND EMPLOYMENT
PROBLEMS IN VENEZUELA: An Analysis of an
Oil Based Economy

> Mostafa F. Hassan

ECONOMIC NATIONALISM IN LATIN AMERICA:
The Quest for Economic Independence

> Shoshana B. Tancer

FAMILY AND OTHER BUSINESS GROUPS IN
ECONOMIC DEVELOPMENT: The Case of
Nicaragua

> Harry W. Strachan

LATIN AMERICA'S NEW INTERNATIONALISM:
The End of Hemispheric Isolation

> edited by Roger W. Fontaine
> and James D. Theberge

MUNICIPAL DEVELOPMENT PROGRAMS IN
LATIN AMERICA: An Intercountry Evaluation
                              Pirie M. Gall

OIL IN THE ECONOMIC DEVELOPMENT OF
VENEZUELA
                    Jorge Salazar-Carrillo

THE UNITED STATES AND MILITARISM IN
CENTRAL AMERICA
                         Don L. Etchison